Kapal Haji

Singapore and the Hajj Journey by Sea

Published by
World Scientific Publishing Co. Pte. Ltd.
5 Toh Tuck Link, Singapore 596224
USA office: 27 Warren Street, Suite 401-402, Hackensack, NJ 07601
UK office: 57 Shelton Street, Covent Garden, London WC2H 9HE

National Library Board, Singapore Cataloguing in Publication Data

Name(s): Green, Anthony, 1947- | Mohd Raman Daud, writer, researcher.
Title: Kapal Haji: Singapore and the Hajj Journey by Sea / Anthony Green, author and research; Mohd Raman Daud, additional text and research.
Description: Singapore: World Scientific Publishing, [2019] |
Includes bibliographical references.
Identifier(s): OCN 1113862721 | ISBN 978-981-12-1253-6 (hardcover)
Subject(s): LCSH: Muslim pilgrims and pilgrimages -- Singapore -- History. |
Muslim pilgrims and Pilgrimages -- Saudi Arabia -- Mecca.
Classification: DDC 297.352--dc23

British Library Cataloguing-in-Publication Data
A catalogue record for this book is available from the British Library.

For any available supplementary material, please visit
https://www.worldscientific.com/worldscibooks/10.1142/11614#t=suppl

Desk Editors: Karimah Samsudin and Rhaimie Wahap

Book concept by connotations

Supported by: National Heritage Board (Singapore) | Majlis Ugama Islam Singapura | Halijah Travels

Design: B.RU Collective
Printed in Singapore

Kapal Haji

Singapore and the Hajj Journey by Sea

Anthony Green

and

Mohd Raman Daud

World Scientific

NEW JERSEY • LONDON • SINGAPORE • BEIJING • SHANGHAI • HONG KONG • TAIPEI • CHENNAI • TOKYO

Contents

Foreword

Hajj is the fifth pillar of Islam. It is a spiritual journey for all Muslims, from the country in which they reside, to the holy city of Mecca. The journey requires the performance of rituals commemorating the life and sacrifices of Prophet Abraham (peace be upon him) and his family, and it is obligatory for Muslims to perform the Hajj at least once in their lifetime, if they can afford this, and if their health permits.

To fulfil the Hajj rituals – the performance of the wuqf at Mount Arafah, the stoning of the devil in Mina, the tawaf (encircling of the Kaaba) and the Sa'i (about a five kilometre walk between Safa and Marwa) – requires physical strength and a great deal of walking.

But aside from the rituals there are profound humanitarian and social principles embedded in the whole Hajj journey, something captured by the scholar Ali Shariati' in his very important book, Hajj. The Hajj teaches values of equality: throughout the Hajj experience, the rich and the poor of all nationalities not only intermingle, but all are required to dress identically (i.e., to be in the state of ihram, where all male pilgrims are required to don two identical pieces of white cloth).

Muslims from the Nusantara region of Southeast Asia have faced additional challenges when undertaking the Hajj journey. Today pilgrims travel by air but in the past, travelling by sea, their journey to Mecca and back could take many months, so pilgrims' stories have taken the definition of "sacrifice" to another level, as they left behind their families for long periods. For those thousands who travelled via seriously overcrowded ships to Mecca mortality rates were high and pilgrims from Jawa (modern day Indonesia) had yet one more layer of difficulty arising from Dutch colonial policies that discouraged this journey for fear they might return home influenced by reformist ideas. The Hajj is a huge meeting place for pilgrims from all over the Muslim world: a place where ideas are exchanged, and these issues are explored in this book.

The scepticism of the colonial powers towards the Hajj was one of the reasons why Singapore, and more specifically Kampong Gelam, became a focal meeting point for pilgrims from across the region. Javanese and others from the Archipelago would come to Singapore and the Straits Settlements first before heading to Mecca, some to avoid detection from Dutch authorities, whilst many others were so poor that they had to work in Singapore and the Malay Peninsula for months in order to fund their onward journey, and Kampong Gelam became a hub for Hajj pilgrims. Businesses providing services to them grew and pilgrim brokers and shops selling goods for pilgrims could all be found in the area. Even today, remnants of this historical role can be found. The name of the small street Haji Lane is one reminder but the shophouses all throughout the area used to provide accommodation for pilgrims in transit. Muslim owned travel agencies dealing with the Hajj can still be found and the name of Hajjah Maimunah, a businesswoman who ran hajj services for pilgrims in the past (and who is referred to in the first chapter of the book), still features in a restaurant here.

In recognition of the significant role Kampong Gelam played for Hajj pilgrims, the Malay Heritage Centre (MHC) held a special exhibition entitled Undangan ke Baitullah: Pilgrims' Stories from the Malay World to Makkah in 2018. It ran from October 2018 to June 2019 and explored the Southeast Asian perspective to the Hajj journey. The exhibition was complemented by a two-day workshop and the "human interest" material in this book was shared there and with museum guides.

I am pleased that Anthony Green and Mohd Raman Daud have made this effort to document this important, once-in-a lifetime, journey for many Muslims. Kapal Haji: Singapore and the Hajj Journey by Sea not only underlines the challenges faced by pilgrims, but also highlights the historical significance of Singapore in the inter-connectedness of the region and specifically the role of Kampong Gelam in the whole process. This was one of the reasons why Kampong Gelam also developed as an intellectual hub for the Malay world, something enhanced by it being a major regional centre for printing. It not only connected people from different parts of that world, but also facilitated the flow of ideas. I am confident that, as much as the local community has supported MHC's efforts to document Singapore's and Kampong Gelam's role as the hub for Hajj pilgrims, many will find Kapal Haji equally fascinating.

The challenges for Hajj pilgrims today are different and require their own levels of patience and sacrifice. While travel time from Southeast Asia to Mecca has been reduced multi fold, from fourteen days via steamship in the last century to less than 10 hours by air, the waiting time for a Hajj visa resulting from the quotas set by the relevant authorities can be up to three decades. This book looks at the conditions from the early part of the nineteenth century and is an important opportunity for us to reflect on the challenges of the Hajj over the years and to count our blessings, and the Malay Heritage Foundation (MHF) is happy to support such efforts.

I wish to congratulate Anthony Green and Mohd Raman Daud for this good work, and look forward to many more books from them documenting our history and the contributions to Singapore and beyond. This book not only provides detailed accounts of those who had to travel by sea to modern day Saudi Arabia, but also includes rich illustrations and will be useful for future generations, who wish to compare contemporary experiences of the Hajj journey with those of their forefathers. I hope that discussions about the Hajj and the significance of Kampong Gelam will not end with this publication but will continue in other forms.

Dr Norshahril Saat
Chairman, Malay Heritage Foundation

Introduction

This book focuses on the journey of a pilgrimage; on those who made it, and on how it was made; on what it cost them and what it might have been like. In this case, it's the journey of hajj pilgrims from Southeast Asia to Jeddah, by sea.

At the heart of every pilgrimage is a destination and a reason to travel there. And at the human heart of the story are the pilgrims. They can, and often did, come from afar. In modern times air travel can link places across the globe within one or two days and in that sense journeying is far easier than it was. But even now that is not true for all and not everyone can afford that choice. And so, many pilgrimages are made overland, and in the case of the Muslim hajj, just occasionally, stories still emerge of pilgrims walking great distances, right across Africa or Central Asia, to the Hejaz, the region that includes Mecca and Medina. But for those living on islands or in lands far across the waters – certainly in the time before air travel – it was always the sea that connected.

The journey from Southeast Asia

And amongst the hajj travellers arriving by sea it was the journey of Muslims living in Southeast Asia, and on through the Philippines and up to China, that was one of the longest. Yet, despite the length of the journey, there were times, particularly in the late 1920s, when Muslims from Southeast Asia – from the

Indonesian Archipelago and the Malay Peninsula – would account for more than half of the non-Arab pilgrims present in Mecca. The desire, the drive, was very strong.

Over centuries Muslims had travelled from this region as individuals or in small groups to perform the hajj, some of them staying on for many years to study the religion and then return to their homelands as teachers and to bring back ideas as to how society should operate. But in the first half of the nineteenth century the establishment of regular sailings made it possible for much larger numbers to sail in what are called in Malay the *kapal haji* – the hajj ships. And this was the norm up to the 1970s when the economics of air travel changed the game.

If the hajj is an article of faith for Muslims it was also something that attracted the interest and attention of a wide range of people. There were those who recognised the need to provide services or who saw business opportunities, whether they were fellow Muslims or people from outside the faith; and there were those whose interest owed more to suspicion, or the desire to ensure that the structures of control and order they had put in place were not threatened.

For much of the time of the *kapal haji*, countries like modern-day Indonesia, Singapore, Brunei, and the lands that now constitute Malaysia, were under colonial rule – Dutch rule in the case of Indonesia, and British rule for the Malay Peninsula, Sabah (then British North Borneo) and Sarawak, and especially for the Straits Settlements: Singapore, Penang, and Malacca. This colonial presence introduced its own pattern of priorities and dynamics so that, if the sea-borne hajj is at the centre we can see a number of forces or interests overlapping.

The Force of Faith

Faith and the desire to perform the hajj and complete the fifth "pillar" of Islam drove the many thousands to undertake the journey. Their path led them through places that offered services and possibilities and connections, and amongst communities that "spoke the same religious and cultural language." It has to be said, however, that if the religious language was the same, that was no guarantee that, along that path, they would not be tricked or robbed or, in the worst cases, stripped of almost everything they had.

The Commercial Instinct

The hajj also presented a business opportunity – firstly for those who sold tickets and who arranged passages and then connections with guides and services in Mecca. These people would be Muslims but the force of faith did not prevent profit being made. For much of the time of the kapal haji the pilgrims were almost like a cargo and the transport of hajj pilgrims was spoken of as "a trade." That trade drew in a wide range of business interests – in the funding or ownership of ships, in insurance or finance or the consigning of freight. This was especially true after the opening of the Suez Canal, with the eventual control of hajj shipping being almost exclusively in the hands of Western interests.

Aside from a brief exception in the 1930s, throughout the history of the hajj from Southeast Asia all the ships that carried pilgrims were essentially cargo ships. Often during that time hajj pilgrims were like a "fill in" when a ship had space. And even when Jeddah was the destination a ship was specifically travelling to, this would be an opportunity for the shipowner (or the ship's captain) to add to his cargo with far more pilgrims than his vessel was judged able to carry.

This use of cargo vessels to carry pilgrims would not really change until 1953 and the introduction of the China Navigation Company ships, *Anking* and *Anshun*.

Forces at work in the sea-borne Hajj

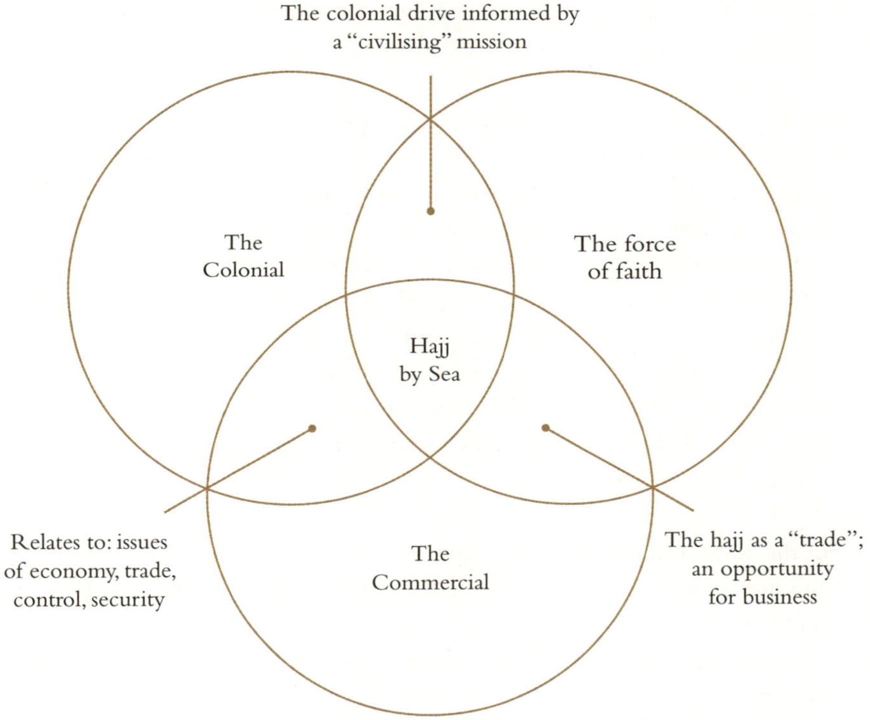

First to benefit from "the trade" were those who owned ships that could make that journey and that were big enough to carry pilgrims, and here it was Hadhrami Arabs who led: those who came originally from the Hadhramaut region in Yemen. But once shipping companies became inter-connected, the trade itself would be effectively controlled by a small group of Western companies. And if Southeast Asian shipowners – principally those Hadhrami Arabs – were significant throughout the nineteenth century the opening of the Suez Canal would mark the beginning of the end of their dominance. Powered vessels – steamships or *kapal api* (literally, "fire ships") – would change everything and that control became entrenched towards the end of the century when a number of companies grouped together to create a monopoly.

And the Colonial View

The third overlapping element that has to be included came from the colonial powers, in this case the British and the Dutch. Colonial interests are in acquiring territories and in developing the control of trade. With that, rules and systems are introduced over lands and peoples and resources.

But the business of colonisation was also a "civilising mission": it was coloured by a clear sense of the superiority of the beliefs of the colonisers over those of the people they now ruled. In the lands where Muslim communities existed – "*Mohammedans*," as they were referred to – the British would often work with, and through, selected individuals or organisations. But public attitudes to Muslims were sometimes very disparaging and the reference to hajj pilgrims, as in chapter 8, as "wretched fanatics" and "wretched fellows, who do not care if they die" are just two small examples. Such references would eventually fade and disappear, and the twentieth century offered interesting occasions where the discipline and behaviour of the pilgrims stirred respectful observations from members of ships' crews.

For the colonial authorities the hajj prompted mixed responses. On the one hand they wanted to be seen as facilitating the hajj for their "*Mohammedan*" subjects. On the other there was a good deal of suspicion, so the Dutch particularly, but also the British, set up surveillance systems and engaged those who could report back.

Mecca and other centres in the region provided places of learning that were the sources for the spread of ideas as to how Islam should best be practised, and how a society in which Muslims lived should best be ordered; ideas that challenged those of the old order – the "kaum tua" – back in the places people had come from, and empowered those who saw the need for a new "young" order – the "kaum muda." Those ideas were brought back amongst some returning hajjis and the distinctions were seen to threaten societal structures that seemed to guarantee colonial stability. The hajj, then, was also an occasion where different attitudes met.

• • • • • • • • • • •

The role of Singapore

Penang became an important centre for hajj pilgrims from the north of Malaya and from across the Straits of Malacca. But at the southern end of the Malay Peninsula Singapore quickly become the administrative centre of the Straits Settlements and was, for the period that this book concentrates on, perhaps the major centre for hajj pilgrims from the region. There were many reasons for this. Many reasons, too, for why a small part of that island – the area called Kampong Glam[1] – became so significant. Singapore and Kampong Glam are a clear focus for this book.

• • • • • • • • • •

Beyond fragments of dry information

In an editorial for Malaysia's *Hari Kebangsaan*, or National Day, at the end of August 2018, The Star newspaper recounted how the website of Malaysia's National Archives – *Arkib Negara* – carried "brief descriptions of the Aug 31 celebrations in certain years from 1958 to 2003." But the newspaper lamented that they were "sedate and sterile accounts that do little to convey the sentiments of the day" or to answer or address the question of what was going on in people's heads. "Unfortunately," said the editorial, "the National Archives is not a repository of emotions. We cannot know Malaysia's mood from fragments of dry information."

The hajj pilgrims have left us almost no accounts to let us understand what their journeys would have been like, particularly in a wooden sailing ship; what the seas were like or the conditions and discomforts on board; what fears they might have had. We can offer possible reasons for this: a great many might not have been able to read or write, and the practice of keeping a journal and writing down thoughts would have been almost non-existent. But, beyond all that, and perhaps most importantly, the understanding is that those who make the hajj go as the "*dhuyyuf*," the guests, of Allah, of God. As guests on this particular journey you accept whatever comes to you, and to write about what you are experiencing may seem like drawing attention to yourself and seeking to highlight this as a kind of achievement.

And yet, if we could have some idea of what the hajj journey might have "cost" in terms of fear or loss, or what it might have brought in terms of learnings, we may better understand the personal significance of the hajj and perhaps respect the commitment of these, mostly nameless, pilgrims.

A central hope in these pages is to try to move beyond "fragments of dry information." The lack of direct personal accounts leads to a search for comparisons and a means of "listening" in another way. But even though it centres on the journey itself, to tell that story means looking at the places hajj pilgrims travelled through, the systems and businesses that developed and the processes that were established.

• • • • • • • • • •

The structure of the book

The timeframe covered is from around the 1830s and the time of sailing ships, into the advent of "steamships" and through to the mid-1970s and the eventual end of the sea-borne hajj from Southeast Asia.

The story begins at the end; that is, by listening to one or two people who travelled on the *kapal haji* in the 1970s, to introduce some features of what happened as individuals from different backgrounds and origins came together and became ship-borne communities; a coming-together that, at times in the history of the hajj, disturbed colonial authorities who saw this and the great gathering in the Hejaz as having the potential to stir anti-colonial sentiment. The focus then moves back to the development of Singapore as a port, to where the pilgrims came from, and the recognition of just how much the sea was the connector for them all.

Singapore offered a place in which prospective hajis would be free from the somewhat feudal relationships that were the norm in the Malay Peninsula or from the relationship with the colonial power that they would know in the Netherlands East Indies, so the differing attitudes of the Dutch and the British to the hajj introduced a significant element into the growth of Singapore as a place of departure. And within Singapore many would find the chance to work to earn money for the pilgrimage. Within the area of Kampong Glam in particular they could meet with pilgrim brokers who were often links in a chain from their place of origin to Mecca and who were able to facilitate their travel onwards. Kampong Glam was an urban setting which would supply many of their needs, and at the end of the nineteenth century it was also the centre for the printing and publication of religious texts and poetry in their own languages; a place of ideas.

The book then looks at the ships they sailed in; who owned them, and some of the incidents of serious overcrowding. It begins in the time of sail; progresses through the great change brought by the Suez Canal, and includes the notorious 1880 incident of an Arab-owned ship that inspired Joseph Conrad's story, *Lord Jim*.

The aim is to catch the feel of the sea journey and what life might have been like on board. But given the lack of actual accounts, chapter 6 offers comparisons with other journeys on wooden sailing ships. This is followed by some images of the experience on land from the 1890s and the end of Ottoman Empire, through to the developments brought in under Ibn Saud in the 1920s. The return journey meant a person changed in some ways, but issues of quarantine from communicable diseases must also be considered, along with the frequency of deaths on board, since so many of those who travelled were old people.

The book closes with a brief "looking back." The last years of the sea-borne hajj came in that thirty-year period from the end of the Second World War, as long-distance passage by sea was winding down and as air travel became the norm.

So, "beginning at the end," we look first at the 1970s ...

• • • • • • • • • • •

[1] The accepted, modern spelling of the Malay word is now "*kampung*." The older spelling "kampong" has been used in this book because that was how it was more consistently spelt throughout the times that this book focuses on.
[2] "*The Star Says*" (editorial), *The Star*, Kuala Lumpur, 31 August 2018, p.2

1

The "last" journeys by sea

The hajj begins with intention and, for Muslims, intentions play a powerful part in how actions are deemed to be judged. The Arabic word for this is *niyyah*. So, in the case of the hajj you first form your *niyyah* to make that journey. And then you work to overcome whatever obstacles are in the way. For some, that intention comes very early in life but to realise it, to make it happen, may take a lifetime of work, and saving, and throughout the history of the hajj by sea from Southeast Asia newspaper reports of the ages of pilgrims revealed just how long it had taken for many to be able to make the journey and, sometimes, what it had cost them, both financially and in other ways. A verse in the Qur'an reminds people, "Be sure, We (meaning God) will test you with something of loss."

The hajj is both an invitation and it's a time of tests.

Islam sets out responsibilities, for which the followers of the faith accept they will be held to account on a Day of Judgement. Some of these are for a community as a whole. If they're not done, the community might be judged to have fallen short. Other responsibilities are for each individual, alone. If the affirmation of faith has been made, the daily prayers offered, the fast observed and the *zakat* (or alms) paid throughout their lives, the hajj remained as a kind of duty of completion; something that had to be performed once in one's lifetime if the means were there. Yet, unless a pilgrim speaks about it in detail, the difficulty in understanding the personal significance of the hajj is that all we can say is, "this is what they did."

What the inner thoughts and motivations were of each hajj pilgrim; what they understood of the place and rites of the pilgrimage, and what they derived from the experience cannot really be known. And for each individual pilgrim the hajj would have a different significance.

The 1830s to the 1970s

For the people of Southeast Asia Michael Laffan has said that the possibilities for undertaking the journey were greatly increased from around the 1830s[1] – a time when some sort of regular sailings were begun. These sea-borne hajj journeys were undertaken in what's known in Malay as the *kapal haji*; and this was the principal way of journeying until the mid 1970s. By that time significant changes had been building in long-distance travel across the globe. Long distance flights had been in place since the 1920s but these were initially only for the very few. The aircraft were not large and they flew slowly. Wars bring rapid technological development and the years following the Second World War saw aircraft finally taking over from ships, so that a 10-hour flight by jet aircraft would come to seem both affordable and far more appealing than 14 days at sea. In many ways the development of the wide-bodied 747 was the big "game-changer."

In 1935 the Dutch airline KLM advertised flights from Batavia (modern day Jakarta) to Amsterdam and then London. The aircraft was a Douglas DC3, carrying perhaps 20 passengers and the journey, with many stops, took five and a half days. Forty years later a Boeing 747-200 might carry 18 times as many people at nearly three times the speed and cover that distance within one day. Passenger travel by sea over longer distances had been slowly losing out and in the time from the end of the Second World War shipowners were having to look around to find a use for the passenger vessels that they had.

The last years of the hajj ships from Singapore and Malaysia were from 1970 to 1976, and the last company to operate was the Kuala Lumpur-based, Hongkong-owned, Great Malaysia Lines. In 1974 one of its ships – the *Malaysia Kita* caught fire off Singapore and was scrapped. Two years later its sister ship, the *Malaysia Raya*, caught fire off Port Klang, Malaysia. It too was scrapped and the last ship to sail that route from the Malay Peninsula was the company's *Eastern Queen* in late 1976.

The numbers of passengers opting to journey to Mecca by sea had dwindled dramatically, the business was not profitable and in 1977 the company stopped trading.

What follows here is a look at some of those pilgrims who travelled in those last years.

A view over the rooftops in Mecca, 1963, taken by Singapore's then President, Yusof Ishak. Yusof Ishak Collection, courtesy of National Archives of Singapore

Intention and preparation

Until his retirement, Maamor bin Sutan Nordin worked for many years for Keretapi Tanah Melayu – Malayan Railways. When he'd started in 1939 (with what was then the Federated Malay States Railway: FMSR) he'd earned 84 cents a day. After four years it rose to $1.20, then $31 per month as a ticket collector. In his working life he recognised that others were sometimes annoyed by him because he was meticulous and, in his own words, "not patient," and in 1972 he felt he did not yet have the calling to perform the hajj: "*Saya belum ada seruan*." Yet one year later he made that journey and the experience changed him.

Aisha Beebee Ajum Angullia – known to her friends as "Betu" – made her hajj trip in 1973. By this time hajj training courses were in place for prospective pilgrims. Not everyone on the ship would have gone through them but the many who did were far more prepared for the rituals and the significances of what lay ahead. Before they even caught sight of a ship, prospective pilgrims might practice the *tawaf*, the anti-clockwise circumambulation of the Kaaba by following an *ustaz* – a religious teacher – around a large box-like model of the real thing, and the *manassik* or rites of the hajj, the sequence of what the pilgrims must do, were explained. In the history of the hajj it hadn't always been like this.

Ustaz Hj Ali Hj Mohamed is the Chairman of the Management Committee of Khadijah Mosque in Singapore. He also made that 14-day journey to Jeddah about this time. He was 25 or 26 and travelled with his mother:

> We know that hajj is an obligatory thing, one of the pillars of Islam. It's not only that . . . it's a duty for a son to bring the mother to God, to Allah. That is one. But to ourselves also, we feel that this is an obligatory thing to us also – to perform the hajj, so you get both: one is your parents, your mother; another is your own person.[2]

The Kaaba in Mecca, 1963, taken by Singapore's then President, Yusof Ishak. Yusof Ishak Collection, courtesy of National Archives of Singapore

When Aisha Angullia travelled, education and opportunities for learning would continue on board the ship. In 1965, for example, it was announced by Haji Ali Rouse, the Pilgrimage Control Officer in Malaysia, that there would be "a stock of religious books – in Malay and Arabic – for the libraries of the hajj ships *Anshun* and *Kuala Lumpur.*"[3]

Outside the hajj season, a ship like *Kuala Lumpur* would be used by its owners on cruises from Australia or New Zealand, so conversion of the vessel for the hajj would include removing "one-armed bandits" – the coin operated slot machines – and anything associated with alcohol. That points to one issue for those whose ships served as pilgrim ships – the hajj was a seasonal thing, so the challenge was always to find uses for them for the rest of the year.

On the hajj the pilgrims would gather together for talks in a space that, in other times, was used as the ship's ballroom. If the weather was rough then those talks might have to be relayed through the vessel's p.a. system by the *guru kapal* – the teacher who was on board to give regular lectures, organised and provided by Tabung Haji, the Malaysian hajj organisation. Tabung Haji itself had been launched by the Malaysian Government in 1963 as a pilgrim savings cooperative, in part to tackle the long-standing practice of people selling everything they had in order to perform the hajj, travelling – many of them – with a kind of wish to end their days in Mecca, but too often returning home in some state of destitution.

In the 1960s and 1970s, for pilgrims from Malaysia and Singapore, travel was both easier and more predictable than it had been in earlier years. The ships that started from Singapore would head up the Straits of Malacca and stop at Port Klang – known up to 1972 as Port Swettenham – and then Penang, and departure times were planned and published well in advance by the Malaysian Pilgrimage Controller, based on the estimates of pilgrim numbers and the actual number of applicants. The Pilgrimage Controller took care of that. It had been very different in 1927 when there was "an unprecedented inrush of pilgrims, mostly from Dutch territory" and a newspaper could report that, "there are still thousands of Mohamedan pilgrims waiting in Singapore for transportation to Jeddah." In times such as this shipping companies had to try to provide extra steamers "at short notice"[4] and in such times – as, here, in September 1907 – pilgrims might find themselves sleeping out beside the dock and under the stars.

> There is a large number of prospective Hadjis on the water front awaiting the arrival of the pilgrim steamer *Perim*, due tomorrow, which is to take them to the Mohammedan holy land.[5]

When Aisha Angullia sailed on the *Malaysia Kita* in 1973 the hajj package cost S$2,000 and was organised by the well-known company of the late Hajjah Maimunah in Singapore. That company's connections between Southeast Asia and Saudi Arabia were well established:

> Our Shaykh in Singapore was Hjh Maimunah but when we reached Mecca our Shaykh was Nafisa Nawawi. Her husband was Hj Mat Top, a Malay man, living in Mekkah.[6]

Departure of the Malaysia Kita, late 1973
Picture courtesy of Aishah Angullia

In the Hejaz they would meet many long-term Meccan residents who had originated from Southeast Asia:

> They speak Arabic very well: all the Indonesian people who are there, the Pattani people, the Thailand people who are there ... but they cannot speak their own language. The Malay is horrible. When they speak their language it's so broken.

These meetings were like a small link with the past. Going back to the seventeenth century and earlier there has been a presence in Mecca of numbers of what came to be called "*Jawah*" or "*Makkawi*" – those who originated from the Southeast Asian lands of the Indonesian Archipelago and the Malay Peninsula. From the countless thousands who travelled over the centuries – first as small numbers of individuals and, in time, as part of larger groups – there were those who stayed on to study and to live: the "*Jawi Meccan*" connection.

In Aisha's case, two things at least stood out for this hajj journey. The first was her age when she formed her intention to travel. Most of those travelling for hajj were old people, "the youngsters a few only." Aisha was 25, going on 26 when she went but she'd already made up her mind to go when she was still at school in Secondary Four – at the age of around 15 or 16.

The kursus haji (hajj course); Aisah Ibrahim (centre) and Aisha Angullia (right) in the second row. Picture courtesy of Aisha Angullia.

> I'm thinking, when people go haji it's a lot of money. Oh God, when are you going? When I get a little bit of money I keep, keep, keep. When it's prayer time I said to my mother, I want to go to hajj.

Her desires weren't shared by her adopted sister, Aisah Ibrahim, but intentions can be quietly contagious. (Her name was also "Aisha" but birth certificates could render different spellings). Aisha Angullia was the one who "drove" the journey at first:

> I said, come, we had no money but we learn first. I said to her that, at the moment we are still strong but we are handicapped. In future, in time, we did not know. Our energy is limited. That's the main point and we prayed hard.

So they began attending a two-year course – a *kursus haji* – in a small *madrasah* in a road that's now disappeared, called Jalan Labu. Their teacher, their *ustaz,* was Ust Osman Jantan, a man who had also served as a *guru kapal*, and at first Aisah Ibrahim "just followed."

> I don't have any intention to go. She said, "Come follow me." I said, "I'm not going hajji," but she said, "Never mind, just follow. One day who knows?"

One year into the course, and somewhat like the change in Maamor bin Sutan Nordin, those feelings altered and she too wanted to perform the hajj. But a second issue stood out – the handicap that Aisha had spoken of. Both of them had had polio when younger.

> The doctor always told me, "You're handicapped people, your energy is like 60-year old people." And I'm thinking Oh God; I'm always thinking God will be helping us. But when we went there, there were people worse than us – without legs; without hands; with one leg; with no legs. But the men can *mengaji*, they can read the Qur'an. I made *tawaf* with one stick. She got callipers plus crutches. I'm without callipers so I always say, *Alhamdulillah*. It's only for the *sa'i* I take a wheelchair.

The ladies on the hajj course. Ust Osman Jantan, their teacher, at the left in the front row; Ust Hafi Hakim on the right of the row. Picture courtesy of Aisha Angullia.

All the hajj course participants. Picture courtesy of Aisha Angullia.

The realisation came that the hajj brings together an extraordinary range of people, and their own physical condition would work in unexpected ways while they were there. Aisah Ibrahim used crutches and was wearing black most of the time. Waiting for her sister she would fall asleep in a corner of the mosque and it seemed to prompt certain responses in those who passed by.

I have two crutches; I lie down; I would wait in one corner for my friend to come out from the mosque but when I wake up there's a lot of money. And I asked the Shaykh, Mat Top, what I should do with this, he said, "Never mind, if you don't want you just give to other people."

The Qur'an says:

"And proclaim the pilgrimage among men: they will come to Thee on foot and on every kind of camel, lean on account of journeys through deep and distant mountain highways."

Surah Al-Hajj, 22: 27

If the cost of the hajj had seemed a real obstacle this was overcome in the second year into the hajj course when Aisha's father asked where they were going.

I said, "I go *kursus haji*." "You want to go to *haji*?" he asked. I said, "I want but I've got no money." "If you really want, I give," so my father gave.

Boarding the ship brought a new challenge. Their brother had taken their luggage down to the lower decks where they were booked to sleep and he realised that they'd have to climb up to an upper deck to eat so he was firm: "You can't stay in this place. You are both handicapped." Negotiations followed with a very good friend on board, Mr Awab. The "A" class cabins were all for the Malaysian staff from Tabung Haji, he was told, but one room was available.

Many "Aishas"

After Port Klang the medical staff from Malaysia came on board the ship and a nurse from Penang joined them in their room. Her name?

> Aisha also! Three Aishas in the room.
> We called her sister because she's a nurse.

And in Saudi Arabia there'd be "another Aisha" when they met and made friends with a lady from South Africa, a lady they kept in touch with for some time afterwards. Meeting others from different parts of the world, interacting, sharing experiences, seems a strong element in their memory of this journey.

> We meet a lot of people in the ship and in the mosque; we share together. This ship carried *jemaah* [community] from Singapore and Malaysia. So we met a lot of Malaysians there.

That sharing included knowledge of the hajj rituals themselves:

> Some of them they don't know anything. They see us sitting down reading so they come and join us, because we took a two-year course. They didn't know the proper way to do some things. They know about *tawaf* but some don't take the course. When they know us they like us both because we're friendly to them; because we cannot keep quiet.

One more advantage the sisters had was linguistic. Speaking Malay and English was a start but the Angullia family name originates in the north-west of India and the extended family has trading links around the Indian Ocean so Urdu and Hindi were part of the capabilities and with a father from Mauritius, Aisha was able to speak a bit of Creole.

Aside from the teaching of rituals the hajj course had laid stress on attitude. They'd been reminded that, on the hajj they would see all kinds of things.

> Our *ustaz* always reminded us, don't say anything about this is strange; don't think you're better than others or laugh at them; you can always help. If anyone is struggling that all belongs to what they do before they go. We cannot laugh at them; cannot say "you have a lot of sin." I think if you don't go to the *kursus* you can always get lost there; maybe you cannot control your anger; you always want to be right.

These were qualities that were emphasised by the older ladies that they spoke to on the ship. "Be patient," they were told. "They were older, so we respected them."

"He's a zam-zam boy. Sometimes behind the masjid; sometimes in front of the masjid he will call us 'Hajjah! Hajjah!' The water inside the leather pouch is very cold. In the afternoon when you come out from the mosque, there were a lot of boys but this one was regular."*

[water from the well of zam-zam]*

Picture courtesy of Aisha Angullia.

Attitude, ability, intention

Some of their fellow pilgrims on the ship were unable to read the *Qur'an* but Aisha Angullia's response was to say to them,

> *Makcik,* [Auntie] no need to read. Just say *Subhannallah, Alhamdulillah, la illa ha illallah, Allahu akhbar.* Allah will accept. Don't worry. I see you

> all can recite this. We don't know how our *haji* will be, correct. I said, it's from the heart. If your niyah is good and your money is clean, then sure you will be ok.

And it wasn't just an inability to read the *Qur'an*. There were everyday issues on board – some that you can get a feel for when looking at the "exploded" view of the ship *TSMS Kuala Lumpur* in chapter 7. Each bunk on the ship had a number but finding your way through the different decks to your own berth could be perplexing, especially for older village folk, probably on a ship or in such a space for the first time. Shipping companies tackled this by painting symbols instead of writing words: in this case, *buah manggis, buah durian, buah rambutan* – mangoes, durians and rambutans. You follow the picture to find your way to your berth. If you were stuck and lost, a Malay-speaking crew member would lead you around and ask, "Does anyone recognise this person?"

Habib Hassan Al-Attas, Imam of Ba'alwie mosque in Singapore experienced that, returning from Jeddah as a young man with his father in the *Malaysia Kita* in early 1972. Boarding the ship, he too saw pictures of tropical fruit painted up around the ship – rambutan, mangosteen, duku and others – with arrows directing clearly where they could be found. These were favourites and after spending many months in Saudi Arabia he was keen to make their acquaintance once again. So, after assisting his father to his cabin, he went out and followed the arrows. He went deck to deck but all that he found were just beds full of pilgrims. Tired and after searching for more than half an hour, he met the Chief Purser, Mr Osnain, and asked where he could get these fruits. Osnain just laughed. "Fruits? Sorry there are no fruits! These are names of '*kampungs*.'" [like villages] With more than one thousand pilgrims on board and so many being illiterate, the familiar was the easiest way to guide them to their sleeping places.[9]

To add to any discomfort in finding your way around, Aisha Angullia remembered it being, "very dark, and hot" inside the ship.

> Daytime they would go up on deck and rest and sleep there. Sometimes the captain would come and say it can be dangerous, you never know how the ship will move. But, *Alhamdulillah*, our journey was very smooth. We went during fasting month, Ramadan. From Singapore it was not yet Ramadan. We reached there in Ramadan. The whole month of Ramadan was in Mecca.

There is a gap of more than three months between Ramadan and the time of the hajj and this, too, made the journey different from modern days when the time spent on hajj is far shorter. And if we trace back to the nineteenth century, and especially in the time of sail, pilgrims would likely be away on hajj for at least a year and always when people travelled from Southeast Asia they took with them supplies of food.

> During our time we had to cook for ourselves. We bring our own food, our own rice in a big box; everything inside; our ingredients, our pots and pans, our *masalah*. We had to bring *batu lesong* [pestle and mortar], dried chillies, dried fish, all our ingredients, *lah*! But when we reached there we see everything already there. We see spices, and a lot of dried fish there. Our box was very heavy but there in Mecca one man picked it up by himself and carried it!

> The *makcik* from Kelantan, they take *ikan bilis*, they make like a pickle, it looked like *ulat*, like worms.

> They make like a salted durian and they bring that. I bring pickle; I bring salted fish, *serunding* [floss] – in a big tin; to eat there for the three months.

In times past when there was no food provided on board, one comment of ships' crews was that by the time the pilgrims were ready to return home, food such as the rice that they'd brought with them from home was often riddled with weevils and unfit for consumption. There was little or no nutritional value left in it for bodies – often, old bodies – that were exhausted after the rigours of the hajj.

Whatever hardships there were on the outward journey seemed far outweighed by the joy of arrival. For the two sisters there was Mecca and the sight of the Kaaba for the first time.

> When we saw the Kaaba we just can't control our tears. It was very nice to see Arafah; when you see you can't imagine what this place is; really meaningful for me.

Ust Hj Ali Hj Mohamed remembers the same kind of reaction; tears that cannot be explained in words.

> Your inner feelings change (approaching the Kaaba), and you don't know how but you start crying. It's different, depending on whether you are nearer or farther away. But of course you forget everything when you see the Kaaba. The only words from you are "*Labbayk Allah.*" *[Here I am, O Allah] – meaning here I am, to serve.*

From Jeddah to Mecca and Medinah the sisters travelled in a group; something that added the pleasant experience of community into what is an individual's undertaking.

> During the three months we were together we were like a family there. It was a bit cramped where we stayed in Mecca but we never

A note in their collection of photographs says, "Photos of friendship, goodwill and fond memories. . . taken in the holy land of Mecca." Picture courtesy of Aisha Angullia.

> mind as long as we are together. We were in the downstairs because the stairs were so big. They all can manage up and down but we two cannot. Upstairs were Afghans.

And then, after the culmination of the hajj at Arafah where Muslims accept that the last sermon of the Prophet Muhammad was given, and in leaving Mecca and boarding the ship to leave Jeddah, the feelings were clear. Just like the tears on arrival, they are feelings that have been echoed by thousands who have made the hajj.

> Very, very sad. You don't know where your tears come from.
>
> We always pray that one day we can come back again but we don't know when we can. We'd stayed there three months. We know a lot of people. We meet friends from all over the world.

That sense of community

What comes through from the account of the sisters is a clear sense of what happens when strangers on a common journey are drawn into a shared space and have time enough together. People met and spoke with one another, the ships became floating communities, and the journey itself became part of the experience and part of the learning.

In these last few years of the history of the kapal haji the pilgrims travelling on ships that left Singapore and touched at ports on the west coast of the Malay Peninsula would almost all be from Malaysia – both East Malaysia and West Malaysia – and from Brunei and Singapore. Those who came from Malaysia would include many who lived in the kinds of rural settings that had by then almost disappeared from an increasingly urbanised Singapore. Despite this there was much in common and many would have shared family links across the Causeway.

But in earlier times, and up to the middle of the twentieth century, both Singapore and Penang had served as gathering points for Muslims from across the Indonesian Archipelago and beyond, so the ship-borne communities would have been formed from backgrounds that were a good deal more diverse. A ship leaving one of these two ports could carry on it pilgrims from anywhere in those lands that are now Indonesia or Malaysia. It might have hajj pilgrims from the Philippines or China or Thailand, and this mixing and interacting was something that, at different times, caused concerns for colonial authorities. Those concerns can be seen in the security reports that the colonial powers commissioned; in the monitoring of some of those who travelled and even in attempts on the part of the Dutch to separate Hadhrami Arab travellers from other "Indonesians," something that we touch on later in this book.

The great draw of the Hajj

Amongst the many questions posed by outside observers is just how much pilgrims of the past, such as those from Southeast Asia, could have understood of the hajj experience if they did not understand Arabic. Questions such as these played their part in leading some colonial administrators and commentators to that mix of perplexed suspicion, misunderstanding and disparagement. And this included the view that the hajj was a place where anti-colonial sentiments could be stirred, so that the hajj was seen as a setting and a platform for "malcontents" to meet.

One of the many distinctive features of the place of Mecca and the Hajj is just how large a cross-section of aspirations, understandings, and of humanity are represented in those who have travelled there. Given those differences, in the meetings and interactions on the *Malaysia Kita* and in Mecca itself, the experience of the two sisters showed a glimpse of how common space was constructed and how working arrangements are created across languages. This was the case throughout the history of the kapal haji. There are many elements involved in understanding, and responses can be difficult to put into words.

Writing of his experience of the hajj in 1979, H.M. Jajuli described his response on entering the Great Mosque – the *Masjid Al-Haram* and seeing the Kaaba:

> This really is the house of God ... My body shakes, my heart pounds. Too weak to walk. I rest my body against a pillar and raise my arms upwards, high up, asking forgiveness, asking God not to judge my wickedness, asking for strength ... After praying, it is as if I am given new strength to approach the Kaaba.

The desire amongst Southeast Asian Muslims to make the hajj led to situations where, according to one source, "during the peak years [of the hajj – in the 1920s] no fewer than 52,000 pilgrims from Indonesia and 12,000 from Malaya congregated at Arafah, comprising well over half of the overseas [ie, non-Saudi] pilgrims present." These are very significant numbers.

The hajj might be seen as a kind of ritual of identity – the inviting of each pilgrim into a re-affirmation of what it means to be human, in terms of their relationship with God and with the rest of Creation. Whatever the individual's understanding of Arabic, from wherever their home in the world, Mecca is the place to which each of the pilgrims has turned in the daily rituals of their shared faith, and their arrival is a kind of culmination of a journey – both the "outer" one, as here on the ship, and the "inner."

In this book we look at a part of that outer journey; at the structures that needed to be put into place; and what it might have demanded.

• • • • • • • • • • • •

1 Laffan, Michael. 2011. *The Makings of Indonesian Islam: Orientalism and the Narration of a Sufi Past.* Princeton, New Jersey: Princeton University Press, p. 88.

2 From an interview with Anthony Green.

3 The Straits Times (hereinafter, ST). 9 January 1965.

4 ST. 1 March 1927.

5 ST. 10 September 1907.

6 All quotations from Hajjah Aisha Angullia and her sister are from an interview with Anthony Green.

7 The *Sa'i* is the ritual of running or hastened walking between the two hills of Safa and Marwah in memory of Hagar, the wife of Prophet Abraham (Ibrahim in Arabic) in her frantic search for water for their son Ishmael.

8 These are phrases of praise and acceptance frequently repeated by Muslims. "Subhannallah" – Glory to God; "Alhamdulillah" – combines the sense of all praise and all thanks being due to God; "La illa ha illallah, Allahu Akhbar – There is none worthy of worship except the One God.

9 Written correspondence from Imam Habib Hassan Al-Attas.

10 Matheson, V. and A.C. Milner. 1984. "Perception of the Haj: Five Malay Texts." *In Research Notes and Discussions Paper No. 46.* Singapore: Institute of Southeast Asian Studies, p. 33.

11 Ahmad Ishak, Md. Sidin and Mohammad Redzuan Othman. 2000. *The Malays in the Middle East.* Kuala Lumpur: University of Malaya Press. Footnote 38, p. 21.

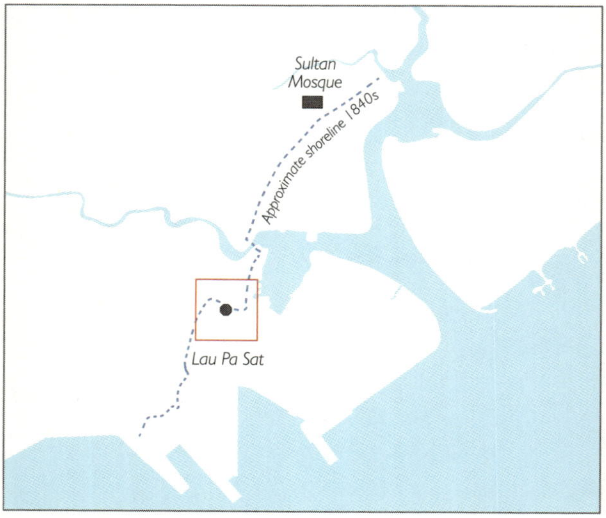

Lau Pa Sat

"The Market House," 17 April 1842. Charles A. Dyce, Watercolour on paper. Courtesy of the National Museum of Singapore, National Heritage Board. In the 1840s the old Telok Ayer Market jutted out into Telok Ayer Bay. The sea and all the trade associated with it was like a physical presence, feeding into the nearby Commercial Square and the city itself. Its successor, the building known as Lau Pa Sat, sits on the same site. But in modern times and after decades of land reclamation that site is firmly inland. The small outline map of the 2019 coastline (left) gives an indicator of the scale of the transformation.

2

Setting the scene:

Singapore as a port and a centre for the Hajj

A number of factors came together for Singapore to develop as a centre for hajj shipping in Southeast Asia. There had to be business networks to provide the infrastructure for shipping but there also had to be a cultural, social and religious setting that could speak the language of the hajj and provide what was needed by the Muslim community from across the region.

"Across the region" because one powerful, additional factor in this was the difference between the attitudes and policies towards Muslims of the colonial powers: the British in Singapore and the Malayan Peninsula, and the Dutch in the Netherlandsd East Indies, or what is modern day Indonesia.

A centre for business

For any place to act as a centre for business it needs to attract the necessary people, and for them to come there need to be compelling reasons. Location is one key driver. There must be opportunities and advantages for trade, and if the place is "young" or newly established, in a relatively short space of time there needs to be a coming together of a wide range of supporting and complementary enterprises: financiers – in this case the ones with the money to support the expense of purchasing ships; docking and repair services; businesses supplying "pure fresh water" for Ship Masters; information networks; and suppliers and markets for all kinds of goods – for ships and shipping companies and for the people passing through.

And for the hajj

To be a centre for hajj pilgrims there need to be factors of "push" and "pull"; of this place making easy what another is making difficult. In this case, Singapore was open to migration for work or transit in a way that the Netherlands East Indies, for long periods, was not. And within Singapore the area that was Kampong Glam brought together a rich mix of opportunities that belied its small size. In modern terms, Kampomg Glam "punched well above its weight."

Singapore as a port

The choice of Singapore as a port came well recommended. In February 1819, just after the arrival of Stamford Raffles in Singapore, a report was published by Captain Daniel Ross of the Bombay Marine. It described the advantages Capt. Ross saw in the Singapore Harbour:

> ... situated four miles to the N. N. E. of St John's Island, in what is commonly called the Singapore Straits, [it] will afford a safe anchorage to ships in all seasons, and being clear of hidden danger, the approach to it is rendered easy by day and night. Its position is also favourable for commanding the navigation of the Straits, the track which the ships pursue being distant about five miles; and it may be expected from its proximity to the Malayan Islands and China Seas, that in a short time numerous vessels will resort to it for commercial purposes.

That expectation that, "in a short time numerous vessels will resort to it for commercial purposes" seems, in hindsight, to be something of an understatement.

And as a free port – a place for business

When George Windsor Earl arrived from Batavia in 1833, his ship, the *Theodora*, with its Danish captain anchored for the night "a short distance from Singapore." It was eight p.m. on the 6th February and the journey from Batavia had taken them forty days.

Later he would make the same journey in just four days "with the monsoon favourable," or eleven days with it contrary. But this time the winds had been mixed and the currents against them and they'd frequently had to anchor. Such were the uncertainties of travelling by sail; uncertainties that could sometimes translate into real difficulties for hajj pilgrims to Jeddah in the days of sailing ships.

During the night a large Chinese junk had stopped close by. He reckoned there must have been "at least five hundred people on board" and when, an hour before sunrise, they began hoisting an enormous main sail, the noise for getting underway "could have been heard miles off."[2]

When daylight came, the town and shipping were enveloped in mist, so it was the morning gun fired from Mount Faber that made clear where they were.

> The rising sun soon cleared away the vapour, and afforded us a view of the "Queen of the Further East." Although so early, there was considerable bustle in the Roads; several ships were standing out under all sail, to proceed on their voyages, and on board the others the crews were aloft loosing the sails to dry.[3]

The sheer number of those ships, junks, and prahus was so great, that he could scarcely bring himself to believe that, fifteen years before this, Singapore had been a quiet place. Inland at that time there had already been gambier plantations, worked mostly by Chinese, but from the sea this forested island would have appeared in 1819 more like a scatter of villages around the coast than a trading port. Yet all the elements were there for trade and business to develop: a deep-water port, a location on what would become the busy sea-lanes at the meeting of the Malacca Straits and the South China Sea, and a very convenient transhipment centre for entrepôt trade, even if a certain amount of that trade came and went unchecked.

Removing "impositions and restrictions"

To the north, in 1786, and under instructions from the British East India Company, Francis Light had taken control of Penang and with that strategic position had developed an important port of call for ships from India headed for the Malacca Straits.

In Penang, Light had noted that if "Malay, Bugis and Chinese will come to reside here, it will become the Exchange of the East if not loaded with impositions and restrictions." Removing "restrictions" was seen as a key, so having Penang as a free port was an inducement.

At the southern end of the Malacca Straits in the contest between the British and the Dutch for commercial advantage and for control, the declaration by Raffles that, from the beginning, Singapore would be a free port must have served as one more attraction.

In the first half of the nineteenth century, newspapers had pages showing market prices of goods and giving details of commodities imported and exported, and often, across the top of such pages were words, like a kind of claim, to state and promote the situation in Singapore:

No duties on imports & exports and no port charges on vessels

Other places had also made such claims. On the way from Batavia George Windsor Earl had called in at the islands around Bintang. Earl remarked that the Dutch had made "Rhio" a free port, "with a view to encourage the natives of the Archipelago to visit it for the disposal of their produce," but there was no appearance of commercial activity when they arrived – just one ship at anchor near the town and no one seeming to be on board. He judged the Dutch move a costly failure, "since the native vessels from the eastward all pass it and proceed to Singapore, which is only forty miles distant."

In 1844 The Free Press in Singapore invited its "mercantile readers" and others "to compare the results produced by a monopoly and exclusion system" [in the Netherlands East Indies] "with those of a free system."[5]

Enterprising Merchants

Earl's feeling was that exemption from port duties alone would not be enough of an attraction for people to sell produce such as gambier and pepper from plantations in the group of islands around Bintang. These plantations were worked by Chinese planters who'd been invited there by Bugis "merchant-aristocrats" in the 1730s.[6] For him, what was also needed were "enterprising merchants," the kind who could attract confidence and under Stamford Raffles, Singapore had been active in identifying the enterprising and inviting them to establish themselves.

In Surabaya Earl had drunk mocha coffee with a man called Seyed Hasan who,

> ... complimented the English on the sound judgment which they had displayed in making Singapore a free port, its excellence being proved by the extensive commerce which the liberal system adopted there had attracted to the settlement.[7]

Those early invitees attracted to Singapore included Arab merchants, particularly those from the Hadhrami diaspora, who would play a key role in supporting the business of the hajj. These were people who had already established shipping networks around the Indonesian archipelago and the Straits of Malacca, and who also maintained connections with the Hadhramaut – their place of family links and family origin – and with the Hejaz; with Mecca and its surroundings. Their ships were large and suited to medium and longer-distance routes and with these connections and capacities they were ideally placed to play a major part in the transportation of hajj pilgrims.

Javanese port records from 1774 – 1777 show that while Arabs accounted for only two per cent of sea captains, "they operated the largest vessels after those of the Dutch East India Company"; vessels that were generally much larger than the ships owned by locally resident Chinese.[8]

But it wasn't just their size. On this occasion Dutch regulations worked in their favour. From 1818, in a move that was aimed mainly at blocking the

British, engagement in coastal shipping could only be by those who were resident in the Dutch colony. You had to be a Dutch subject to fly the Dutch tricolour. Many Hadhrami Arabs were in this category and in this situation the pace of development of their fleets was considerable. From owning 22 per cent of the registered tonnage of European rigged ships in 1820, they claimed ownership of 50 per cent by 1850.

Stepping ashore

What, then, was Singapore becoming? When Earl arrived there the sense of bustling activity that he had felt from the sea was intensified once they'd anchored:

> ... after breakfast I got into one of the numerous Malay *sampans* which surrounded [the ship], and in the course of five minutes had entered the creek and landed on the commercial wharf ... The wharfs were absolutely crowded with natives from all parts of India; vast numbers of Chinese labourers were dragging bales and boxes out of the merchants' warehouses and putting them into boats, where they were received by *kling*[9] boatmen from the Coromandel coast. At the landing-place the Malay *sampan* boys (who resign the laborious employment in the cargo-boats to the *klings*) were plying for hire; and on stepping on shore I was received by an obsequious Madras *dubash*, who offered to conduct 'master' to any part of the town to which he might wish to go.
>
> *[dubash: translator or interpreter]*

The "commercial wharf" he speaks of would have been somewhere along the short stretch from the Singapore River to the old Telok Ayer Market, which pushed out into the sea. This small area directly served the business centre of Commercial Square – now called Raffles Place – and until some time after the 1850s this was where the coastline ran. And both here and at Kampong Glam – then written as Campong Glam – cargoes were brought ashore, most of them at least.

Lt. Jackson's "Plan of the Town of Singapore" 1828. Survey Department Collection, courtesy of National Archives of Singapore.

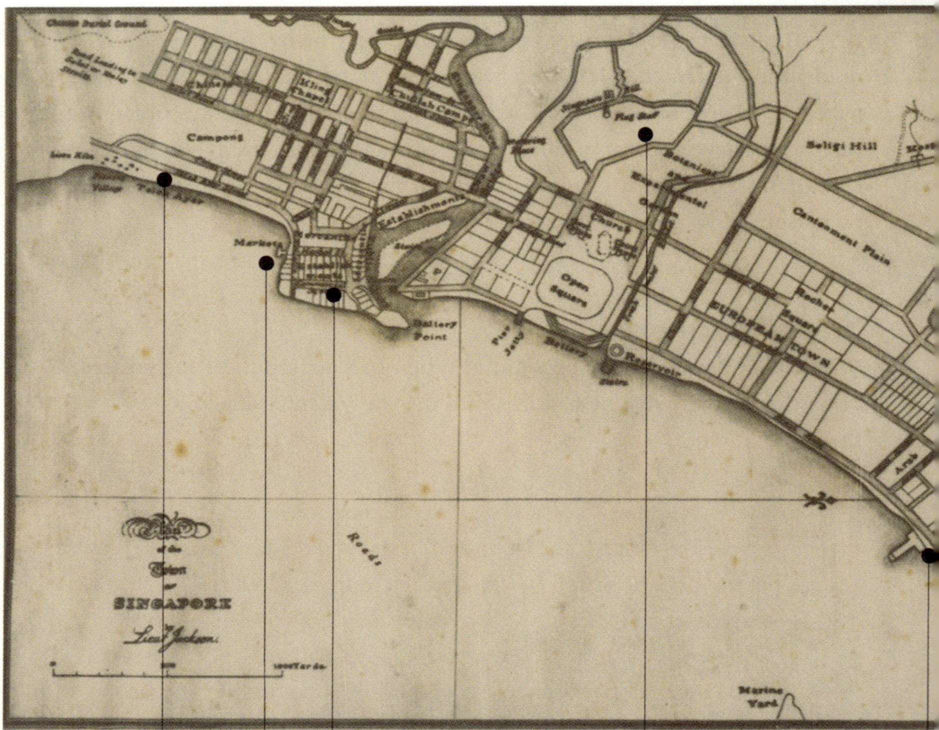

Telok Ayer Bay, fronted by Telok Ayer Street.

The Telok Ayer Market: predecessor of what is now Lau Pa Sat.

Commercial Square: now known as Raffles Place, in the Central Business District. It's in this area that George Windsor Earl would have disembarked in 1833.

Flagpost at Fort Canning (then called Government Hill), important for business communication with shipping.

Beach Road and the axis from the sea, through the Sultan's compound and the mosque.

Modern ports have a kind of sameness to them. Mechanised, automated cargo handling delivers impressive efficiency but rows of containers reveal nothing of what's inside. And aside from a flag on a ship's stern or the name of the port of registry there's little sense of where it has come from. Here, though, in Commercial Square and along the Singapore River, the sights, and noise – and, very likely, the smells – that would have greeted the new arrival must have seemed like a kind of organised chaos.

Sights, smells, sounds to greet the visitors

A list in *The Singapore Free Press and Mercantile Advertiser* in September 1841 detailed some of the vessels that had arrived in the previous year and gives a sense of the cargoes they carried and where they'd come from: Dutch and "Arab" ships, British and Danish brigs, Portuguese barques and Spanish schooners. And their cargoes?

- *Capt Bakar La Hamoody,* from "Bally" [Bali] – 4,500 pls [piculs] rice, 80 pls tobacco, 20 pls bêche de mer [sea cucumbers, known as *gamat,* in Malay], ¼ pl tortoiseshell, 40 ponies;

- Portuguese barque *Uniam,* Capt Remedios from Macao – 267 baskets tobacco, silk piece goods, 86½ pls raw silk, 80 pls galingals [galangal, or *langkuas* in Malay], 38½ pls sugar candy, 58 jars soy, 1 bx musk, 2,100 umbrellas, 189 pls tea, 600 gallons red and 1,200 gals madeira wine, 10,220 Spanish dollars;

- Arab ship *Futtay Rahman,* Capt Rahman, from Muskat – 1,515 pls and 1,000 jars dates, 12 pls coffee, 100 btls rose water, 10 cor turban, 1 cor carpets, 7,000 Spanish dollars.

- Dutch ship *Lord Minto*, Capt Aboobakar, from Palembang – 248 pls rattan, 135 pls coffee, 55 pls pepper, 2½ pls elephants teeth [probably tusks], 16 pls tobacco. 15 pls tallow, 7 pls betelnuts, 38 buncals gold dust, 42¼ buncals silverware, 26,960 guilders, 4 pls dragon's blood [Bright red resin used as varnish, medicine and dye, produced from rattan palms, and known as *jerang* or *djerang*].

The goods were an extraordinary mix: bees wax, saltpetre, betel nut, sherry, salt pork, sardines, Spanish dollars, tamarinds, rice, ghee, Java tobacco, salempores [a cotton from the Coromandel], indigo, "battick" handkerchiefs, chintz, raw silk, teak planks, arrack, castor oil, saffron, vermilion, rattans, copperware, tin, brasswire, spy glasses ... Patna and Benares opium by a British barque from Calcutta; gold dust and diamonds from Sambas in Borneo; birds' nests and fish maws from Palembang; 5,300 dollars, 596,000 "segars" [cigars], cowries and tortoiseshell by a Spanish brig from Manila. The list goes on.

"Native" shipping

But there are considerations that stand out from this. However detailed the lists of cargoes, "native traders" seemed often like another, parallel economy. To quote George Windsor Earl again:

> The Bugis, Chinese, and other native traders, do not land their goods for sale, but hold markets on their junks and prahus during their stay in port; and the traders established in the town go on board and purchase the goods which they require in small quantities, sometimes not exceeding in value four or five dollars.

In any listing in the English-language papers of shipping movements through the harbour, the names, tonnages, types of vessel, places of origin, consignees and next destination were all given, along with the name of the ship's master, so long as this man was European. In other cases, where the master was a "native" there was either a blank or the word "*Nakoda*" or "*Nacoda*."

> *From the Straits Times:*
> **Departures**
> **Monday 7th Dec. 1874**
> British barque, *Mary & Emma*, Nacoda, for Jeddah
>
> **March 1st 1883**
> Arrived, a brig from the westward under Dutch colours; belongs to some Arabs.

... and Kampong Glam

The trading records above relate mainly to European concerns and what was traded through Commercial Square, but around the Kallang River and in the area now known as *Kampung* (or *Kampong*) *Glam* and formerly known as *Seduyong*,[11] a range of activities existed. Through its identifiable social priorities, this location would come to be the point of attraction for aspiring or intending hajj pilgrims arriving in Singapore. It spoke a kind of "language" they could understand and the character and priorities of this area would be significantly different in a number of respects from the dominant, commercial culture and dynamics of the rest of Singapore.

Arab ships

In that mix of commerce in nineteenth century Singapore we find comments from Europeans on their impressions of the "Arab ships" from the Netherlands East Indies. This 1846 comment is from G.F. Davidson:

> Singapore is annually visited by a large fleet of vessels from all parts of Java: the most important of these are what are commonly called Arab ships, that is, ships fitted out and owned by Arabs residing in Java. They carry the Dutch flag, are commanded by Arabs, and manned by Javanese ... These Arab ships are built of teak, ranging from one hundred and fifty to five hundred tons per register, and are altogether remarkably fine vessels.[12]

... and Hajj sailings

Arab shipowners based in Dutch ports "captured the bulk of business with the British settlements in Malaya from the 1830s" and, it's been alleged, "independent Muslim rulers ... accorded Hadhrami *sayyid* shipowners a remission of duties, on account of their 'superior sanctity,'"[13] sayyids being those who claim descent from the Prophet Muhammed. One early ship-owning Hadhrami to arrive in Singapore was Syed Abdul Rahman Alsagoff (or al-Saqqâf) who arrived with his son, Syed Ahmad, in 1824 and it was Syed Ahmad who "initiate[d] a regular pilgrim service to Jiddah in the 1850s."[14]

And it seems clear that it was Arab ship owners who were recognised by the English language press as central in the transport of hajj pilgrims from Singapore.

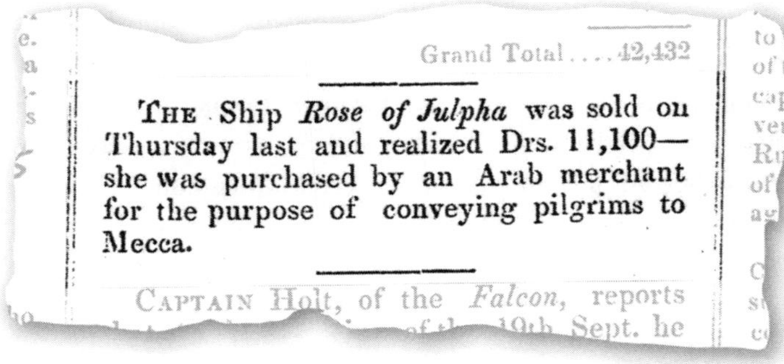
Grand Total....42,432

THE Ship *Rose of Julpha* was sold on Thursday last and realized Drs. 11,100— she was purchased by an Arab merchant for the purpose of conveying pilgrims to Mecca.

CAPTAIN Holt, of the *Falcon*, reports

October 1855: a Singapore newspaper reports a ship bought to carry hajj pilgrims.

A December 1855 article in the Singapore Free Press and Mercantile Advertiser was quite specific about which vessels were engaged in carrying the pilgrims to "Juddah" and who owned those ships. In recording that they were "now taking their departure" it described them as, "the Arab ships which annually carry pilgrims from this [meaning Singapore] to Arabia." In that year, according to the newspaper there were eight of them and they'd be carrying "from two thousand to thousand five hundred passengers in all."[15]

This raises the question about just why so many pilgrims would be travelling through Singapore, since this number did not originate from the island itself or from the Malay Peninsula, and it introduces the next element in the development of Singapore as a hub for hajj shipping: the near discouragement of the hajj by the NEI authorities in Indonesia. And that leads to the large issue of suspicion of the hajj – particularly by the Dutch but later also by the British – and the question of how the colonial authorities regarded the hajj, the situation in Mecca and the potential effects and influences that the time spent in the Hejaz might have on those making the journey.

Dutch Controls

In 1825 the NEI government in Batavia set conditions and regulations for anyone wishing to undertake the hajj. A special passport had to be bought at a cost of *fl* 110 (110 Dutch Guilders). But, just as water, when blocked, will always find a new course, would-be pilgrims would simply find a way around the restriction by travelling through Sumatra or Singapore and in 1852 the rule was abandoned. Seven years later, a new rule meant that each haji had to prove they had "sufficient funds to undertake the pilgrimage and support families left behind."

That requirement for "sufficient funds" was in marked contrast to the experience within the Hejaz where colonial authorities struggled with considerable numbers of hajj pilgrims – especially from India – who arrived without money enough to return home and who often ended up destitute and starving, and begging for repatriation, in front of the British consulate in Jeddah, only – in some cases – to return to the Hejaz in some subsequent year.

The Dutch regulations demanded that once they arrived in Jeddah the pilgrims had to report to the Dutch Consul and on their return, and before they could adopt the title and dress of a *haji*,[16] they would be questioned by Javanese officials to confirm that they had actually gone to Mecca, as opposed to spending time in a place such as Singapore and claiming that they had completed the hajj, a situation that led to applying that oft-repeated labelling of such people as "*Haji Singapura*."

A source of passengers

Internally, within Java, communications networks were improving by the beginning of the nineteenth century. Michael Laffan points to the completion of the Great Post Road in 1808, connecting Anyer in the west of Java with Panarukan at the eastern end so that, by the 1840s, *pondoks* near the main towns became key points of intellectual exchange for religious students. From there advanced students could connect with greater numbers of Arab scholars in the larger ports. That led to "two major destinations in this network, ... Surabaya ... and Singapore."[17] For its part in this web of connections Singapore would also come to be a very significant centre for Malay-language printing and publication; a centre for the spread of religious literature, at a time when different religious interpretations were competing with one another.

Arab shipping links provided regular connections out of Java and Sumatra but for a prospective hajj pilgrim or student of Islam seeking to reach the Hejaz there were many ways of getting from Indonesia to a less obstructive Singapore. G.E. Davidson also mentions another group of "native traders" – the Bugis, who he described as being next in importance to the Chinese as traders, and who he recognised as "essentially a maritime people."

> On an average two hundred of these boats come to Singapore in the fall of each year, each manned by about thirty men.[18]

He acknowledges the level of illicit trade for which "the coast of Java offers many facilities in its numerous small rivers, with which the Arab shipmaster is intimately acquainted." And in the journeys of all of these ships carrying cargoes there was the opportunity for prospective pilgrims to travel quite easily from the Indonesian islands to places where the opportunity to make the hajj pilgrimage would be less constrained by officialdom.

The disincentives put in place by the Dutch to control the hajj served in turn as powerful incentives for the development of a hajj trade under its British-ruled neighbour. But attitudes also have to be remarked on. In his exhaustive recording of Malay printing and publishing, Ian Proudfoot cites a comment at the end of the nineteenth century by the Dutch scholar Christiaan Snouck Hurgronje who served as an advisor to the Netherlands East Indies. In "*Ambtelijke Adviezen*" (Official Advice) Snouck contrasted Dutch policy with the policies in British territories: "*waar hadji en goeroe ... als de Engelschman*" – where "a *haji* or a *guru* [could] circulate in the Malay lands as freely as an Englishman, coming to police notice only if he breaks the law."[19]

Proudfoot adds that,

> For Arabs resident in the Netherlands Indies a bitter grievance was their legal classification as Foreign Orientals, subject to pass laws, while the Japanese were given European privileges.[20]

Years later, in the 1920s and 1930s, something of this would emerge in the policies of the "*Kongsi Tiga*" – the three Dutch shipping companies in Indonesia that worked together to maintain a monopoly over sailings from the Netherlands East Indies to Jeddah, and who also "systematically [segregated] passengers along racial, ethnic, and class lines," since they were "worried that 'dangerous' passengers, such as Hadrami Arabs and Meccan sheikhs, would influence the general 'spirit' of Indonesian pilgrims onboard by encouraging anti-colonial, nationalistic, and pan-Islamic sentiments."[21]

Trade and trading vessels – Networks of companies linking together

With the opening up of Singapore from 1819, Asian traders – the Arabs, Chinese, Indians and Bugis – were joined in fairly quick succession by the establishment of trading houses by Europeans who saw the very considerable business opportunities. In the space of the next sixty years it would be Europeans who would effectively remove the advantages that Asian ship-owners had enjoyed, and would, in fact, gain a monopoly over the business of the hajj itself.

There are many examples. Alexander Guthrie arrived in Singapore in 1821 and set up business in 1823 to sell British goods and act as an agent for shipping and banking. The merchant, Edward Boustead, arrived in March 1828 from China and, though no longer operating in Singapore, the import and export and shipping business of the company Paterson Simons can be traced back to 1821.

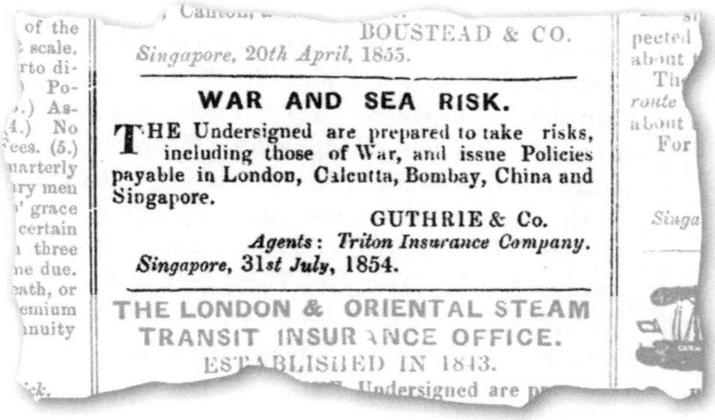

BOUSTEAD & CO.

Singapore, 20th April, 1855.

WAR AND SEA RISK.

THE Undersigned are prepared to take risks, including those of War, and issue Policies payable in London, Calcutta, Bombay, China and Singapore.

GUTHRIE & Co.

Agents: Triton Insurance Company.

Singapore, 31st July, 1854.

THE LONDON & ORIENTAL STEAM TRANSIT INSURANCE OFFICE.

ESTABLISHED IN 1843.

Seaborne trade was a vital core of economic life. Securing that life against threats opened up business opportunities. In this example the trading house of Guthrie & Co offering "War and Sea Risk" insurance.

Some of these names appear often in shipping related documents – as consignees; as providers of mortgages; as sources for ships; as providers of insurance; and as "connectors": people involved somewhere in the chains of supply or sourcing of vessels or cargoes.

A FAMILY HOTEL ADJOINING.

NOTICE.—LLOYDS.

WE request that particulars of all cases of shipwreck be communicated to us by the Master or survivors on their reaching this Port, for the information of the Underwriters in London.

SYME and CO—*Lloyd's Agents.*

***Singapore, 20th May* 1851.**

As a service "Masters of Vessels" could, for a small charge, pay Syme & Co to send a telegram to Lloyds in London, reporting their ship's safe arrival.

Co[illegible] merchants, Ship masters and Supercargoes buying for other markets will be treated with on the most liberal terms.

S. M. PUCKRIDGE.

COMMERCIAL SQUARE.

SHIP CHANDLER.

AND GENERAL STORE DEALER.

S. M. P. begs to announce to Ship-owners, Merchants, Commanders of vessels, and the Public generally, that he has always on hand every description of ship and cabin stores at the lowest prices.

Canvas, Twine, Europe and Calcutta—Cordage. Bunting, Blocks, Paint oils, Wood and Lamp oil, Varnishes, Turpentine, Tar, Pitch and Rosin, Soap and Candles, Gunpowder. Cheroots and Tobacco. Glassware. Salt provisions. Flour in Barrel. Vinegar and Lime Juice. Oilman's, Grocery and Dry stores. Wines, Beer, Porter, Brandy, Whiskey, Gin, Old Tom, Arrack, &c. &c.

Shipping supplied with Fresh Water, Firewood and Sea Stock with all despatch.

Ship Chandlers – many based in or near Commercial Square – advertised long, detailed lists of all of the items they could supply for ships and their crews. This is a small part of an advertisement in the 1860s. S.M.Puckridge had been operating since at least the 1840s when they were advertising their service of accurately setting "chronometers" and – a very different service – providing "soda water and lemonade." The accurate setting of chronometers was essential in order to calculate longitude when at sea.

On at least two occasions in 1872 Guthrie & Co. were named as consignees for newly built steamships from Glasgow that had called at Jeddah on their way to Singapore: the *Ban Yong Seng*, on delivery to Chinese owners in May, and the somewhat ill-fated Alsagoff ship, named *Jeddah*, on delivery in November. In the case of the *S. S. Jeddah* and ships run by the Alsagoff family, the involvement of the Guthrie company seems to have involved much more than merely acting as consignees, something that is touched on in chapter 8.

Built in 1852 or 1853, the *Fathool Carrim*, a sailing ship of 1,216 tons and one of the largest at that time to arrive in Jeddah,[22] was owned by Syed Massim (or Mohsen) Al Joofree, another Hadhrami ship owner and trader. But the ship registration records for the *Fathool Carrim* record a mortgage "dated 15th February 1865 for $4,259 & cents 82" under the names "William Wemyss Ker, William Paterson & Henry Minchin Simons of Singapore, Merchants, trading under the firm or style of Paterson Simons."

Paterson Simons were again listed as mortgagees for the 659-ton sailing ship, *Kangaroo,* a vessel with a dubious record for safety and seaworthiness, owned by "Hadjee Mahomed Allie of Singapore, Trader" in 1861, and built at Sunderland, County Durham in England in 1853.

Business was business. The mortgagees were many and varied and cut across any lines of race. The 1861 Ship Registry listed the 888-ton *Faidthul Illah* as another ship being owned by Syed Ahmad Alsagoff. Its mortgagees included "Tan Quee Lan" and "Lee Bong Lim," (perhaps "Sze Bong Lim") both variously listed as traders or merchants.

Paterson Simons developed a wide range of interests. The company traces back to a business set up in Singapore in 1821. Ker arrived in Singapore in 1828 and Paterson and Simons were admitted as partners in 1853. They began with import-export but spread to include agencies for shipping lines, insurance companies, governments and more. They traded rubber, tin, gambier, copra and, importantly, pioneered the export of gutta-percha, a product that's still used in root canal treatment and was once used in submarine communication cables, where it provided an insulator "that would not crumble underwater."

The submarine cables laid globally grew from about 15,000 nautical miles in 1866 to over 200,000 nautical miles by 1900. Insulated by a sheath of gutta percha, this global cable network was often referred to in the 19th century as the "nervous system" of the British Empire and of world commerce, as it constituted a key means by which modern technology extended its reach around the world.[23]

Whilst not directly involved in the business of the hajj they provide an example of just how much profit could be made out of the trade and products of Southeast Asia and how businesses were connected. When they were not sailing to Jeddah the ships of the Alsagoff or Aljoofree families were sailing for ports all around the region. The core business of Paterson Simons was trade and cargo in the same way as Arab traders but, as the 1905 advertisement belowindicates, their links included Jeddah and the Red Sea.

---

s.s. "Den of Airlie"
(Captain J. Gumming) now in port will leave for
Jeddah and Red Sea ports on or about the 19th instant.
For Freight etc. Apply to
PATERSON, SIMONS & CO., Agents.
Sept 15
(advertisement 18 Sep 1905)

Docks

Harbours and docks compete with one another in claims to provide the best, or quickest, or most convenient service. The first graving dock (or dry dock) in Singapore was constructed in 1859. By 1852 the P&O had its own private wharf at what is now Keppel Harbour. The Tanjong Pagar Dock Company was set up in 1865 and the Victoria Dock in 1868.

With the arrival of larger numbers of ships powered by steam, coaling stations were needed. Coal came from Japan, Australia, India and Wales, with some more locally from Borneo, Sumatra and Sarawak. To supply a coal-burning ship in the 1920s, nothing was mechanised. Pairs of "coolies" – presumably Chinese labourers – would carry a basket of coal between them on a bamboo pole, each basket weighing 160lbs. (72.5kg); 14 baskets equalling 0.9 tonnes. The harbour record in 1921 was to re-supply a man-of-war with 21,000 baskets (1,370 tonnes) in this way in just five hours.

The relevance of these odd statistics is to reinforce just how intense and driven was the commercial activity of Singapore. And in the 1920s, when about 12,000 pilgrims were recorded as embarking at these wharves annually, and with many of them coming from small islands or communities across the region, one can wonder what impression they would have formed of the out-and-out industry and energy before them.[24]

Steamships and changing fortunes

An announcement in the Straits Times in September 1872 for the Singapore Steamship Company reveals another example of the business connections that existed but in its timing it also pointed, ironically, to impending changes in the hajj business that would take this out of the hands of Arab and Asian owners.

By this stage the company was run by Syed Ahmad's son, Syed Mohammed Alsagoff, known as *Nong Cik*, but looking at the picture of the company's experiences it can be said that whilst pilgrim numbers were increasing, the advent of steamships would open up Arab ship owners to a level of competition to which they would be unable to respond. The 1872 report said that the company,

> . . . is establishing a line of steamers to run between Singapore and Jeddah, for the purpose of carrying pilgrims. There are, we understand, steamers building at home for this line, but the Company some time ago purchased the steamer *Sunfoo*, which having completed her then existing engagement is now to be taken over by them and

will proceed to Jeddah shortly. The undertaking is one that ought to receive encouragement, as the Company send small steamers down to the Dutch ports to bring intending pilgrims to Singapore.[25]

If the aim was to "establish" a line of steamers it has to be said that it was never achieved and in the course of just twelve years – between 1872 and February 1885 – the Singapore Steamship Company would experience significant setbacks. Before moving on to discuss this though, one phrase in this brief report might deserve a remark: in the light of any discussion of the hajj as provoking anti-colonial sentiment, the idea of "steamers building *at home*" seems a tiny indicator of colonial identity and orientations. Southeast Asia was not "home" to the colonial mindset. It was, however, home to others.

The *Sunfoo* had been bought for £35,000 in June of that year with the intention to use it on the hajj route but it appears to have been used just twice for that purpose – in September and then in December – stopping at Malacca and Penang on one of those voyages. In 1873 James Guthrie of Guthrie and Co. had joined with others to form a shipping line with mail and passenger services connecting Southeast Asia and China with Australia. This was the Eastern & Australasian Mail Steamship Co. and the *Sunfoo* was sailed from Singapore to Australia that year with Guthrie and Co. as consignees and at least two of the captains were masters who had sailed for the Alsagoffs also sailed for Guthrie and Co. Whether the Singapore Steamship Company had sold the ship to Guthrie at that stage is not clear but on a voyage to Hong Kong in March 1874 the ship struck a reef and was wrecked.[26]

Another setback to the Alsagoffs came a year later. At 4.45 am on 1 October 1875, their hajj steamer, the *S.S. Medina*, was stranded on rocks south of Hudaida in the Red Sea and started to break up. Four days later the master and crew abandoned the ship. Passengers had to be transferred to another pilgrim ship, the *S.S. Timor* but only after the *Medina*'s master was forced to agree to a kind of salvage fee of £4,000. In the process of transferring to the *Timor* some of the pilgrims had their money stolen – in one case, quite a significant amount – and they protested vigorously through the Dutch authorities but, more significantly for the Alsagoff company itself, a court case ensued because they claimed that "the agreement had been extracted from the master of the *Medina* under duress." Whilst the court in Britain upheld their claim, the attention that court cases bring is not something that companies normally welcome, and they would face another experience of negative publicity within five years.

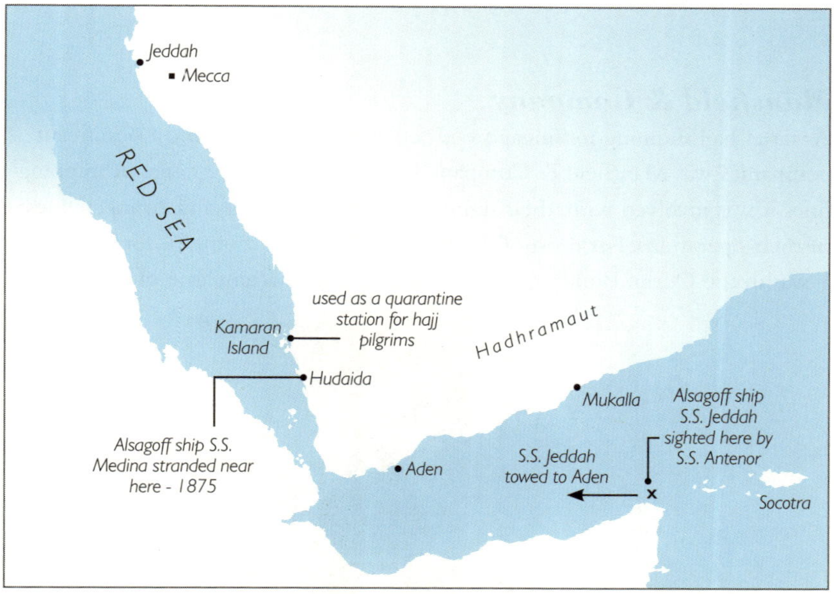

Which brings us to the ship, *Jeddah*. When Syed Mohammed ordered his steamer that was being built "at home" and wanted some changes in the design, the confirmation to the shipbuilder that the price for the changes was acceptable came from Guthrie and company. And there is a comment here that is telling. When the order for the vessel was placed with the Scottish shipyard written in upper case were the words, "TIME IS AN OBJECT."[27] Just what exactly was intended by that phrase cannot be known for sure but Syed Mohammed was a businessman and he must have been able to read the signs. So it should be noted that on 17 November 1869, less than two years before he ordered his ship, the Suez Canal had been opened, creating a sea route that would carve distance and time out of the journey between Asia and Europe.

With Suez and the development of reliable, long-distance steamships the control of sea routes would shift still further and European shipping companies would come to dominate.

In 1880 the *Jeddah* would be involved in an incident that caused a good degree of public outrage and indignation, and this will be spoken of in chapter 8. Here though, one more company needs to be introduced.

Mansfield & Company

As far as hajj shipping in Singapore is concerned one of the most significant companies was Mansfield & Company, both in terms of the range of shipping lines it was involved with, their significance, and the scope and connectedness of their operations. For most of their time in business, "home" – for Mansfields – was in the Ocean Building in Singapore and this became one of the key

The Ocean Building in the 1930s; the home of Mansfields. Picture sourced from Blue Funnel and Glen Line Bulletin; reproduced courtesy of John Swire & Sons Limited.

centres of hajj shipping activity, although in 1870 they moved for a time to De Souza Street, by modern-day Raffles Place. There, from the corner of the office,

> ... it was possible to see Fort Canning Flagstaff from one window. As the House Flag at Fort Canning was the only indication of the arrival of a ship, this viewpoint was invaluable in those days.[28]

That flagstaff still stands, though now unadorned and skeleton-like, but in the nineteenth century it was an important communication device for those on land and for ships arriving. Information flowed through these arms.

All shipping companies had a "house flag" so the ship's owners could be identified. This is the Alfred Holt house flag on the S.S. Tyndareus, being taken down in Hong Kong where the ship went to be scrapped in 1960. Picture by permission of John Spain.

Flags, Messaging, and Business Communication

The Fort Canning flagstaff as it stands now. Photograph – Anthony Green.

Flags played a key role, as is clear from a complaint to the newspaper in August 1874:

SIR,—The trees on Fort Canning Hill have within the past few years grown to such dimensions that they interrupt the view of the Flagstaff from many of the residences at Tanglin,—mine among the number, though situated at the top of a high hill immediately in the rear of the Fort,—and it is impossible to make out the signals that are almost constantly displayed, which is so necessary for business men to watch closely.

Ships arriving in a port had to identify themselves and a failure to do so could lead to a financial penalty. A vessel passing the port could also communicate, as in September 1886, when the steamer *Bancoora* could signal to the flagstaff her name and owners; that she had a shipment of horses, westbound, from Australia for Calcutta; and that all was well on board.

Accurate information (and business advantage) depended on a degree of vigilance and the proper use of telescopes, and criticism came when those at the flagstaff got it wrong – as, for instance, hoisting "the P. & O. Flag . . . when the French steamer was coming in," and not correcting that until the ship was entering the harbour. Or for using the wrong set of signals: the Marryatt Code of Signals when they'd been replaced by the Commercial Code.

But at sea, from ship to ship, flag signals could range from a request to report the reassuring "all well" to messages of far greater urgency; an urgency that is clear in the example of the *Jeddah* that we describe in a later chapter.

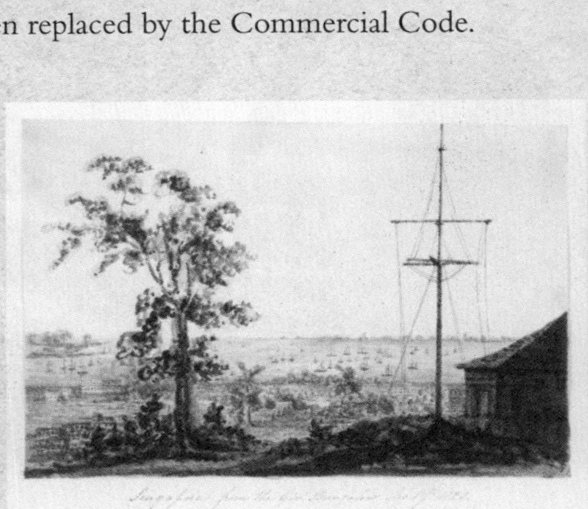

1828 painting by James Marianne of "Singapore from the Govt Bungalow" (on what was then called Government Hill). Courtesy of the National Museum of Singapore, National Heritage Board.

Mansfields was the company that founded Malayan Airways Ltd in 1947 – the precursor of today's Singapore Airlines and Malaysian Airlines System. In 1934 they became the agents for Imperial Airways when their air service from London to Singapore was inaugurated, and in 1934 the agents for QANTAS when their service from Australia linked with Imperial. Together with their extensive shipping links around Southeast Asia Mansfields played a significant part in travel through the region.

There are many examples of people – whether well-informed or just following a hunch – who have made what turned out to be very sound business decisions. In 1859, George Mansfield set up in Singapore as a ships' chandler. Four years later, in 1863, he died on a visit to London and his brother, Walter Mansfield travelled to Singapore to wind up his estate and take over the business. Then, in November 1865 George Mansfield's 16-year old son travelled alone to Singapore to join his uncle.

The next year, 1866, the Alfred Holt & Company ship *Agamemnon* inaugurated their service "to the Far East" for their Blue Funnel Line. At Singapore the ship was consigned to Syme & Company who were the agents for Lloyds, but Holt thought they were "unduly expensive." Captain Middleton, the ship's master, recommended that if the agency were to be transferred it should be to Walter Mansfield. And so it was agreed that Mansfields would be offered the agency for Blue Funnel Line.

In 1923 another Mansfield – George John Mansfield – recalled the doubts he'd heard expressed at the time:

> My recollection takes me back to 1867 when I saw the old *Agamemnon* just arrived in Singapore, lying in the harbour. No one had any idea in those days of the probable growth of the Blue Funnel Line, except my uncle, Walter Mansfield, who as an old Liverpudlian, recognised who A. Holt was! A great friend . . . thought otherwise and told me, a youngster, 'Have a look at that ship for she won't be here again—she can't pay or stand up against the P. & O. Co.' —and about 18 months afterwards he was dead and my uncle was agent.[29]

Aside from the Blue Funnel Line, Mansfields became agents for the China Navigation Company (CNCo) of Hong Kong, the company run by John Swires, and for a number of coastal operators including the Straits Steamship Company – the "little white fleet" as it was sometimes known. Holts and CNCo had close business connections and understandings.

Importantly, the business of the "carriage of pilgrims between the Straits and Jeddah ... was carried on in connection with Alsagoff & Company, who acted as the passage broker."[30] This meant that tickets had to be bought through the Alsagoff company, something that led to at least one court case when a pilgrim broker tried to buy tickets directly from Mansfields.

• • • • • • • • • • •

The sea connects

The vast majority of us live our lives on land. The sea is, for many, something unknown and maybe even to be feared. But it's a well-worn saying that the sea connects. For those who live on islands and for many coastal dwellers, the sea is the lifeline and up to the middle of the twentieth century coastal shipping was a very significant means of getting around in the Malay Peninsula, across to Sabah and Sarawak and the Southern Philippines, and around Indonesia.

From Malacca to Singapore, by sea

In January 1927, as the hajj approached, a news comment said:

> Malacca is daily witnessing the departure from the jetty of many Malays from all parts of the Settlement for Singapore on the pilgrimage to Mecca. More than 400 persons in the Central District have taken out pilgrim passes.[31]

Even in a smaller way, connections were across water. Until the construction of the Causeway from Johore in Southern Malaya and the opening of the railway line in October 1923 any goods or passengers travelling from the

Peninsula to Singapore had to cross by ferry. The road followed eight months later.

A sense of the scope of coastal shipping can be seen in the map of "services maintained by Straits Steamship Company Ltd., 1935," shown on the next page. Companies like the Straits Steamship Company had a network that, as the time for the hajj approached, could serve as a kind of feeder service for the hajj ships leaving for Jeddah. Add to that the fact that this was another company represented by Mansfields in Singapore, and the result is a close and very effective linkage.

This use of the sea was there even in small, local settings. Interviewed in 2007, Haji Mohamed Suppien Haji Mokree remembered that even in the late 1960s in a place like Sembawang in the north-east of Singapore, if there was a funeral the quickest way to get to the nearest cemetery was to take the body by sampan around the coast rather than by land.[32]

Coastal shipping – the time before roads

Small ships don't need big ports and all around Southeast Asia small ships came to river mouths and jetties.

Straits Steamship and its subsidiaries – the Sarawak Steamship Company in Kuching and the Sabah Steamship Company in Sandakan – were described as "linking ports and parts of the territory that otherwise were completely isolated from each other"[33] and as "venturing into every minor creek and waterway to provide for trade to and from the outside world."[34] A Straits Steamship vessel would arrive in Sandakan from Singapore on a Saturday afternoon, and a Sabah vessel would leave on the Monday, sailing south. Other, fortnightly, sailings would go north and across to Jolo and Zamboanga in the southern Philippines. Since the Straits Steamship network and their associated companies were linked with Holts, Mansfields were their agents and Singapore was their point of orientation. With services to the southern Philippines, this was one of the ways in which the so-called "Moro"[35] Muslims of that region could make the hajj journey, linking with ships in Singapore.

K.G.Tregonning wrote that,

> ... with the arrival of the Sabah Steamship vessels, captained by their own faith and managed by non-ideologically inclined Britons, the way to Mecca was clear. From Sultans downwards, the Suluks joyously responded.
>
> Sabah Steamship Company employed mainly Malays from Brunei or Labuan as *serangs*, or captains. They had a very familiar knowledge of the whole coast [i.e., north Borneo] from Kuching to Tawau, having lived there fishing and sailing all their lives. Their reputation as sailors was second to none ...[36]

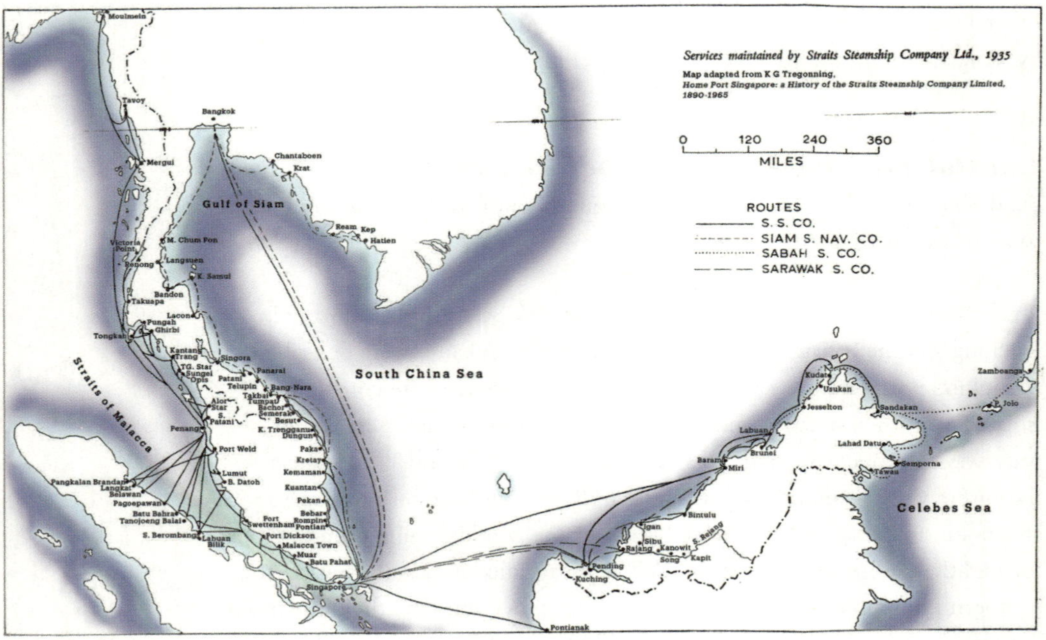

Image by Umar Green.

This kind of connectivity highlights another aspect of the interactions between communities in Southeast Asia; in this case, the multi-religious and multi-cultural complexion of the society.

> From the late nineteenth century in particular ... and with land travel still inadequate, a most astonishing number were found lying on their rattan mats or squatting in groups on the decks of the Straits ships ... a Buddhist monk next to a Muslim *hadji*; Sikhs; Malays; a half-naked Dyak; and a Dusun policeman; a Murut and a Suluk; a Javanese and an Achinese; Muslims returning from Mecca, a Nepalese seller of precious stones, a Tamil rubber tapper, an Arab coming from his shop in Tunis, and above all, Chinese ...[37]

In time Straits Steamship took over "the runs up the East Coast of the Malay Peninsula and northwards to Bangkok" from the Siam Steam Navigation Company, whose "experienced Danish Masters" had sailed the coast through many years without a single loss."[38]

Since the company's ships were, carrying both cargo and passengers, like so many ships that feature in the hajj journeys, it deserves recording that a major cargo carried by Straits Steamship from Kuala Trengganu in the 1930s was dried fish – sometimes "as much as $50,000 worth" for consumption in Singapore. The smell on board may have been interesting![39]

And for prospective hajj pilgrims, if the need to travel fell during the north-east monsoon, the journey would be more difficult. K. G. Tregonning described it in this way:

> The east coast of the Malayan Peninsula faced the fury of the north-east monsoon. The full effect was felt in early December, when it was *katup kuala*, or the closing of the river mouth and the end of all fishing for the Malay people ... Heavy rains, strong winds and pounding seas would lash the villages and beaches and play havoc with the schedules of the small craft from Singapore. Often they had to seek shelter

behind the Perhentian Islands, Pulau Tioman or elsewhere. Since they were not equipped with wireless telegraphy, from the point of view of the Singapore office they would vanish into the blue.[40]

... unable to stop crowds

The mention of "experienced Danish masters" introduces another side-story into the hajj experience. One of the long-serving companies in Southeast Asian coastal shipping was the East Asiatic Company based in Copenhagen but with operations centred on Bangkok. Their ships ran down the east coast of the Isthmus of Kra and the Malay Peninsula, stopping at small river mouths and picking up cargo and passengers along the way. An incident with one of their ships in 1906 provides a nice example of how the irresistible force of hajj intentions could meet the immovable object of shipping company timetables and lead to a classic case of apparently unstoppable overcrowding. When connections to get you to your destination are not strong or frequent you take every chance you can get.

In September of that year the East Asiatic Company's shipmaster, Captain Danholt, found himself in a Singapore court, prosecuted for arriving with a ship loaded far beyond its licensed number of passengers. The Senior Boarding Officer of the Master Attendant's Department had found about 240 passengers on board and realised that the space usually occupied by passengers was already taken up by 149 cattle and 109 pigs – a challenging, and perhaps unpleasant, mix!

Danholt's ship, the *Chakrabhongs* had arrived at Khota Bahru in Kelantan from Bangkok. She'd barely cast anchor when "over two hundred pilgrims rushed on board and took up their quarters to come to Singapore." A witness, Mr. John Lindeberg, said he saw a "real struggle" going on. "As soon as the natives were driven from one side of the ship they swarmed up the other and would not leave."

The fare from Kelantan to Singapore was $4 but for this perhaps unavoidable misdemeanour Danholt was fined $50 and $5 for every passenger in excess carried – "the excess number the Court holding to be 207," the penalty the Company had to pay coming to $1,085.

His defence lawyer, Mr. Allen promised to appeal and argued that, "it was well known that these natives when going on a pilgrimage fought and struggled to get aboard the ship they meant to go by. The Captain was powerless to make them leave the ship."[41]

The Office of the Master Attendant

At all ports under the control of the British Empire a Master Attendant would be appointed to supervise all aspects of shipping in that port. In Singapore the Master Attendant's pier was by the Post Office building – now the Fullerton Hotel – and in front of his office. As far as ships were concerned, that supervision called for surveying and registering them, and determining whether or not they were seaworthy and what their carrying capacities were. And yet there were times in the nineteenth century when that scrutiny seemed to fall short.

Connections: Penang or Singapore?

From the early nineteenth century the two main points of departure for the kapal haji were Penang and Singapore. As the first port of call on the Malay Peninsula for ships coming from the Indian Ocean, Penang became a major hajj port for pilgrims from across the Malacca Straits in Sumatra, from the peninsula itself, and from places further north. So when the ship *Anking* left Penang in May 1960 its passenger list included 50 from Thailand and 24 from Cambodia.[42]

But for any prospective pilgrim from the northerly, east coast states of the Malay Peninsula – Pahang, Terengganu, Kelantan – the question is of what route would you take to board a hajj ship?

If most of the development of the Malay Peninsula from about 1750 onwards was along the west coast of the peninsula, when it came to transport up and down the east coast, from Johore in the south to Kelantan in the north the road options were very limited.

As late as December 1964, if pilgrims from Kelantan and the north-east states intended to go to Penang to catch the pilgrim ships in the following year, the Pilgrimage Control Officer in Penang, Haji Ali Rouse could be advising them to obtain border passes to travel via Thailand. "The passes, he said, should be valid for at least six months."[43]

This was before the development of a full network of roads down the east coast or across the peninsula.

Before the 215 kilometre long East-West Highway from Kelantan was opened in 1982 the journey across to the west of the Malay Peninsula was about 1,000 kilometres. The difference made by the new road was clearly considerable. That is perhaps one reason why a steady stream of pilgrims travelled each year from the east coast states to take a hajj ship from Singapore.

Writing in 1951 one observer commented on the lack of a single, uninterrupted road up the sparsely populated coast. The road was like a series of sections:

> It may surprise most people that even today there is no through communication between Johore and Kelantan except by sea. Road communication ceases abruptly some 70 miles north of Johore Bahru and there is no other motorable road communication except from Pekan (Pahang) to Khota Bahru (Kelantan) and most of this was constructed during the Japanese regime.[44]

The present coastal route runs beside the South China Sea but it took until independence from Britain for a road to be completed. Yet for many, during the years of the kapal haji, that would not be an easy journey. Even allowing for the fact that dates of birth given on birth certificates were not always accurate, many of these people were old, some very old.

Who travelled these roads?

In April 1963 the oldest pilgrim was said to be Che Mek binte Osman from Kelantan, the 101-year-old wife of a fisherman, "who had to be helped aboard." Time and again the ages stand out from the newspaper accounts. A 1967 account of the return journey of the ship *Kuala Lumpur* reads:

> Oldest pilgrim, aged 103, dies on return voyage. Haji Mahmood bin Haji Raoh died in the pilgrim ship *Kuala Lumpur* soon after the vessel left Jeddah on its return voyage.
>
> The death of Haji Mahmood, of Nibong Tebal and three other pilgrims was announced here [Penang] today when the *Kuala Lumpur* arrived ...
>
> The other three pilgrims – Haji Ariff bin Tambi, 84, of Malacca, Hajjah Khatijah binte Haji Yusoff, 64, of Kubang Semang, Province Wellesley, and Hajjah Niyah binte Salleh, 69, of Tampin, Negri Sembilan – died while the ship was in the Indian Ocean. [45]

In June of that year, the oldest pilgrim returning on the *Anshun* was Inche Dasin bin Osman, 102, from Singapore.

This list of ages adds a layer to our reckoning of the challenge of the journey.

Bridges down the east coast of the Malayan Peninsula

It was only in December 1961, just four years after Malaysia's independence from Britain, that a Straits Times report from Kuantan in Pahang would announce a tender that had been awarded to a French company to construct four concrete bridges across rivers on the east coast of the Malayan Peninsula. These were named as being at Kemaman, Dungun, Paka and Kuang. The promise was that they would "greatly reduce the present delay crossing the rivers," and once completed, the report said, "there will be only two more ferries, at Marang and Losong."[46]

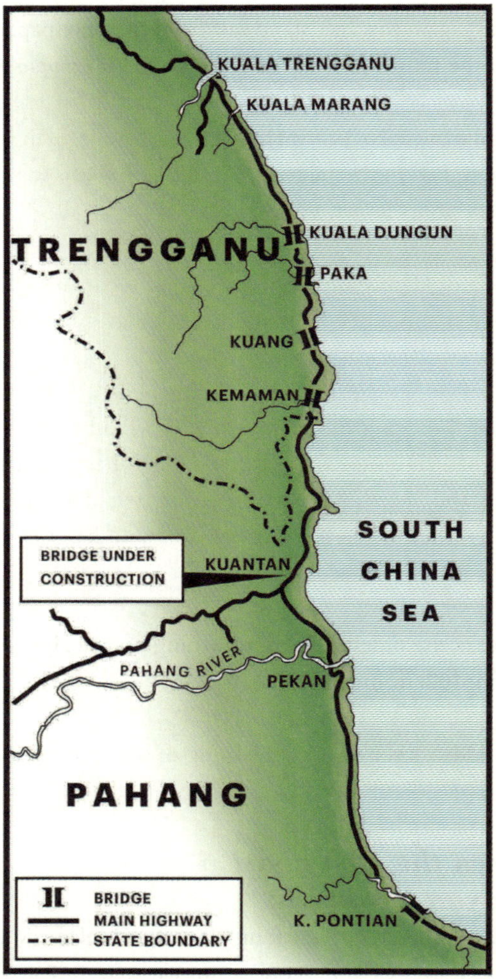

In 1961 a contract was signed for bridges to be built over rivers to replace a series of ferries in Terengganu and Pahang on the east coast of the Malayan Peninsula. (The information here is as adapted from that given in a Straits Times report, December 1961) Image by Umar Green

What that means is that through the 1950s on their journey south from Kelantan people just like the 101-year-old Che Mek would have had to experience a journey interrupted by ferry after ferry. A small matter, perhaps, but another indicator of the effort to which people went on their hajj journeys. Road transport might have made for a speedier journey than a coastal steamer but there were still ferries to take across rivers.

And the matters in place for the hajj

The shipping links to and from Singapore and around the region were comprehensive. What then would happen once prospective pilgrims arrived in Singapore? The principal focal point would be Kampong Glam. It offered accommodation, hajj services, and a place of cultural and spiritual support. First, though, the question is, "who travelled?"

• • • • • • • • • •

[1] Report dated 7 Feb 1819, published in "Calcutta Journal." Quoted in: Wright, Arnold (ed.). 1908. 20th Century Impressions of British Malaya. London: Lloyd's Greater Britain Publishing Company, p. 25.

[2] Earl, George Windsor. 1837. *The Eastern Seas*. London: Wm. H. Allen & Co. pp. 141 – 142.

[3] Ibid.

[4] "The Straits ports are wholly free from duties on imports and exports . . and the only tax or duty to which shipping entering the port is liable, consists of a very moderate one of 3 cents or 1½ d [a penny and a half] per register ton [sic], in support of aids to navigation." In ST. 1 July 1861, p. 2.

[5] The Singapore Free Press and Mercantile Advertiser, (hereinafter referred to as SFPMA). 1 August 1844, p. 2.

[6] Imran bin Tajudeen. "Reading the Traditional City of Maritime Southeast Asia." In *Journal of Southeast Asian Architecture Vol 8*, Singapore, 2005. p. 15.

[7] Earl. p. 68.

[8] Clarence-Smith, William Gervase. 2002. "The Rise and Fall of Hadhrami Shipping in the India Ocean, c.1750 – c.1940." In *Ships and the Development of Maritime Technology in the Indian Ocean*, ed David Parkin and Ruth Barnes. London: Routledge Curzon, p. 230.

[9] The term *kling*, now accepted as being derogatory, was used to speak of people from South Asia, particularly India.

[10] Earl. op cit. pp. 145 – 146.

[11] Information from Imran bin Tajudeen, op cit. p. 1.

[12] Davidson, G.F. 1846. *Trade and Travel in the Far East*, or, *Recollections of Twenty-One Years passed in Java, Singapore, Australia and China*. London: Madden & Malcolm, p. 62.

[13] Clarence-Smith, op cit.

[14] Ibid.

[15] SFPMA. 6 December 1855, p. 2.

[16] Ricklefs, M.C. 2007. *Polarising Javanese Society*. Singapore: NUS Press, p. 58.

[17] Laffan. p. 47.

[18] Davidson. op cit.

[19] Proudfoot, Ian. 1993. *Early Malay Printed Books*. Kuala Lumpur: Academy of Malay Studies & the Library University of Malaya, Perpustakaan Negara Malaysia, p. 7.

[20] Proudfoot, footnote 26, p. 65.

[21] Alexanderson, Kris. 2014. "A Dark State of Affairs": Hajj Networks, Pan-Islamism, and Dutch Colonial Surveillance during the Interwar Period. In *Journal of Social History vol. 47* no. 4. pp. 1021–1041 URL: doi:10.1093/jsh/shu020 Oxford University Press (accessed 4 August 2018).

[22] According to its one-time Captain, William Henry Kidley, this was the largest ship that had been seen at Suez in those days, when the Suez Canal had not yet been opened. Kidley carried

pilgrims to Mecca in the 1860s. Recorded in *The Star, Lyttleton, New Zealand, 10 March 1906.* Source: https://www.encyclopedia-titanica.org/community/threads/news-from-1906-1929-retirement-death-of-capt-kidley.25530/.

[23] http://eresources.nlb.gov.sg/infopedia/articles/SIP_358_2005-01-06.html?s=gutta-percha.

[24] These details are taken from: Singapore Harbour Board, *A Short History of the Port of Singapore,* Raffles Library, Singapore 1921. http://pasirpanjang.org/Singapore_Docks.pdf Accessed 1 May 2018.

[25] ST. 7 September 1872, p. 3.

[26] The relationship between Alsagoff and Guthrie is not clear. In one website, the ship *Jeddah* is referred to as "Guthrie's Jeddah." (See: http://www.red-duster.co.uk/wp/2016/02/25/shire-line-3/).

[27] Information from National Maritime Museum, Greenwich, London.

[28] *The History of Mansfield & Company – Part 1, 1868-1924,*'by A. J. & C. E. W.'; re-printed in the Blue Funnel and Glen Lines Staff Bulletin, Jan 1952, p. 6.

[29] Ibid. p. 1.

[30] Ibid. p. 5.

[31] ST. 11 January 1927, p. 8.

[32] Personal interview with Anthony Green.

[33] Tregonning, K. G. 1967. *Home Port Singapore – A History of the Straits Steamship Company Limited, 1890-1965.*" Singapore: Oxford University Press, pp. 116-117.

[34] http://sarawaksteamship.com/fleets.html.

[35] The term "Moro" came into use by the Spanish during their time in the Philippines, as a generic term for all Muslims. It came from the Spanish experience of Muslims in Spain before the *Reconquista* as being "Moors" (from North Africa), in much the same way as the British referring to Muslims as "Turks."

[36] Tregonning. op cit. pp. 116-117.

[37] Ibid. pp. 95-96.

[38] Ibid. p. 154.

[39] Ibid. p. 159.

[40] Ibid. p. 155.

[41] SFPMA. 5 September 1906, p. 8.

[42] ST. 12 May 1960.

[43] ST. 8 December 1964.

[44] Foreman, J.E.A, 1986. *Transport in Malaya*, Oxford: Bodleian Library.

[45] ST. 15 April 1967, p. 14.

[46] ST. 27 November 1961.

3

Who travelled? And when?

In January 1854 *The Overland Free Press* reported that, "Upwards of three thousand natives of the Indian Archipelago have this season sailed from Singapore bound for Arabia, there to perform the pilgrimage to Mecca."

The date of the report was equivalent to the Islamic date 3 Rabiulakhir 1270AH, almost four months after the culmination of the previous hajj. As we've already suggested, in modern times, flying to and from Saudi Arabia, a hajj pilgrim might be away from their home for just three to four weeks. But what this shows is just how far in advance pilgrims in the past had to set out and that, in turn, might prompt the question of just how long they would be away from home.

Monsoons and sea conditions

The season the report referred to was the "season" for hajj travels and describing it in that way suggests that the numbers of hajj pilgrims annually travelling through Singapore from the Netherlands East Indies was sufficient to be well recognised as a real presence in the local calendar.

But, more importantly, "the season" also implied the monsoons. In the time of the sailing ships the earliest departure of hajj ships from Singapore was the end of October and the latest was around the end of January. This is the time of the north-east monsoon.

Alan Villiers, the great writer on sailing ships – the "windships," as he called them – said that,

> Of the three great oceans, the Indian was, upon the whole, always the most kindly to sailing ships . . . Though the least of the three great oceans . . . it is, in many ways, the most interesting.[2]

In part that "kindliness" of the Indian Ocean came from "the dependable monsoons which made possible the sailing commerce of the ancient East,"[3] of which, "the northeast [monsoon] ... is as gracious, as clear, as balmy as a permanent trade."[4]

Returning could be a different matter. If a hajj ship were returning in the southwest monsoon in mid-year, seas were far more likely to be rough. This report from June 1897 gives an indicator:

> Early this month, heavy weather prevailed in the Indian Ocean especially off the island of Socotra. The pilgrim steamer *Sultan* foundered near the coast there. Ten persons were drowned. The chief cook on the *Chingwo*, bound from Liverpool for Singapore, was washed overboard and drowned in the storm.[5]

A ship at sea – the Southwest Monsoon in the Indian Ocean. Picture from John Marshall.

This likelihood of a rough sea in the southwest monsoon is important when we match that with the likely weakness through exhaustion of the returning pilgrims at the end of the hajj.

As the nineteenth century progressed, pilgrim numbers from Southeast Asia increased. An 1854 report noted that,

> ... the numbers of these pious pilgrims have much increased since the Dutch government removed the restrictions in the shape of a tax &c., which formerly proved serious impediments in the way of poorer classes in Java becoming Hadjis.[6]

Aside from "natives" of the "Indian Archipelago" – what's now Indonesia – Singapore also attracted aspiring pilgrims from a large part of the Malay Peninsula, and well beyond, through the Philippines and up to China.

In 1926 Captain J.H. Brown travelled as Mate on the Blue Funnel ship *S.S. Priam* from Jeddah to Batavia by way of Padang on the west coast of Sumatra. Looking back forty years later, he described,

> ... a party of 150 Mohammedan Chinese from North China . . . small in stature, rosy cheeks, thin bow legs, not so easy to handle as the Javanese, they had spirit lamps and plenty of live chickens. The women in their black shrouds gave one a bit of a shock meeting them at night when making the rounds.[7]

If these pilgrims returning to China were travelling via Batavia there were also Chinese pilgrims travelling through Singapore. Vernon Elliott served as a Radio Officer on two voyages in the late 1940s – "in the old, coal burning steamers *Atreus* and *Rhesus*."

> Our passengers were Malay in the majority, but with Moros and other Filipinos, and some Northern Chinese ... The North Chinese liked to do their own "chow," as shown in one of the pictures.[8]

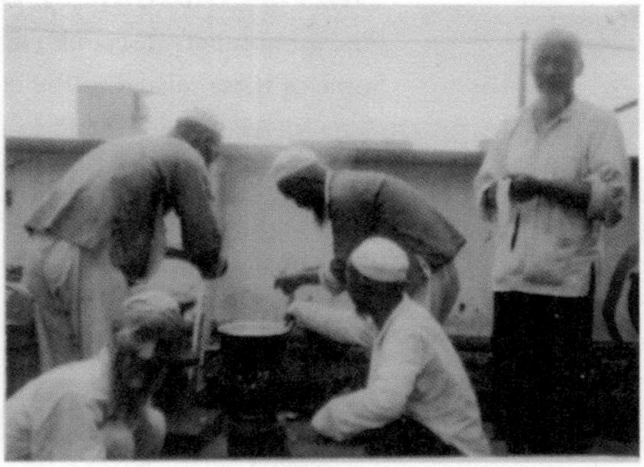

Pilgrims from North China travelling via Singapore in 1948. Pictures by permission of crew member Vernon Elliott, who wrote: "Sorry about the quality but these were taken with an old 'Box Brownie.'"

In the 1854 report the vessels they travelled on were said to "generally belong to Arab traders or [be] chartered by them." And the passage-money paid by most of these pilgrims, "who in general are poor," was said to be ten dollars each.[9] For this the pilgrims were to be supplied with water and firewood for cooking their food, although the food was something that they had to provide themselves. Food – or the lack of it – would be a real issue on ships sailing from ports controlled by the British. Cooking would take place on deck but this always added an element of risk, especially in a wooden sailing ship. Fires did break out, and one significance of the regular reports of the overcrowding of pilgrim ships was that it would have been impossible for there to have been space for all pilgrims to be on the upper deck, so small fires would be lit on the lower deck. This practice was something that ships' crews still had to look out for as late as the 1960s on a hajj ship like the *Kuala Lumpur* where, in their rounds of inspection below decks, crew members would check to ensure that fires were not being lit.

The rise and fall of pilgrim numbers

Pilgrim numbers rose and fell at different times in direct response to events. Some of these related to the economic circumstances of the people intending to travel. And some related to events going on in the world.

War in the Hejaz in the first half of the 1920s was one cause of a fall in numbers and the eventual control of Mecca by Ibn Saud and his forces was something that he was keen to publicise as permitting the prospect of a safe hajj. In 1926 the following report was published:

> Aneta Press Bureau learns from the Kongsie Tiga in Batavia, that Sultan Ibn Saud has sent the following telegram to one of the largest firms of pilgrim brokers in Singapore :– "Please inform all pilgrims throughout the Philippines and Malaya that thanks to the Almighty's mercy there now prevails throughout the whole of the Hedjaz peace and rest. Every pilgrim has complete freedom in the exercising of his religious duties and in visiting the holy mosque of Mohamed. Trusting in God, I guarantee absolute safety to all pilgrims during their sojourn and journies [sic] in the Holy Land and the Hedjaz. The rumours published by our enemies are unfounded and basely calculated to impede the exercising of religious duties for personal benefit and to stay in the holy places." The telegram was signed Abdul Aziz bin Saud, King of the Hedjaz, Sultan of the Nedj and Mulhakataha.[10]

The Economy and its Effects on Pilgrim numbers

At different times over the years the economy affected the numbers of pilgrims. The Great Depression was one cause and this is how one person who'd grown up in Malaya remembered the effects of the Depression:

> ... there had occurred the Great Crash of 1929 on Wall Street, followed by the slump. The rubber industry, itself highly cyclical, was plunged into recession. The price of rubber fell from 73 cents per pound in 1925 to 28 cents in 1928 and then to less that 3 cents in 1932.[11]

Late harvests of rice in Malaya or weather that affected the crop and reduced income were other issues.

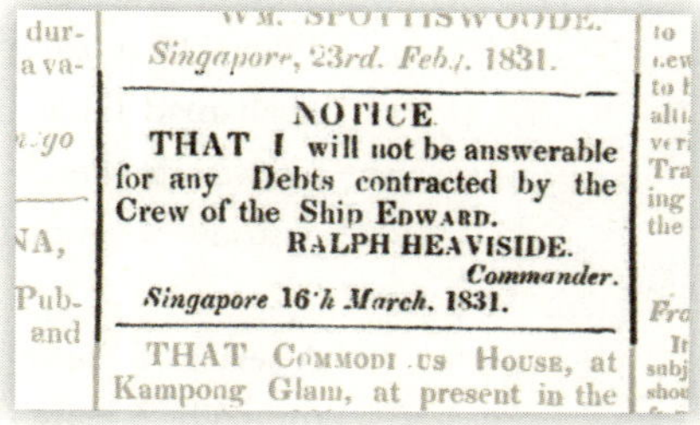

WM. SPOTTISWOODE.
Singapore, 23rd. Feb., 1831.

NOTICE

THAT I will not be answerable for any Debts contracted by the Crew of the Ship EDWARD.

RALPH HEAVISIDE.
Commander.
Singapore 16th March, 1831.

THAT COMMODIOUS HOUSE, at Kampong Glam, at present in the

It was not unusual for a ship's master to place an advertisment such as this in the newspapers of the port in which they were docked. Money was a temptation, thefts occurred, and wages might not always seem sufficient to support the situation in which a member of the crew found himself.

And threats along the way

From time immemorial, those who carry valuable things have always stirred a predatory interest in others, and it's clear that those who had saved for the pilgrimage and were carrying money or gold or other valuables with them became attractive targets from the time they left home, in the foreign ports they passed through, in the ships on which they travelled, and even when they arrived in the Hejaz. Some would be carrying gold or far more money than those around them were earning and the ones who targeted them ranged from gangs to individuals. The predators might be identified as Muslims or they might not. A number of colonial office reports from the Hejaz speak of pilgrims being robbed by Bedouins who took from them everything they had, even clothes. And those who tricked them might even be people whose business it was to make things easy for them – people operating as pilgrim brokers – or, as below, they might even be people claiming to be travelling on the same journey.

In December 1845 a Straits Times report, headed, "Serious attempt at gang robbery with violence," described an attack by a gang of Chinese:

> Yesterday morning about 2 o'clock the neighbourhoods of Campong Java and Glam were thrown into a state of considerable excitement in consequence of an attack made by a numerous Gang of Chinese on the House of a Javanese situated at Campong Java. It would appear that the attacking party had obtained information that the Javanese above mentioned was about to proceed on pilgrimage to Mecca, and that he had about one pound weight of gold dust in his possession.[12]

In December 1870 an account was published[13] of four Javanese, who had arrived from Palembang on their way to Mecca, and how they'd been "taken suddenly ill in a house in Clyde Street." It appeared that the men had been drinking ginger tea made in a small copper kettle." A 12-year old, Assan Hooden died, followed by two others, Hajee Jamalooden and Nooreman.

They'd been carrying "between $3,000 and $4,000." The fourth man, Hadjee Mohamad Tahar, had lodged in the same house and claimed also to be on his way to Mecca but with only eighteen dollars on him he was detained in custody on suspicion of having poisoned the others.

A series of claims and responses were published in the Singapore press at that time. The Straits Times Overland Journal published an article from the *New Batavia Handelsblad*, which offered a caution for intending pilgrims from Java. It claimed that they are "fleeced in the holy city, involved in debt, and do not come back until they have worked for years in the spice gardens of the Straits Settlements. This "abuse," said the newspaper, "can only be countracted [sic] by the stationing of a Dutch Consul at Mecca, and consultation with the Straits Government." A series of small, "to-and-fro" propaganda battles like this were played out in published communications between the Dutch and the British, each seeming to present itself as the best protector of the Muslims in their colonial possession.

This "working for years in the spice gardens of the Straits Settlements" may have referred to claims made against Syed Mohammad Alsagoff. There seemed to be a fairly common practice for money to be advanced to pilgrims stranded in the Hejaz who were without the means to return. This was a very real problem, even more so for destitute Muslims from India. In the case of Muslims from Java or the Straits Settlements, Syed Mohammad Alsagoff was one of those who would have people work in his plantations at Kukup in Johore in return for the advance, until they had paid this money off. Claims were made that this was a system akin to some kind of slavery, and that pilgrims were having to work beyond the time necessary for repayment of the debt. Syed Mohammad wrote to the press to explain what he did and to defend himself firmly against the accusations.

In 1907 "an elderly Malay dame" on her way to Mecca reported to the police, that she had,

> ... slept with a belt containing twenty(?)-five sovereigns, five gold American dollars and $150 in local coin under her pillow. She has made a report to the police and its contents were removed while she slept. [14]

When the Alsagoff ship *Medina* ran aground in the Red Sea on the way to Jeddah in 1875 its pilgrim passengers had to be transferred to another ship, the *S.S. Timor.* In the process a number of them discovered that money had been taken from their trunks or luggage.

Seven pilgrims from the *Medina* together lost a total of $1,341, while three men on the *Timor* had money stolen. One of them, "Abdel Halim bin Abdel Mallick" had $2,416 taken from his trunk, a very considerable sum since, of the other two men, one had $37 and the other $800. In Abdel Halim's words,

> A pilgrim called Abdalla heard money jingling in the hold, thereupon he went below and saw two sailors run away ... I brought the trunk from the hold upon deck, and in the presence of Captain Brown and the supercargo of the "Medina" I counted the money and found a deficit of $2,416. Begging for help to recover that stolen sum, I sign this paper ..."

For those who were critical of the situation these possibilities for becoming a victim could lead to messages of caution:

> In a satirical poem, written in 1867, Raden Muhammad Husayn of Krawaang had repeatedly warned the elite sons of 'Sunda and Jawa' of the financial burdens of the pilgrimage, of the dangers of being robbed en route, or worse, of ending up as a coolie in Singapore, Japan or Malabar.[15]

Haji Singapura... and beyond...

It's situations like this that led to the oft-repeated label for those who set out from their home in Indonesia to perform the hajj but did not get too far. Some became known as Haji Singapura if they only made it as far as Singapore.

In the same vein there are anecdotes of pilgrims being referred to as Haji Penang, when Penang was the furthest they reached on their hajj journey. Some might make it further but still not as far as Mecca. In June 1861 the

Sultan of Terengganu arrived in Singapore "with a numerous retinue" which, according to other reports, included a number of ladies. The Sultan was clearly not in that category of pilgrims paying ten dollars and getting water and firewood.

> The Sultan of Tringanu arrived here on the 26th current with a numerous retinue and was received at the landing place by the Hon, the Governor and the Resident Councillor. His Highness took up his abode at a house in Campong Glam which had been engaged for him by the local government. The Sultan, we understand, is so far on his way to Mecca, which like a devout Mahometan he considers it his duty to visit. The Government of Tringanu has been committed to his brother. Considering the difficulties which are to subsist with Siam, it appears to us that His Highness might have chosen a more auspicious time for his pilgrimage, but he probably considers his purpose so meritorious that it will secure him against any worldly misfortunes.[16]

Where he stayed in Kampong Glam we do not know but he and his party then sailed in a steamship to Ceylon. Unable to obtain any cabin accommodation on a ship to Aden and Suez and worried about being away from his state for too long, he returned to Singapore, where he chartered a steamer, the *Chow Phya* for $600 to go back to Terengganu.[17]

Pilgrim brokers

In all these references to deceits and mischief it should be said that, for the most part, the network of pilgrim brokers provided an important and necessary link, both back to the place from which the pilgrims had come, and onwards to connections with men of similar origin in the Hejaz.

Instances arose where pilgrims were cheated but Kampong Glam in Singapore became a very significant centre for all kinds of services in support of pilgrims and we talk more about this in the next chapter. If cheating were widespread its reputation would have suffered.

The hajj voyage – a journey of meetings

Lacking passenger manifests we cannot know the identities or explore the backgrounds and personal concerns of the people who travelled through and from Singapore and Penang to Mecca. And since conversations are almost always private matters, we can only speculate on what people might have spoken about together.

The European officers of the Blue Funnel hajj ship S.S. Ajax in 1910, itself a cargo ship. The ship's doctor, F.W. Hogarth, is seated, cross-legged on the right at the front. Some idea of the hajj passengers they would have been carrying comes from the images on the following pages, even though these photographs had been taken just over twenty years earlier. One impression to draw is of a hajj ship being like a temporary home or an encounter between two quite different cultures and priorities. Picture sourced from the Blue Funnel and Glen Line Bulletin; reproduced courtesy of John Swire & Sons Limited.

This speculation might be dismissed as a futile exercise but floating communities are formed when people travel together on a long journey at sea and people interact and speak together; perhaps especially so when they have a shared faith and are focused on a common experience. This needs to be set in the context of colonial suspicion against hajj pilgrims, and the assumption or fear that the hajj could be a platform for the discussion or spread of views that might translate into anti-colonial sentiment. If the concern was that this would be a significant focus for pilgrims then ship-board conversations were to be watched.

Part of that concern with the potential "political overtones" of the hajj was with the ideas about Islam and its teachings on priorities and on how best to live that might be spread amongst Muslims and be carried back with them.

Hajj pilgrims from across the Indonesian Archipelago

In 1888 the Dutch scholar Christiaan Snouck Hurgronje took a series of photographs in Jeddah and Mecca with a special focus on pilgrims from the Dutch East Indies. Here we use some of those images to give a sense of the journeys these pilgrims would have had to have made. For many it would first be by one or more small sailing vessels before ultimately joining a steamship, and travelling from Java or Sumatra, or via Singapore or Penang.

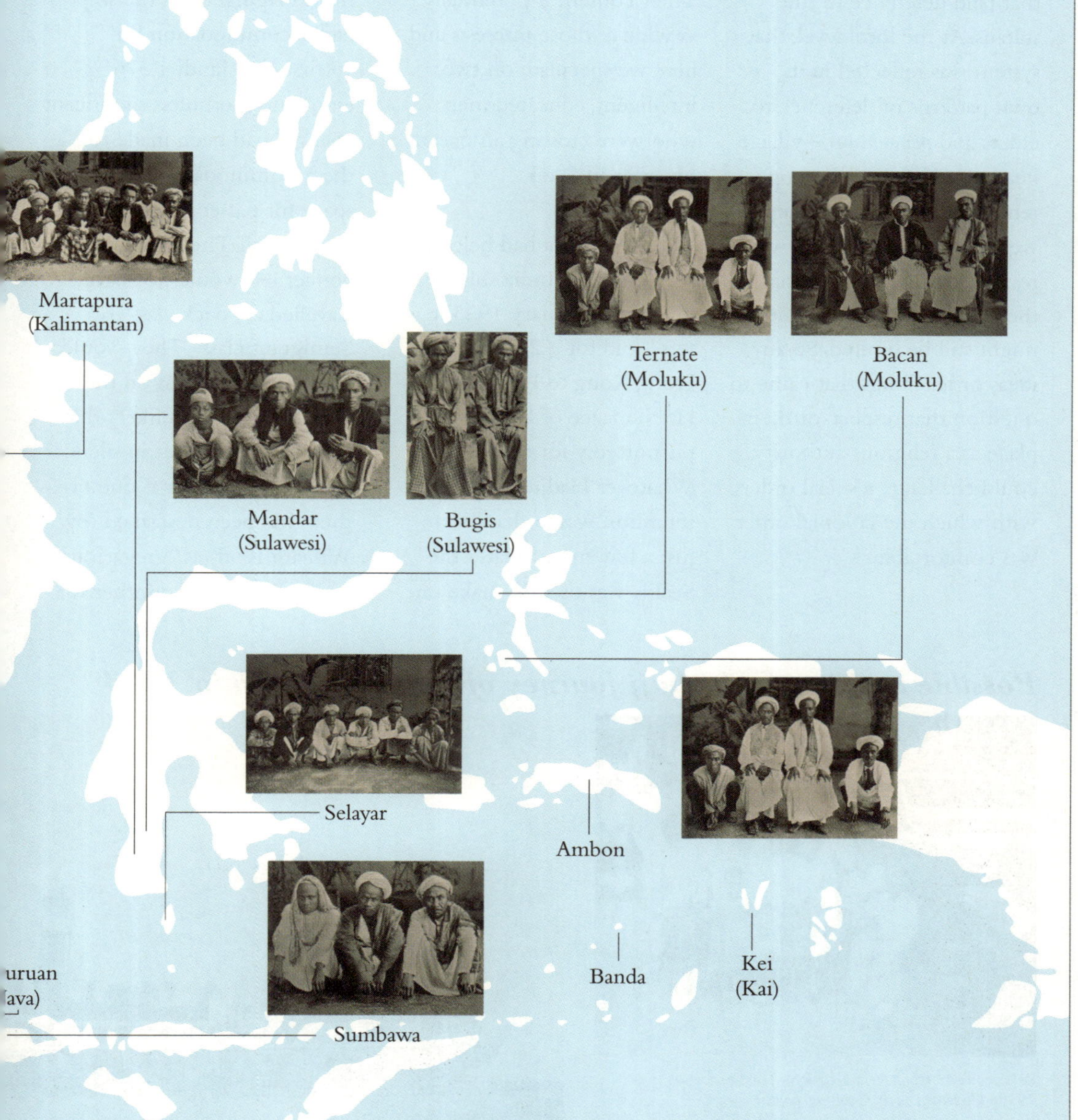

All images are in the public domain and are taken from the Qatar Digital Library (https://images.qdl.qa/iiif/images/81055/vdc_100022547736.0x000001/1781.b.6_).

In the Malay Peninsula the social order in colonial times owed a good deal to a system that paid deference to the sultans. At the local level, that system was reflected in its own patterns of deference to elders and *penguhulus* – village headmen. When such people returned from the hajj they were often accorded a new respect, despite the fact that their knowledge of the faith might still be limited. So any ideas or teachings that came to question that respect, or their place as a religious authority, could challenge a social order with which the colonial order was comfortable.

But conversations are shaped by the personal concerns and experiences of the speakers. Their content is potentially as wide as those interests and here we speculate on two, intelligent, educated men who were crossing an ocean together in 1923.

The *S.S. Sealda* had belonged to the British India shipping line but in January 1923 it was "sold for £20,000 at Hong Kong to Hadjee M. H. Nemazee of Bombay," purportedly for demolition. Whatever Hadjee Nemazee's intention was, or had been, just a few months later the Sealda was used to make one hajj journey from Jeddah to Penang and Singapore.

In its original form the ship had accommodation for "9 first class [and] 1,376 emigrants" so unless significant changes had been made to the accommodation, the space for passengers in cabins was limited. The two men concerned would not have travelled as "deck class" or "emigrant class." They would have been in cabins on the ship. It is highly unlikely that they would have sat in silence together, especially if one of them has been described (by William Roff) as "gregarious and sociable" and another is a

Possible meetings – the hajj journey of the S.S. Sealda in 1923

Dr Mohamed Ibrahim (centre, back row) and his family in the 1930s. He served as ship's surgeon on this voyage.

Standing beside him, his elbow on the car, and looking almost through the camera is his son Ahmed Ibrahim. He would go on to become Singapore's first Attorney-General.

Picture by permission of Ibrahim Tahir.

The S.S.Sealda – bought by H.M.Nemazie of Hong Kong and used for one hajj journey in 1923. © P&O Heritage Collection www.poheritage.com

man with a record of social involvement.

Travelling as ship's surgeon was Dr Mohamed Ibrahim bin Shaykh Ismail. His son, Ahmad Ibrahim, at that time just seven years old, would go on to win First-Class Honours at Cambridge University, be a member of the Singapore Legislative Assembly in the 1950s, and, in time, become the State Advocate-General of Singapore and then independent Singapore's first Attorney-General and a driving force behind the teaching of law in Malaysian universities.

Dr Mohamed Ibrahim was a man very active in Islamic organisations, and with a clear sense of social purpose. His was a family that was fully involved with life – religiously and in terms of the wider society.

On the return trip from Jeddah to Singapore another significant passenger was Abdul Majid bin Zainuddin. He had earlier postponed his intended hajj trip for his daughter's wedding, but he'd then been approached by the Criminal Investigation Branch of the Federated Malay State Police "as the government wanted someone trustworthy to do something for them."[19]

That "trustworthy" thing was to serve as the Malayan Pilgrimage Officer, based in Jeddah. Abdul Majid had chosen to travel on a Nemazee (or Namazie) ship "in the belief that, unlike Blue Funnel, they provided food for their pilgrim passengers, but discovered to his consternation that this was true only for Netherlands Indies pilgrims picked up at Batavia." He was fortunate because he found a sympathetic crew but the experience may have influenced his views. In his subsequent recommendations to the Straits Settlements he stressed that ships from Malayan ports should provide food for the pilgrims. Before this, passengers had had to take their own.

Born in 1887, Abdul Majid Zainuddin travelled on the Hajj in 1923, before he took up his post as the first Malay Pilgrimage Officer in 1924.

Abdul Majid would take up his post in 1924 and serve for sixteen years but returning to Malaya after this first visit to Mecca in 1923 to perform the hajj "he submitted a written report that much impressed the government."[20]

The British had come to feel the need for a representative to be stationed in Jeddah for the interests of pilgrims from the Straits Settlements – to monitor the situation and their comings and goings.[21] Up till then any of their concerns over pilgrims from the region had been handled by Dr Abdul Razzack from India. Yet if Abdul Majid was meant to "keep an eye on a variety of Malay and Muslim movements," in Roff's words, "he was not in fact a very energetic or successful spy" and "scarcely had the personality to become an 'under-cover agent.'"[22] His reports on the social conditions of the hajj, however, were thorough and well received. Dr Mohamed Ibrahim's own work had a real social concern and social involvement. The prospect of two such educated co-travellers being together on this ship for two weeks; of their meeting and having time to speak, invites all kinds of interesting scenarios.

Once again in this book questions are raised that cannot be answered but any sweeping application of colonial suspicion would seem to fail to respect the range of concerns, backgrounds and intentions of the people who travelled.

When cultures meet

Ships are like moving societies, divided in different ways, with a wide range of lives lived side by side. It was not just a case of Muslims from a variety of origins being together. Those relationships and connections that developed in the floating communities have already been mentioned.

But the hajj journey is interesting for other interactions that it offered. Throughout the history of the hajj ships, comments made and perceptions held by Western individuals towards the pilgrims were mixed – sometimes neutral, sometimes positive, at other times less so. Throughout the nineteenth century we can read comments that are dismissive, even derogatory. These opinions weren't held by everyone but they existed. At many times in the twentieth century, however, and particularly after the Second World War when the colonial tide had turned, one can read examples of increased openness, even respect.

In general, the policy of shipping companies was that crews and passengers should not mix. First class passengers and VIPs would meet with the captain and other senior officers, and any committee of hajj representatives would also meet regularly. When Ustaz Hj Ali travelled as a young man in the 1970s he was invited to be a member of one of those committees, but for most pilgrims there would be limited contact – each group kept to themselves. And yet it would be odd to have no interaction even if brief. Captain J.H. Brown's recollections of his 1926 voyage included the following observations:

> On passage the Pilgrims just sat about, a few possibly reading the Koran, but I never saw them reading books. They were a simple folk. Prayer at sunset was the most important thing of the day, even in port with steam winches working and coolies shouting, their prayers were carried out regardless. A muster of all Pilgrims was organised for manifest purposes, and for some this would be the only appearance on deck for the whole passage. They usually turned out in their finest gear, bright coloured sarongs and headscarves; children (156 on this trip) in all their best.
>
> I always found the Javanese very easy to handle, polite and clean in their personal habits, and the mustering for manifest checking always orderly... I sometimes cut up a bar of soap and gave small pieces to the children; the freshwater taps were unlocked so that only a trickle was available and the children enjoyed this.[23]

And Vernon Elliott adds some comments on children on board in 1948:

> Most of us picked up a few words and phrases [of Malay]. As you can see from the photos the crew were very attached to the many young children, and gave them sweets and chocolate.

(Right) Children on board a hajj ship in 1948. Pictures by permission of Vernon Elliott. Whilst the vast majority of pilgrims were old, children also travelled, as did infants, since there were many occasions of women giving birth on board.

In exchange, children might teach the crew to count in Malay. But the fact that the hajj voyages brought together people from very varied backgrounds could create interesting situations.

• • • • • • • • • • •

Curious meetings... and a footnote

As a very young man in 1948 Charlie Service from Northern Ireland served as Fourth Engineer on the Blue Funnel ship, *M. V. Prometheus*, on a voyage from Tanjong Priok, Java, to Jeddah, and he recalls a meeting that must count as unusual:

> The only one I had a talk with was a Turkish millionaire fella. He was a well educated fella. But he had done that trip out east so that he could do the hajj with these people. Why he did that I'm not sure, but he had the same conditions as they had, but he could come and . . . we had a yarn on number three hatch – I don't think he was ever in my cabin. We had a yarn on number three hatch on a tropic night. And he was explaining to me the Qur'an, you know. It was very interestin'; it was very interestin'.[24]

The voyage of Charlie Service was just three years after the end of a hugely destructive war that had unsettled millions. The world was now apparently at peace. The pilgrims themselves had been under Japanese occupation but were now on a journey that made clear sense to them because it ordered their understanding of life and purpose. The phrase "Alhamdulillah" – all praise is due to God – is commonly uttered by Muslims, signifying a quiet, an acknowledgment, and a complete acceptance, and it seems to be that most approached the journey in that way.

But journeys don't have the same significance for everyone and when people from very different backgrounds come together into the same space there is the question of what each one sees when they look at the other.

If the pilgrims were seen by many of the crew members as quiet and accepting, the crews of the hajj ships themselves came from different worlds and included men and women who had lived through very recent and violent experiences of war. Charlie Service spoke of the Chief Engineer on his ship.

> We embarked 1,200 pilgrims at Tanjong Priok, Java. We had three doctors on board, two Dutch and one elderly English, Dr Barton, who had been on Hadji ships prewar. On the morning after departure it was found that the Chief Engineer H. N. Jones was missing and we had to turn back to where he was last seen but unfortunately there was no trace.[25]

This would have been on 15 Aug 1948. Mr. Jones – "a very gentle man" – had served with the company for 36 years but he'd also been down below in the engine room of the Blue Funnel ship *Troilus* when merchant ships had been pressed into war service. In June, 1942 she was one of only two out of six merchant ships sailing in the Mediterranean convoy to get through to Malta, after attacks by torpedo bombers and cruisers, and a passage through a minefield. For his part he was one of those mariners who received awards, in his case, the OBE for "Good Service in the *Troilus*, June, 1942" though, according to Charlie Service, "he never mentioned his wartime service."

Writing fifty years after the voyage, Charlie Service said,

> My cabin was next to the Ch. Eng, and on the night he disappeared I can still see his cap on top of his bed.

Just as it is impossible to know of the hopes and intentions of the pilgrims on this hajj ship, so it's impossible to know how far a voyage such as this with a placid group of pilgrims might have impacted on individuals adjusting to peace from a recent experience of war and danger and violent loss. The contrast would be considerable. We cannot know how Mr Jones died or what thoughts he would have had. His is just one more of the many unremembered footnotes in the story of these travelling communities.

[1] SFPMA, 3 January 1854, p. 1.

[2] Villiers, Alan. 1952. *Monsoon Seas – The Story of the Indian Ocean.* McGraw-Hill, New York, p. 3.

[3] Ibid. p. 2.

[4] Ibid. p. 7.

[5] ST. 26 June 1897, p. 2.

[6] SFPMA. 3 January 1854, p. 1.

[7] Brown, Capt. J. H. "Pilgrims' Progress." in *the Bulletin of the Blue Funnel and Glen Lines*, July 1966, pp. 285-286.

[8] Elliott, Vernon. Personal correspondence with Anthony Green.

[9] At this time Spanish dollars would have likely been the currency.

[10] ST. 22 February 1926, p. 10.

[11] Barnes, Ken. 2008. *A Rough Passage: Memories of Empire – Volume 1 and Volume 2.* Radcliffe Press, p. 10.

[12] ST. 31 December 1845.

[13] ST. 17 December 1870.

[14] Eastern Daily Mail and Straits Morning Advertiser. 16 October 1907, p. 2.

[15] Laffan. p. 53.

[16] Singapore Free Press 12 June 1961, p. 6, Reporting on events "100 years ago"; i.e., in June 1861.

[17] SFPMA. 6 September 1861, p. 1.

[18] Roff, William R. 2009A. "The Conduct of the Hajj from Malaya." In *Studies on Islam and Society in Southeast Asia.* NUS Press, Singapore, p. 317.

[19] Roff, William R. (ed). 1978. *The Wandering Thoughts of a Dying Man – The Life and Times of Haji Abdul Majid bin Zainuddin.* Kuala Lumpur: Oxford University Press, p. 146.

[20] Ibid. p. xi.

[21] "The duties were set out in a memorandum by René Onraet, head of the Political Intelligence Bureau, dated 10 October 1924: (i) registration of pilgrims; (ii) registration and retention of return tickets; (iii) assistance to pilgrims; (iv) check against female slavery; (v) assistance to British Agent, Jeddah; and (vi) 'assistance in detecting and countering any political movement, e.g. the possible communist activities of the newly-established Soviet agency in Jeddah.'" Ibid. Footnote 62, p. 146.

[22] Ibid. p. xii.

[23] Op cit. p. 286.

[24] Service, Charlie. Personal correspondence with Anthony Green.

[25] Ibid.

In 1823, the British East India Company authorised Major William Farquhar, the British Resident of Singapore, to advance "such further sums as may be sufficient for the completion of a respectable mosque near the dwelling of the Sultan." In this watercolour the painter, Thomson, may have taken a little artistic licence with the figures in the foreground.

J.T. (John Turnbull) Thomson, 1821-1884, Malay Mosque, Campong Glam, Singapore, 1846, watercolour on paper: 153 x 227mm, 92/1155, given by the Hall-Jones family, Invercargill, 1992, Hocken Collections, Uare Taoka o Hākena, University of Otago.

4

Singapore and Kampong Glam:

What is this place we have come to?

George Windsor Earl had been impressed by the energy and thriving commercial feel of Singapore in 1833, and as the nineteenth century pushed on it would be increasingly busy. But one can wonder what impression Singapore would have made on people arriving from their homes in the Indonesian Archipelago or the Malay Peninsula.

That energy and industry to which Earl had responded meant a focus and a set of priorities that set Singapore apart in many ways from other places in the region, so that William Roff could also suggest that "Singapore . . . represented for Malays" a world that was "alien and highly competitive." Yet within Singapore,

> ... there was to set against this the richly variegated and socially more familiar life of Kampong Glam and the other Malayo-Muslim areas of the city. Free movement between the Indonesian archipelago and the peninsula was of very long standing... for the first time, and increasingly in the last quarter of the century, large numbers of Indonesians, especially Javanese, came to Malaya to work as either indentured or free labour or as peasant settlers, and others came as sojourners, for a purpose bound up with the first, the pilgrimage to Mecca. For many of these people Singapore was to be at the very least a stopping place, and often a permanent home.[1]

The idea that "free movement between the Indonesian archipelago and the Malay Peninsula was of very long standing" hints at a history that goes

The former Sultan Mosque – the "masjid lama" – as shown in the painting on the previous page but here photographed some time before the 1920s. Picture courtesy of Sultan Mosque, Singapore.

back long before the Western presence in the region. In relation to the hajj, however, the opportunity for Singapore to be used by "sojourners" as a "stopping place" becomes the point of interest, and it's this area of Kampong (now Kampung) Glam that we turn to for its part in the kapal haji story.

What then did Singapore – and Kampong Glam – offer to anyone intending to undertake the hajj? What work did they do, those people who came to this place?

Getting money for the hajj: records, and their absence

The British bureaucracy kept fastidious records for the matters deemed to be of concern, so the Government Gazettes in the early twentieth Century can reveal an odd range of detailed statistics, such as how many rats were killed in a specific period or how much money was made from the sale of night soil. In connection with the hajj we can know, for example, how much the Malay Pilgrimage Officer in Jeddah received as a monthly salary; what some his expenses were, and how much was spent on the small boat for his office.[2]

We can find among shipping records that Randolph Campbell, Mate of the ship *Antenor* in 1880 when it rescued the Alsagoff ship, *Jeddah*, was paid

£7 0s 0d per month, or that Thomas Healey, the Third Steward, received £1 5s 0d (One pound, five shillings and zero pence) so we get a sense of relative "purchasing power." In the case of companies run by John Swire in Hong Kong we can discover that in 1876 a seaman such as James Allan had his wife, Sarah Allan, mark his pay agreement with an "X" to show "her mark" (and signify that she was illiterate) to confirm that she had received a cash advance for him.[3]

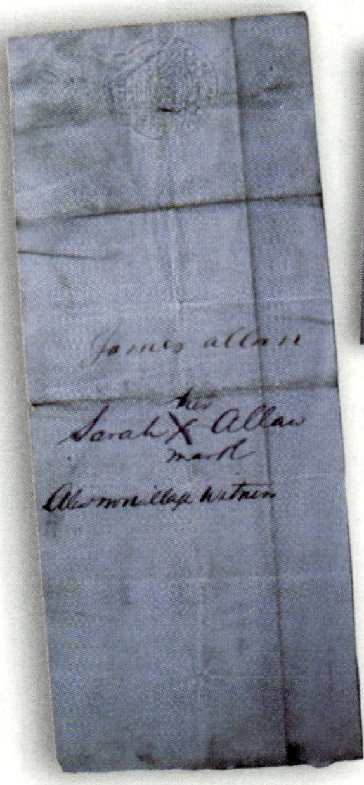
James allan
her
Sarah X Allan
mark

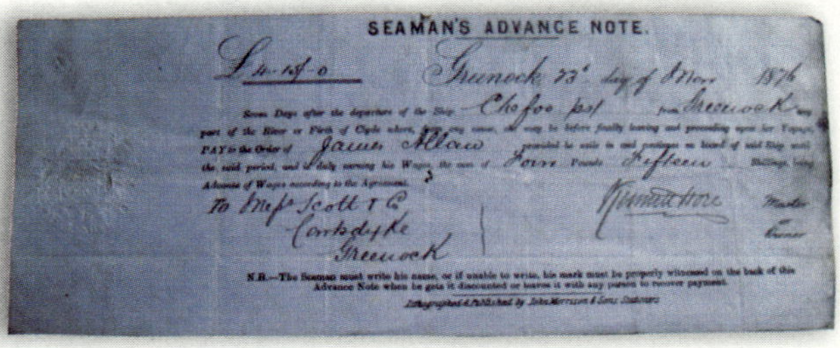
SEAMAN'S ADVANCE NOTE.

1876 Seaman's note for advance of pay; Issued at Greenock to a seaman on S.S. Chefoo, 23-25 March 1876. On the reverse side his wife has marked her receipt of the money with a cross, indicating that she cannot write. Source: JSS IV 1/5 Box A17. (C) John Swire & Sons.

Pay agreements, rates of pay, home addresses, and the date they would join the steamer – all this is available to build up a picture of the daily life of ordinary European working people such as those employed on ships. But for those classified as "natives" information like this has not come to light and was probably never kept.

If there is very little of that sort of information or that level of detail, all we can point to are some of the areas in which they may have found employment. We know that the numbers of these pilgrims from Java and other places continued to increase as the nineteenth century progressed. For many, the British-controlled territories of Singapore and Malaya were the places to earn the money for the hajj.

The options for employment

An 1861 comment spoke of "the importance of the Javanese Lascar to the trade of Singapore."[4] In this case Javanese were spoken of as providing ships' crews. Though the term "lascar" was used, it normally denoted seamen from India and is now considered negative and perhaps derogatory. Whether any Javanese seamen used their presence in Singapore as a springboard for the hajj is not confirmed. If so the numbers would have been few though it is known that Muslim sailors serving on hajj ships in the twentieth Century were sometimes given permission to leave the ship at Jeddah before it went on to Suez so that they could perform the hajj.

In 1836 Malay sampans were crewed by between three to five men. They carried whatever was needed between ship and shore at a charge of sixty cents a day and for $30 a day "they would convey letters to Penang, nearly four hundred miles."[5]

It seems doubtful that this kind of occupation would be engaged in by someone wishing to save for the pilgrimage since there would be times when little or nothing might be earned. Once again, an occupation such as this could not account for the sheer numbers of arrivals, and the need for consistent, regular employment.

Whatever the situation, if a 1902 newspaper claim is to be believed, there would seem to have been considerable opportunities for labour. A report on the debate in the Dutch Parliament on the Java Budget cited the comments of the Minister for the Colonies talking about "the present economic distress in Java" and proposing the promotion of industries, the extension of agriculture and "emigration to other possessions." In response the writer in Singapore hoped that:

> ... the Straits may be considered as one of the other "possessions" for we could do with a few tens of thousands as labourers in the Native States, and others in the Colony itself.[6]

Plantations

There were plantations to provide work and many of these involved contract labour. In 1884, for example,

> Robert Liddelow charged 14 Malays with breach of contract to work on the Pioneer Estate, Johore Lama. 13 appeared in the dock, the other being down with small pox. The prisoners all pleaded not guilty, but the signing of the contracts being proved, the case was adjourned.[7]

In Singapore itself there were pepper plantations and, until the 1860s when disease wiped them out, there were nutmeg plantations. The 1,000-acre Perseverance Estate was situated "at the commencement of the Changie [sic] Road, about three miles out of Singapore, and within a hundred yards of the Gaylang [sic] tramway terminus." Planted with citronella and lemon grasses, this land enabled a factory with sixteen stills to produce citronella oil and patchouli oil, the former being "an invaluable cure for rheumatism and . . . an excellent preventive against attacks of mosquitoes."[8]

The Alsagoff family also owned the Express Saw Mill Company, "one of the largest saw-mills in the East" and employed "as many as two hundred men at Cocub [Kukup in Johore] and forty in Singapore."[9]

And there were many estates owned and run by Chinese, dating back to the time before the arrival of Raffles, where gambier plantations existed both in the middle of the island, and close to the Singapore River although it appears that these were mostly using Chinese labour. But the larger landmass of the Malay Peninsula would have offered far more opportunities for workers from a more rural background.

Just as Hainanese Chinese in Southeast Asia traditionally had a strong presence as cooks, many Javanese tended to work as gardeners and many Baweanese with horses or, later, as drivers. So, in many references Javanese working in Singapore were referred to as *tukang kebun* or gardener and on the hajj ships they were often labelled or listed in that way. Captain J.H. Brown's recollection of his voyage in 1926 was that,

> They were invariably classified as farmers or gardeners . . . they were simple folk and their outlook "Ta' Apa," short for "Tidak Mengapa," "Not to worry."[10]

His recollection is supported by others.

And if there was not enough money?

It is now accepted that those who set out on the hajj should do so free of debt, and not leave behind anyone for whom they were responsible in a state of likely debt. That was not always the position taken and a steady stream seemed to have borrowed money to travel or, more often, to have had to borrow money to return. A system of working to pay off debts then developed.

An 1855 account described how hajj pilgrims, "remain in Arabia about two years on average, and by the time they wish to leave, their funds are generally exhausted."[11]

The report then spoke of how they might "borrow money from the Nakoda of the pilgrim vessel in which they mean to return." He would be repaid the debt and the passage money, of ten dollars per head, on arrival at Singapore by some other person; the debt would then be passed, and the pilgrims would repay it by monthly instalments, "no doubt with a very large profit."

> There are several such persons in Singapore who carry on a large business in this line, one of the most noted being a female named Che or Inche Timah. In some cases these persons even advance the passage money to Arabia as well as back, and the debt of the pilgrims is of course in such cases much larger and a longer period is required to work it off. It seems to be an understood thing that the pilgrims who become indebted as above are not to quit Singapore until their debts are discharged, and they therefore seek employment as coolies on plantations, &c. &c, each month bringing the greater part of their wages to their creditor. [12]

Twenty-six years later this problem of debt and destitution continued. In the case of Syed Mohammed Alsagoff; he either carried pilgrims back from Jeddah on his own ships or paid for them to travel on other people's, but in July 1881 a case was heard of complaints against him. 52 returned pilgrims out of a group of around 100 whose passages back from Jeddah were paid by him were complaining of the contract under which they worked for "$3½" per month at the plantation in Mt Pleasant to pay back the $40 passage. [13] When told they must go to the Alsagoff estate in "Cocob" – now Kukup – in Johore they refused and some ran to another plantation in the east of Singapore, where they were arrested.

Three days after this was published, the newspaper ran an account from Syed Mohamed, defending his position and explaining the expenses he incurred from ticket costs and from promissory notes to cover the level of indebtedness. The quality of labour that this gave him was very varied. It was not like selecting the best employees because he took them "indiscriminately."

• • • • • • • • • •

Pilgrim Brokers

What Singapore, specifically Kampong Glam, offered were linkages to ships to Jeddah and to pilgrim guides in Mecca; shops that would supply what was needed; a free dispensary, at some stage, established by a Hadhrami family; and, always, accommodation for the time they had to wait.

In the first part of the twentieth century one problem lay in the sheer number of pilgrims looking for ships to take them to Jeddah. This was particularly so in the peak years for pilgrim numbers in the mid-to late-1920s. When the Malay Pilgrimage Officer Haji Abdul Majid submitted his report in 1927 he commented on pilgrims from Sumatra speaking of a "three months enforced wait in Singapore owing to the block of pilgrims" and that they only travelled via Singapore because of there being "not sufficient N.E.I. shipping available."

In Singapore – just as in Penang, to the north – one service that was crucial for transiting pilgrims was that of pilgrim brokers, with the term Shayk Haji also commonly used for these people. In 1962 the list of registered brokers numbered twenty-five, with the vast majority of those located within Kampong Glam. Brokers would often specialise in dealing with pilgrims from a specific area, so a pilgrim from Kalimantan, for example – from Pontianak or Banjarmasin – might be directed to a broker whose family originated from that place.

A pilgrim broker's signboard. Singapore, twentieth century. Malay Heritage Foundation Collection. Image courtesy of Malay Heritage Centre, National Heritage Board. Para 235 (1) of the Pilgrim Ordinances required all who supplied lodging or accommodation to display such a sign.

Tickets, passes, medical services

Whilst there were occasional abuses in the brokerage system many who lived in Singapore and in Kampong Glam in the time when pilgrims passed through recall that time as one when, in a sense, pilgrims came and went through people's houses.

The grandfather of former Member of Parliament and Parliament Speaker, Abdullah Tarmugi was a pilgrim broker:

> I can't really put the dates down, as I knew him to be doing it since I was a small boy! His name was Hj Abdul Latiff. He was a first generation immigrant from Ponorogo in Java. We lived at 12-3 Palembang Road, Singapore 7. The house is gone now, but Masjid Fatimah, which is near our old house, still stands. There were at least two other such brokers in the vicinity of where we lived. He operated

from our house and really didn't have a separate office! He ran a provision shop at the front of our house which also served as a 'hotel' of sorts! If I remember, the other brokers also had provision shops at their houses-cum-hotel houses! This was convenient, as the pilgrims bought their provisions for the voyage from the shop! Most, if not all the pilgrims were Javanese living in Malaysia, Johor, mostly.

Our house was a hub of activity during the hajj season. A week or so before the ships sailed, the pilgrims and their relatives and friends would descend on our house and stay until the ships sailed. During this period, our house was a veritable hostel or hotel. The pilgrims and whomever came with them to send them off, were given full board and lodging! I suppose the pilgrims paid a fee for all this! A few days before the ships set sail, the pilgrims would be busy packing wooden crates with provisions – canned food, rice, coffee, etc, even kerosene stoves – to be brought with them on the voyage to Mecca.[14]

The recollections of Hajjah Hasnah binte Sahlan from the Oral History Archives:

They called this place Kampong Haji because there were so many hajjis here and there were a lot of Shaykh Hajis here. There were many tailors and seamstresses here. At the corner there was Kampong Intan. At the junction there was Kampong Tembaga. Kandahar Street did not have a kampong name. Kampong Tembaga had the tembaga [copper] smiths and they sold copper pots. Kampong Pasir Gembur was at Jalan Sultan. In the whole area there were a lot of Javanese, but most people were local and they married within the kampong. The kampong at Jalan Sultan had a lot of Javanese, they sold satay. We did not sell satay in Kampong Haji.[15]

My grandfather was a Shaykh Haji. His name was Sidek. Most of the hajjis came from Pahang, Muar, Sambas, Klang . . . The Hajis stayed in our house and ate with us. They stayed till their ship came, usually about 10 days. When the Hajis returned from Mecca, they would stay with us a few days and then go back to their countries.[16]

Hj Sidek Siraj, Pilgrimage Officer

From the "busy-ness" of people's homes and with pilgrims staying in houses in the area the impression comes across that what the pilgrims received went some way beyond just what might be expected of "business relationships." The passage of the hajj pilgrims through Singapore was part of the life-blood of the community.

Hj Sidek captured amongst the crowd at the departure of a ship in 1955. Ministry of Information and the Arts Collection, courtesy of National Archives of Singapore.

Hj Sidek Siraj was Head of Haj and Commissioner of Oaths in 1962 and the Pilgrimage Officer from 1960 to 1969. That meant close coordination with the Malaysian Government, more so when Singapore was part of Malaysia, from 1963 to 1965. Hj Sidek's role was in the issuance of passports and in working with Mansfields as the agent for the ships and with the sheikh hajis. His would be the signature on the haj passes issued throughout the 1960s.

Hj Sidek Siraj on a hajj ship. Picture by permission of Hanna Taufik Siraj.

His family recall[17] that he would often accept late applicants and also source accommodation in Mecca for them, preferably the cheapest accommodation so that they'd be able to go without worries about having little money to spare. He'd ask them to put an "X" as their signature and he would sign to confirm as witness.

But since the majority were illiterate he would also teach them basic reading, often at home to tutor them, so they could pass the test and be approved for a visa. These were pilgrims from Kelantan, Terengganu, Pahang and Johore. If the pilgrims were brought back to his home for further help with their applications, it became something of a family affair and his children would be involved in helping to fill out the forms.

The old character of Kampong Glam

The name "Arab Street" is often taken as synonymous with this area but it suggests a certain geographical connection that doesn't fully gel with the longer history. Imran bin Tajudeen is one of those who have worked on reconstructing the past of the place.[18] This was a past that existed before Stamford Raffles re-ordered the patterns of just where different communities should live, in some cases, breaking through walls to push roads (Victoria Street and North Bridge Road) through those old orders of hierarchy and society, and cutting "the Sultan's sea frontage" in half. And it was the Bugis who were already settled in the area who,

> ... experienced the full impact of Raffles' policies ...in June 1819 when Raffles desired that "the European town ....should extend along the beach ....as far eastward as practicable, including as much of the ground already cleared by the Bugguese [sic] as can possibly be required in that direction."[19]

The historical significance of this area lay with Malay and Bugis and Southeast Asian trade and settlement, and Imran Tajudeen lists a series of name changes that have altered the perception of how the place is seen.

There were old street names in use by the "local community of Southeast Asia indigenes and the immigrant Hokkien and Cantonese" but in the early 1840s these were replaced with "English ones." Historically, to the Malays, he argues, place names indicated the significance of areas in terms of kampong or compound, and therefore community or activity, rather than with street or road names. In 1887 other names were given and then, in 1912, the residents were invited to give new street names which, he notes, were influenced by "the craze for Persian *bangsawan* or opera troupes and their Arabo-Persian romances," so that Arab street names like Bussorah, meaning Basra, and Baghdad Street appear.

Within Kampong Glam Imran Tajudeen identifies areas associated with Terengganu and Pahang traders from the east coast of the Malay Peninsula; a strong Javanese presence "associated with the mosque, craftsmen and artisans and the performing arts"; and Banjarese (from Banjarmasin in Borneo) in the diamond and gem trade. In front of the Sutan's *istana* or palace, a Javanese bachelor house – *rumah bujangan* – had stood for a very long time.

Around the Istana there was Pahang Street where businessmen, traders, tailors and *capal*–makers[20] operated. The south part of Bussorah Street and Baghdad Street was "Kampong Tembaga": the coppersmith's compound; and an ironsmiths' zone was at the southern part of Sultan Gate. And around Kampong Glam were dotted the houses of pilgrim brokers and houses for the lodging of pilgrims. Arab Street, notes Imran, was known to the Hokkien Chinese as *Jiawa Koi* (Javanese Street). The Javanese presence was very evident.

As early as 1822, that presence in Singapore warranted the appointment of a representative from their community to the town committee. It would be the Javanese who would become central figures in the very significant printing and publishing industry that developed in Kampong Glam, making Singapore the regional centre for printing and publishing towards the end of the nineteenth century.

As a small indicator of relative numbers, in 1852, when a large fire broke out in 23, Arab Street, "Kampong Jawa," and spread quickly among the attap and wooden houses, 135 houses were burnt, "of which 101 were inconsiderable inhabited by Javanese, 21 by Malays, 8 by Chinese and 5 by Klings."[21]

It must be stressed that this was never an exclusively Malay or Javanese area. It was bounded by the sea and by the Kallang River, which was a centre for shipbuilding and ship repairing. The bark from the gelam[22] tree was used for caulking ships' hulls and the area also hosted other small businesses that served ships. In 1924 the Superintendent of the Fire Brigade inspected two shophouses in Palembang Road which each had an unlicensed "smithy and foundry" in them.

> 1 April 1924 – a memorandum from the Superintendent of the Fire Brigade License for a Smithy and Foundry at No 19 Palembang Rd for Tan Ah Kow.
>
> Inspected a "fairly large foundry . . . at present appears to be turning out a considerable amount of work. One small engine installed. Is in a residential area and should be warned that license is unlikely to be renewed indefinitely." [23]

Another on 5 April 1924:

> A Smithy and Foundry license being granted to Leong Ah Yoon, 34, Palembang Road. (Installed machinery without permission).
>
> This is what is classed as Heavy Industry. There is an oil engine driving planers, drilling and other large machine tools, also a number of large lathes. At the back is a small foundry and moulding shop. The engine was producing great vibration on the ground, building, and it appeared to me, vibration in adjoining buildings. This engine is small, but appeared to be running at its top capacity. The engine, bedplate, and foundation block were visibly vibrating. This engine was also making considerable noise.
>
> Except on the frontage, this foundry and workshop adjoins purely residential buildings. The proprietor of the Pilgrims Hostel two doors away, and other persons who I was told were adjacent occupiers, complained pretty vigorously of the noise and the vibration – which, they stated, habitually continued 7 days a week and often all night.[24]

A chain of links

Beyond Kampong Glam there would be work for prospective pilgrims arriving here from the Peninsula to the north or from what is now modern-day Indonesia. Within this small area, would be so much that was familiar: communities of shared origin, and processes and people to help their journey. But the significance of this place was not just for those arriving. Around the end of the nineteenth Century it was what was spreading out from Singapore: printing, publishing, entertainment and ideas.

Bussorah Street in Kampong Glam, looking towards the rebuilt Masjid Sultan that was completed in 1928. Here, a man walks barefoot down the street in the late 1920s or early 1930s. Image by courtesy of Glen Christian.

[1] Roff, William R. 1980. *The Origins of Malay Nationalism*. Kuala Lumpur: University of Malaya Press, pp. 35-36.

[2] This information is available in the 1920s reports from Jeddah held in the UK National Archives.

[3] John Swire Archive. JSS IV 1/5 Box A17. London: SOAS (School of Oriental and African Studies).

[4] Roff. 1980, pp. 35-36.

[5] ST. 30 March 1861, p. 2.

[6] Buckley, p. 311.

[7] SFPMA, 31 December 1902.

[8] ST. 8 March 1884, p. 12.

[9] Wright. 1908, p. 664.

[10] Ibid. p. 707.

[11] Brown. p. 286.

[12] SFPMA. 6 December 1855, p. 2.

[13] STOJ. 28 July 1881.

[14] From an email communication with Anthony Green.

[15] National Archives of Singapore. (Hereinafter referred to as NAS). Acc. No. 560, Reel 1.

[16] NAS. Acc. No. 560, Reel 2.

[17] Personal communication with Hanna Taufik Siraj, granddaughter of Hj Sidek and, through her, to Hj Sidek's daughter – Hana Taufik's aunt.

[18] Much of this information is taken from Imran bin Tajudeen, *Reading the Traditional City of Maritime Southeast Asia: Reconstructing the 19th Century Port Town at Gelam-Rochor-Kallang, Singapore*, in Journal of Southeast Architecture Vol 8 (2005).

[19] Ibid. p. 16.

[20] Makers of the traditional Malay leather sandals; the *capal.*

[21] Buckley, Charles Burton. 1984. *An Anecdotal History of Old Times in Singapore: 1819-1867.* Singapore: OUP. p. 563. "Klings" here is the term used to refer to Indians. It is now considered derogatory.

[22] A tree known as *melaleuca leucadendron* or *melaleuca cajaputi.*

[23] NAS. File no. S.I.T. 331/24, dated 5/1/1924.

[24] NAS. File no. S.I.T. 111/24, dated 5/1/1924.

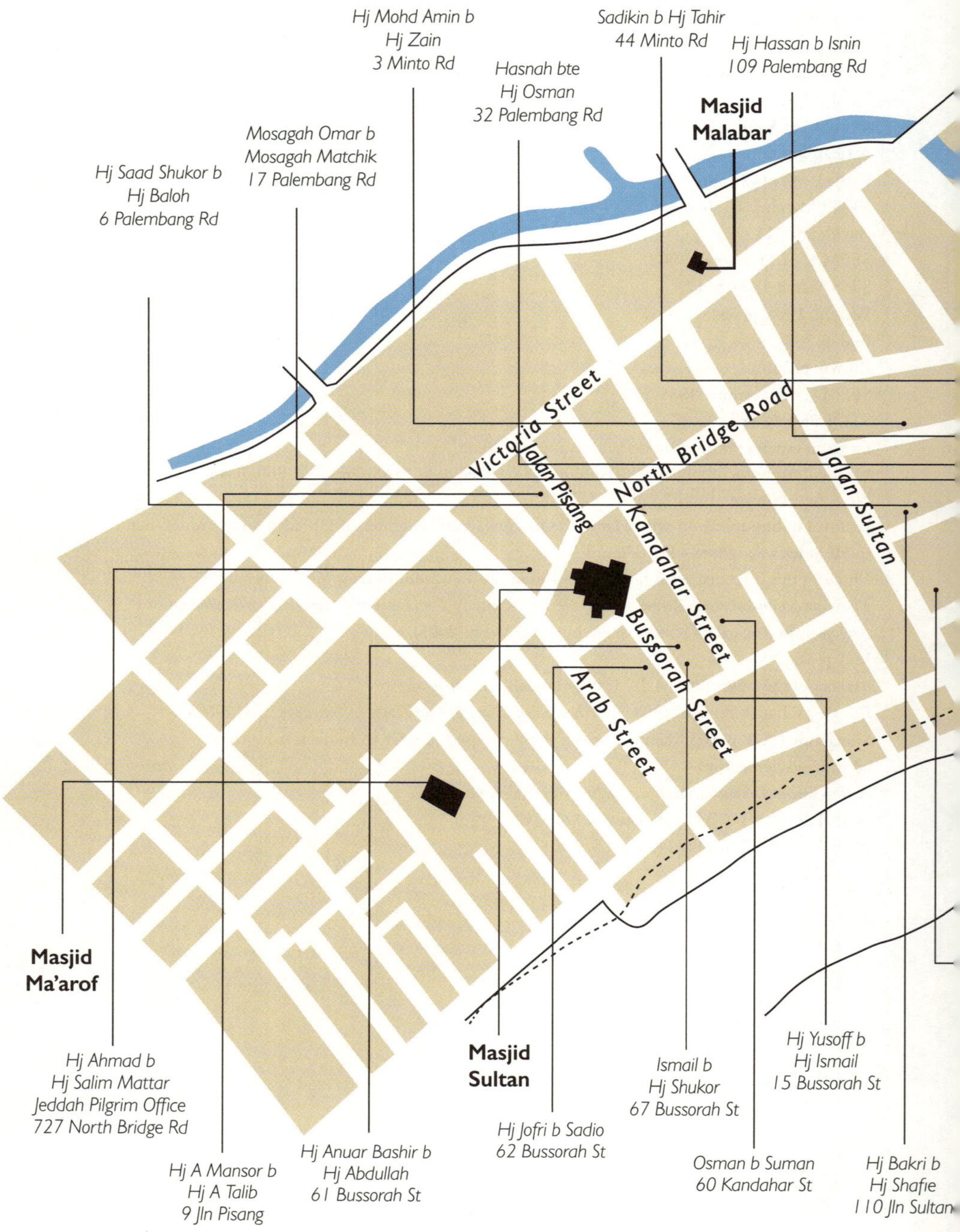
Hj Mohd Amin b
Hj Zain
3 Minto Rd
Sadikin b Hj Tahir
44 Minto Rd
Hj Hassan b Isnin
109 Palembang Rd
Hasnah bte
Hj Osman
32 Palembang Rd
Masjid
Malabar
Mosagah Omar b
Mosagah Matchik
17 Palembang Rd
Hj Saad Shukor b
Hj Baloh
6 Palembang Rd
Victoria Street
North Bridge Road
Jalan Pisang
Jalan Sultan
Kandahar Street
Bussorah Street
Arab Street
Masjid
Ma'arof
Hj Ahmad b
Hj Salim Mattar
Jeddah Pilgrim Office
727 North Bridge Rd
Hj A Mansor b
Hj A Talib
9 Jln Pisang
Hj Anuar Bashir b
Hj Abdullah
61 Bussorah St
Masjid
Sultan
Hj Jofri b Sadio
62 Bussorah St
Ismail b
Hj Shukor
67 Bussorah St
Osman b Suman
60 Kandahar St
Hj Yusoff b
Hj Ismail
15 Bussorah St
Hj Bakri b
Hj Shafie
110 Jln Sultan

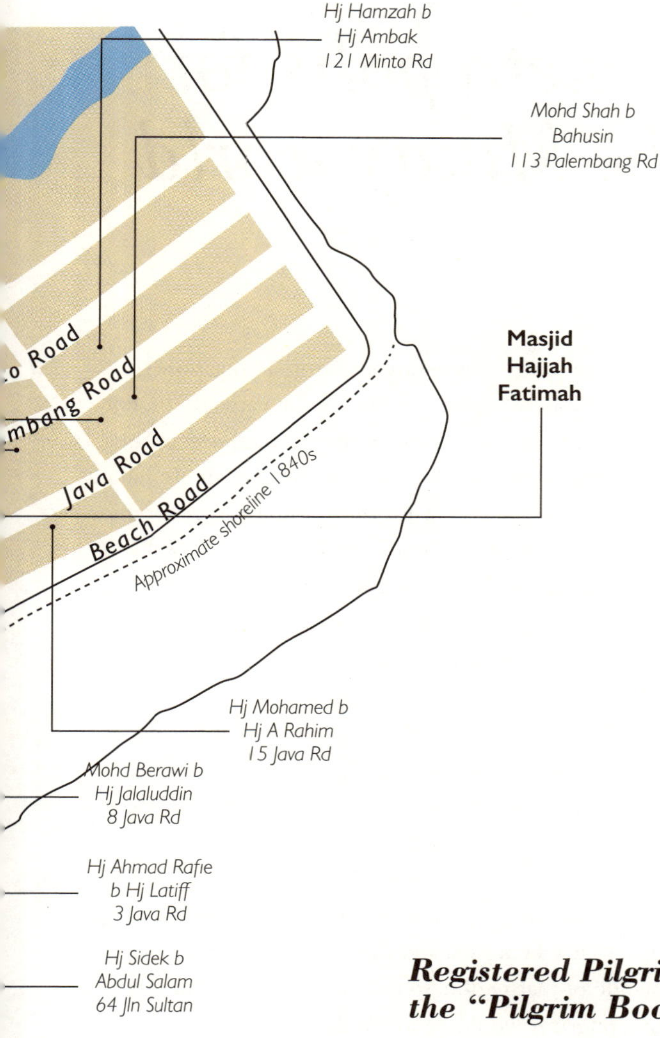

Registered Pilgrim Brokers from the "Pilgrim Book 1962"

Pilgrim brokers came and went. Some operated from other parts of the island, but these names give an indicator of the numbers operating in Kg Glam. (The names are as given in the "Pilgrim Book"; locations within streets are approximate)

5

A metropolis for the Malay world

The rise and eventual shrinking of the hajj business mirrored Singapore's key role within the Malay world between the 1830s and the early 1970s. For Muslims, transactions associated with the hajj clearly represented one of the most thriving businesses and the centre for this was Kampong Glam. In talking about nineteenth century Singapore as a focus for the cultural and economic energies of that wide span "from Kedah and Acheh to the Celebes," William Roff offers a comparison which he concedes cannot be taken too far. He likens it to Malacca in the fifteenth, "in its role as a metropolis" for this area. What it brought together in this one urban setting was,

> ... a great variety of Malaysian and Muslim peoples from differing social and economic backgrounds but sharing a lingua franca and important elements of a common culture, and often freed from the hampering restraints of a traditional social system.[1]

By "Malaysian" Roff was not referring to the modern political understanding of that adjective, but to the Malay Peninsula and the Indonesian Archipelago – Nusantara – and the people of that region, so that in Singapore, and more especially, Kampong Glam, pilgrims would be in familiar territory, in terms of language, food, religious community and more. Familiar, yet different. They would be out of some of the constraints of their places of origin. In the Malayan Peninsula there was a social order based on a concept of *Kerajaan* – "the condition of having a *raja*."[2] This was not the case in Singapore. And for those from the archipelago there would be some clear differences between lives lived under Dutch and British ways of working.

The previous chapter asked what Singapore and Kampong Glam offered to anyone intending to undertake the hajj. But there are more questions that can be introduced, though again these are questions that cannot lead to answers. We can wonder just what impression this place might have made on individual pilgrims passing through, and whether this had any effect on their thinking. A modern hajj journey takes the pilgrim from an airport of departure to one of arrival, in the close – almost exclusive – presence of others bound for Mecca. But this journey by sea would take a hajj pilgrim through a variety of spaces and places, each with their attractions and distractions, and not everything that they would see or hear would lend itself to a focus on the hajj.

What follows suggests just something of the tone and life of Singapore and Kampong Glam.

A free port for ideas

Within that small area there were the mosques of course: the old mosque built for the Sultan; Masjid Hajjah Fatimah, built by that wealthy trading lady; and, after 1870, a mosque in Clyde Street. But here and across Singapore there was also entertainment: theatre, troupes for *bangsawan* (Malay opera), music, and even cinema.

Yet if Singapore was a free port for commerce it was also something of a free port for ideas. Urban settings can be fertile grounds for such things and Singapore offered a place for political discussion and the discussion of religion. Michael Laffan notes that in 1873 the Dutch began their "three-decade attempt to subdue Aceh" and he adds that, in contrast, in Singapore, "the pilgrim, the jurist, and the Sufi could all meet."[3] But the importance went well beyond a meeting place for discussion. The strength of printing and publishing meant that religious ideas could be spread from here across the region, and given Singapore's position as a major shipping and trading centre, it was "ideally sited for the dissemination of information into the peninsula and archipelago."[4]

So, printing and publishing and bookselling feature strongly in any measure of the place of Kampong Glam and Singapore.

The Malay Publishing Industry

Printing in the island began with the arrival of the Danish missionary, the Reverend Claudius Henry Thomsen, and his work with Abdullah bin Abdul Kadir (better known as Munsyi Abdullah), the Malay teacher and translator from Malacca. The two men had collaborated on a number of Malay-language works and, in 1823, along with another missionary, Samuel Milton, Thomsen established Mission Press, the first approved printing press in Singapore.

Munsyi Abdullah is regarded as both a pioneer and mentor of modern printing in the Malay world.[5] He was involved in the translation of works into Malay and in the operation of the press owned by Rev. Keasberry, an American Christian missionary, and his original literary works, including his major work, *Hikayat Abdullah* (Memoir of Abdullah) – part autobiography, part personal views – were also published by Keasberry.

By the 1860s, the first indigenous Malay/Muslim printers and publishers had emerged in Singapore,[6] in some competition with European and Baba Peranakan (Straits-born Chinese) publishers. The latter were responsible for translating many Chinese literary works, including those in the Hokkien dialect, into Malay, and for publishing Baba Peranakan *syair* and *pantun,*[7] although this Baba printing has been said to be "always an ad hoc affair."[8]

Spreading religious ideas

For a Muslim audience the breakthrough in printing came with the use of lithography. Although the technology had been introduced by Christian missionaries, in the hands of Muslim printers the limestone "allowed for the replication of the calligraphic styles favored for the Qur'anic text"[9] since the scribe could hand-write directly on to the stone, with the inscription then transferred onto paper. Handwritten manuscripts have "an elegance"[10] that was not felt to be there in the typographic productions that European missionaries had brought with them. These were "offerings that were deemed barely palatable from an aesthetic point of view."[11] But with a lithograph, multiple copies of a text could be printed economically in a way that reproduced the manuscript format. Production spread very quickly with texts, not necessarily always religious, but expected to appeal to a Malay audience, and from the 1840s onwards, printing presses purchased in Singapore were being used in Palembang, Sumatra; in Surabaya, and in Riau.

Specialised work for a few

Ian Proudfoot writes of a man named Encik Ibrahim Riau who, whilst "not a very significant printer in his own right" has a claim to significance in that, at 720 North Bridge Road, between Jalan Kubur and Jalan Kledek, for twenty years from 1889, he became the leading lithographic copyist in Singapore.

His position adds a small footnote to the earlier discussion on the work available in Singapore. Ibrahim, it seems, assumed the role described by the Dutch scholar, Snouck Hurgronje, when he reported that Singapore printers generally retained "a destitute haji or some other person with a good writing hand" in their service, and had them copy out for lithographic transfer, works of which the printer had a copy and for which he knew there was demand.[12] So, in the story of the hajj journey, we have one more area of work that might have provided an income for a tiny number of hajj pilgrims, in this case those returning.

The Javanese

Proudfoot stresses that the "principal lithographers in Singapore were of Javanese extraction,"[13] so the early Malay printing and publishing houses were established in the main by immigrants from the north coast of Java who had settled in the immediate vicinity of Sultan Mosque. The majority of these were clustered tightly around Jalan Sultan and Bussorah Street, the road that leads directly to the mosque frontage. This was where the potential customers were, and many Islamic pamphlets, and religious books known as *kitab kuning* (using yellow tinted paper), were published there and distributed widely.

Across in the Netherlands East Indies, Hurgronje saw that those who sought a more scholarly path were moving from Batavia "toward the north coast, where students would be offered a richer and more varied diet of works printed at

Singapore."[14] One more reason for the significance of Singapore compared to the archipelago was that,

> ... the Netherlands East Indies government applied draconian press laws, which obliged printers to deposit large bonds with the government and required pre-publication censorship.[15]

Throughout the region levels of "private literacy" in the nineteenth century – ie, personal literacy – were low and the great increase in commercial book production was not matched by an equivalent rise in literacy rates. Even so, there was a real capacity for the consumption of literary material, even if much of that was through listening – to elders of the village or travelling, professional storytellers. And in 1901, for example, it could still be said that, "newspapers written in the new prose continued to be enjoyed by group audiences, in coffee shops."[16] Any mention of literacy should note that listening to a reading is an important way of engaging. Communities like this were closer to oral traditions and the heard word operates with the involvement of the reader and listener together.

Malay as the Lingua Franca

For centuries Malay was the language of diplomacy and trade in Maritime Southeast Asia, and usage such as this, together with the interest shown by non-Malay publishers in producing books in Malay, all highlighted its role as the lingua franca of the region. Early in the nineteenth century William Marsden, an official of the East India Company, said that, "every person, of whatever nation, who frequents a port of trade must negotiate his business in this tongue."[17] In the eighteenth century, François Valentijn had compared Malay with "French and Latin in Europe" and suggested that,

> If you don't understand this language you are not considered a very broadly educated man in the east.[18]

Literature was "a further aspect of Malay uniformity . . . heard rather than read."[19] In Sumatra, Marsden had noted a striking consistency of style of writing in a range of material he received from across the archipelago and, some distance away in Kalimantan (Borneo), Dutch scholar W. Kern noted that,

> Bandjarese, [sic] the dialect of Bandjarmasin in south-east Borneo, had "never been used as a literary language. Even in private correspondence people always use, or at least try to use, Literary Malay."[20]

The prolific printers

Two of the most prolific Malay printers in mid- to late- nineteenth century Singapore were Haji Muhammad Said bin Haji Arsyad of Semarang and Haji Muhammad Siraj bin Haji Salih of Rembang. It was the practice at the time to mention, after their names, their places of origin, both Semarang and Rembang being towns in Java. Haji Muhammad Said and his sons published more than 200 Malay-language publications between 1873 and 1918. In the same period, Haji Muhammad Siraj published around 80 books. In 1868 one Singapore bookshop of Malay books had an inventory of 1,000 books.

In the following two decades the Malay printing industry in Singapore bloomed, with activity peaking in the 1880s. Haji Muhammad Said remained the leading printer alongside other second-generation printers, such as Haji Muhammad Siraj and his brother, Haji Muhammad Sidik; Haji Muhammad Amin bin Abdullah; and Haji Muhammad Taib bin Zain.

Haji Muhammad Said had four sons, all groomed in the book printing business. In 1892, the family set up a branch office in Penang and opened a bookshop there, and by 1898 this was run by one of the sons, Haji Muhammad Majtahid.

... and the competition

After 1900, the output of Malay lithographic printing declined and by the mid-1920s Singapore's advantage as a Malay printing hub fell away. Competition came from at least two sources. In several cities such as Penang and Batavia there was the availability of cutting-edge, letterpress printing machines and knowledgeable operators. Added to this, publications imported from India and the Middle East by Malay booksellers flooded the regional market and the competition affected many local publishers. But if the flow of books outwards fell away, the flow of pilgrims passing through Singapore in the 1920s was still very significant. Writing in the 1970s William Roff said, "The year 1927 saw the largest pilgrimage ever undertaken from Malaya, still unsurpassed in size."[21]

So, like others at the beginning of the twentieth century, the family business of Haji Muhammad Said shifted its focus from printing to retailing books. Haji Abdullah, another son, assumed the main responsibility of running the bookshop in Singapore and marketing its publications. By 1912, their bookshop was advertising Malay books printed in Mecca, Istanbul, Russia, Egypt and Bombay, and men like Haji Muhammad Said, Haji Muhammad Siraj and others were also notable for their distinctly entrepreneurial spirit.

> Sirs, if you want to buy this book
> Just drop in at my shop and take a look.
> Sealed and stamped, it costs a small amount:
> Ten cents; and by the dozen I discount.
> So come in, sirs, as your merry way you wend.
> And you, too, brothers; – and kindly bring a friend.
>
> Found in *Kumbang Cumbuan* (1890), printed by Haji Muhammad Said.
> Translated by Ian Proudfoot.[22]

Newspapers and Magazines

The next key platform for spreading ideas came with newspapers and magazines, and Singapore was credited with producing, in the year 1876, one of the earliest weekly newspapers in the Malay world. This Jawi[23] scripted paper was published every Monday and called *Jawi Peranakkan*. Its owner and founding editor was Munsyi Muhammad Said bin Dada Muhyiddin, a Penang-born Indian Peranakan. When he passed away, Haji Muhammad Siraj bin Haji Salih helmed the paper from 1889 to 1891.

It carried official government notices, letters from readers, editorials and syair (poems), and was in circulation until 1895. In his various correspondences in English, Haji Muhammad Siraj signed off as H.M. Sirat, for reasons known only to himself. He was an astute businessman with a strong network of acquaintances ranging from royalty to editors of The Singapore Free Press and The Straits Times.

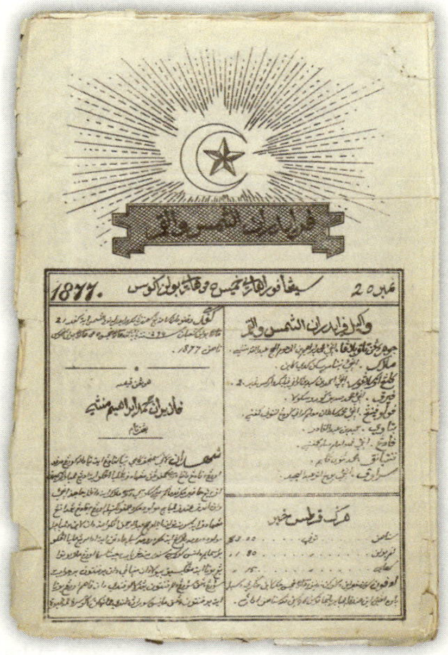

Peridaran al-Shams wa-al-Qamar, issue no.20, 30 August 1877. Wellcome Library, Malay collection / Hervey collection / Pamphlets / 1. A weekly newspaper which, according to Annabel Teh Gallop, was first published 19 April 1877, and "whose editor had studied with Keasberry and Abdullah Munsyi." It seems to have died out after a short run.

From 1876 to 1941, there were 147 Malay newspapers and magazines published in Malaya and the Straits Settlements (Singapore, Malacca and Penang), with 68 produced in Singapore and 36 in Penang.

Muslim Mindsets and Malay Nationalism

In many ways this was a community developing a voice for itself with new opportunities for expression of identity. In November 1874 the Master Attendant in Singapore had written a report on the overcrowding of four pilgrim ships that had left that port. In it he included a table with columns to indicate the numbers of pilgrims permitted on each ship and the numbers actually taken. Two columns indicating where they were from were headed "No. of Netherland Pilgrims" and "No. of English Pilgrims." A small detail, this idea of "English pilgrims," but these were like labels of convenience; they could not reflect the reality of how a people would see themselves, so one more issue of interest in late nineteenth century Singapore – and a force that ties in with the growth of newspapers – was the rise of Malay nationalism.

Malays who had graduated from Al-Azhar University in Cairo brought home new ideas. They combined these with a call for changes in the mindset with regard to religious views and practices that were confused with Malay *adat* (customs). These people were dubbed *Kaum Muda* (Young Turks) by the traditionalists who were against them and who, themselves, were later known as *Kaum Tua* (the older set), and in 1906 a monthly magazine with reformist

JAWI PERANAKKAN.

Jawi Peranakkan, vol.5, no.214, 28 March 1881 – the oldest surviving issue. British Library, OP 434.

ideas appeared on the scene. This was *Al-Imam*. It ran for three years and was largely influenced by the magazine, *Al-Manar*, edited by Rashid Rida and published in Cairo.

Amongst the staunchest exponents of the *Kaum Muda* ideas was Syed Syaikh Syed Ahmad Al-Hadi (1867-1934). Apart from publishing journals, he also published books and novels with reformist themes, particularly on women's emancipation. These *Kaum Muda* and *Kaum Tua* debates or polemics would continue up to the late 1950s. Writing about the British presence in India, John Slight has said that,

> Official policy [towards Muslims] combined a degree of suspicion with "a strategy of cooperation with a wide range of elite Indian Muslim leaders ... and a degree of sensitivity to what officials termed 'Muslim opinion'"[24]

Something similar was present in the approach taken by the British in Southeast Asia and ideas such as those of the *Kaum Muda* offered a challenge to a social order with which the colonial presence felt a kind of comfort. How many passing pilgrims read or heard these arguments while on their journey or whilst in Mecca we cannot know. The core intention was the hajj but thoughts and impressions would be carried in these travelling communities.

And a political Party

In Singapore a remarkable turning point came when Mohd Eunos Abdullah, a former student of Raffles Institution and a civil servant, was challenged by *The Singapore Free Press* to lead a Malay newspaper called *Utusan Melayu*. Eunos has been hailed by William Roff as "the Father of Malay Journalism"[25] for his progressive ideas and his management of the paper, which was circulated even to Sumatra. He was made a Justice of Peace and was the first Malay to be appointed to the Legislative Assembly, a relatively influential position in that time. He persuaded the British to allow the setting up of the Malay Institute to provide remedial classes to uplift the educational level of the Malays.

His significance in this story is that, with several like-minded Malays such as the Bugis tycoon, Ambo Sooloh, and Tengku Abdul Kadir who belonged to the Kampong Glam royal family, he established the first quasi-political body in the Malay world, called Kesatuan Melayu Singapura (KMS or Singapore Malays Union) in 1926. KMS was formed in the premises of the Istana Kampong Glam, the former home of the first sultan of modern Singapore, Sultan Hussein Shah.

The aim was to increase the role of Malays in public life, uphold Malay interests before the colonial authorities, and promote higher and technical education for Malays. It was seen as a beacon of hope in galvanising the spirit of Malay nationalism. It also introduced a new dynamic in being critical of some of the Arab community and the Indian Peranakans for marginalising the general concerns of the Malays.

Two decades later in 1939, KMS members pooled their resources to establish a newspaper that was wholly-owned by Malays, *Utusan Melayu*. Its managing editor was Yusof Ishak, a man who would become Singapore's first *Yang di-Pertuan Negara* (Head of State) in 1959 and its first President in 1965.

The Malay Intelligentsia

The period from the 1950s to the 1970s was a significant one in Singapore, with *Utusan* regaining its premier position as the Malay voice of people seeking *Merdeka* (independence) for Malaya and Singapore. It had many top thinkers and literary figures among its staff. These critical and formative years were remembered by Haji Sulaiman Jeem:

> In the 1950's, Singapore still retained its role as a thriving hub of Malay music, film and printing activities. It was also the centre of Malay intelligentsia who hailed from many parts of the Malay world of Southeast Asia.[26]

Haji Sulaiman had worked as a proof reader with *Qalam* Press whose owner – the Riau-born Syed Abdullah Abdul Hamid Al-Edrus – edited the monthly magazine "*Majalah Qalam*", which published progressive ideas from the Reform Movement. He was an ardent supporter of Egypt's Ikhwanul Muslimun (Islamic Brotherhood) and used his magazine to spread the ideas of *Kaum Muda* in the region.

Another tide of change, and one opposed by Edrus, was the movement to use Romanised letters – *tulisan rumi* – for the Malay language, something that was adopted across the region and that played a unifying role, even if people in different places "agreed to disagree" on certain spellings.

This movement was championed by the majority of associations, including the group known as *Angkatan Sasterawan '50* (ASAS 50), attending the 3rd Malay Language and Literary Conference, convened in Johor Bahru and Singapore. Founded in 1950, the motto of ASAS 50 was *Seni Untuk Masyarakat* (essentially, art for the people). The group was inspired by the Indonesian writers' movement, *Angkatan '45*, and the essence of much of the writings that came from this concerned making a better life for people.

Whilst these issues are not directly involved with the organisation or administration of the hajj, they all concern ideas and the movement of ideas across the region. Ideas spread through interactions between people, and the movement of hajj pilgrims played its part in delivering those interactions.

Beach Road, Singapore in 1947. The Marlborough Theatre on the right and the Alhambra on the left. The Marlborough was where the "first Malay talkie" movie was screened in 1934. Tan Kok Kheng Collection, courtesy of National Archives of Singapore.

Entertainment and Language

For a prospective pilgrim in transit to Jeddah and Mecca, once the hajj connections were made, Singapore also offered something different. It drew in composers, musicians, singers and actors who came in droves. Two significant composers hailed from Sumatra: Pak Zubir Said and Pak Ahmad Jaafar, and it was Pak Ahmad who summed up Singapore as "very attractive with its glittering lights, not to mention *kopi susu* (coffee with milk) and butter" – small luxuries not always found elsewhere, but small details can last longer in the memory.

The two men came to Singapore to work with bangsawan troupes and later at night clubs, cabarets and two film production studios, Shaw Brothers and Cathay Keris. Penang was the birth place of bangsawan but in the late nineteenth century it had blossomed in Singapore, its performers being involved in the birth of Singapore's Malay recording and film industries.

The first movie shown in Singapore – a Hollywood silent film – was in 1898. But on 27 March 1934 there was screened at the Marlborough Theatre on Beach road a "SPECIAL GREAT TREAT FOR HARI RAYA HAJI." The advertisement, with its description of the "TREAT" in upper case, was generous with its adjectives. This was:

> An extraordinary super production and glorious de luxe attraction for all... The first spectacular Colossal Malay Talkie. Numerous Beautiful Egyptian Dances ...Songs and Dialogues in Classical Malay... A soul-stirring spectacular portrayal of true love.[27]

This was *Leila Majnun*, a story which dates back to a twelfth century Persian tale that the English poet Lord Byron had called "the Romeo and Juliet of the East." It was produced by an Indian company in Singapore and starred a number of people that included top bangsawan performers. It set in motion a movie industry that led to a demand for music, songs and dances. It attracted foreign recording companies such as HMV and EMI and generated several local ones but came to an end in the 1970's when the Malay recording industry moved to a new centre, Kuala Lumpur.

It was to this "very attractive" place that hajj pilgrims would come and through it that they would pass.

[1] Roff. 1980, p. 32.

[2] Milner, Anthony. 2016. *Kerajaan: Malay Political Culture on the Eve of Colonial Rule*. Petaling Jaya, Malaysia. Strategic Information and Information Centre, p. 169.

[3] Laffan. 2011. p. 53. Michael Laffan's book gives a detailed insight into titles that were published and how religious ideas were contested across the region through printed works, many of which were produced in Singapore.

[4] Proudfoot. p. 7.

[5] Rahmat, Hadijah. 2012.

[6] Proudfoot, I. (1993). *Early Malay printed books: A provisional account of materials published in the Singapore-Malaysia area up to 1920.* Kuala Lumpur: Academy of Malay Studies and the Library, University of Malaya.

[7] Syair and pantun are both four-lined forms of poetry in Malay. In a pantun the four lines are alternating, roughly rhyming, with an a-b-a-b rhyme scheme. The first and second lines may appear to be disconnected in meaning from the third and fourth, but the link comes through allusion or through the association of feeling through the traditional meaning of the symbols that are used. A syair has four-line stanzas, each one rhymed a-a-a-a and presents a continuous idea from one stanza to the next.

[8] Proudfoot. p. 20.

[9] Laffan. p. 55.

[10] An adjective that we have taken from an online essay: http://s-pores.com/2017/01/the-intellectual-legacy-of-kampung-glam-by-fadli-fawzi-and-faris-joraimi/ (Accessed October 2018)

[11] Laffan. p. 55.

[12] Proudfoot. 1993, p. 42.

[13] Proudfoot. p. 62.

[14] Laffan. p. 142.

[15] Proudfoot. p. 7.

[16] Proudfoot. p. 18.

[17] Milner. p. 5.

[18] Ibid.

[19] Milner. p. 6.

[20] Ibid.

[21] Roff. 2009A, p. 323.

[22] Taken from a display panel in the exhibition *"Tales of The Malay World: Manuscripts and Early Books"* at the National Library, Singapore, October 2017.

[23] Jawi is an Arabic script used for writing Malay and other languages in Maritime Southeast Asia. It was largely replaced by a Latin alphabet called Rumi as the official Malay script in Indonesia, Malaysia and Singapore but it is still used extensively across the region.

[24] Slight, John. 2015. *The British Empire and the Hajj* – 1865-1956. Cambridge, Massachusetts: Harvard University Press, p. 26.

[25] Ibid.

[26] Hj Sulaiman, interviewed by Mohd Ramad Daud at Baalwie Mosque, Singapore. May, 2018.

The Qur'an says:

"And proclaim the pilgrimage among men: they will come to Thee on foot and on every kind of camel, lean on account of journeys through deep and distant mountain highways."

Surah Al-Hajj, 22: 27

6

The ships they sailed in:

The days of sail

A freight of some description

Throughout the history of hajj travel by sea, and until the 1950s, there were almost no dedicated passenger vessels. For the greater part of that time pilgrims were, effectively, just another cargo: a "freight," so that a newspaper report like this in 1880 could appear:

> The conveyance of these devotees has been found to be a profitable trade, and many a captain who has failed to get a freight of any other description has done a good thing in pilgrims for his owners. They are usually taken as deck passengers, paying from two pounds to four pounds a piece for the voyage. In return for this, the captain finds them only with fresh water and fuel. They bring their own provisions, principally of a vegetable kind.[1]

And so there were many occasions when ships' masters would not only "take on deck passengers" but would fill up with as many of them as they could. This seemed to be both common practice and common knowledge. It was recognised by authorities in the Straits Settlements and letters were written to newspapers bemoaning the situation, though it took a very long time before any sort of mechanisms were put in place to try to prevent it. Realistically, it would not be until the last 25 years of the kapal haji when they would finally become passenger ships with proper, assigned sleeping places. Then, aside from those in cabins, most passengers would sleep in bunks just as soldiers would on a troopship.

Being a deck passenger would mean just that – sleeping on a deck; above, in the open, or down below. In the days of steamships the decks were steel although at one stage the regulations for pilgrim ships required the steel to be sheathed with wood; a requirement that was subsequently abandoned.

• • • • • • • • • •

Suez – Before and After

One clear distinction in hajj shipping is between the time before the opening of the Suez Canal in November 1869 and the time after. Before Suez, the ships that carried hajj pilgrims were sailing vessels. Arab shipowners dominated the business and Jeddah was a destination in the Red Sea with little significance to Europeans.

That would change completely after Suez, although the "windships" would not suddenly disappear. In the Singapore harbour in July 1881, for example, there were three "men of war," 20 "steamers," and 31 sailing vessels – Portuguese, British, German, Siamese, American, Norwegian, Danish. For hajj shipping, the balance of ownership and the control of that trade would now shift.

• • • • • • • • • •

The hajj in the time of sail

In Southeast Asia throughout the eighteenth century almost all of the sailing vessels that were used for the hajj were wooden-hulled, with three masts and two decks. These were ships rigged in European fashion with their sails generally configured as barques. In the early part of that period, on a small number of occasions, according to the records available, brigs – smaller ships with just two masts – also sailed to Jeddah.

A brig – a two-masted ship with the sails on both masts "square rigged." Some brigs sailed to Jeddah from Southeast Asia up to the early 19th century. Most sailing ships after that time were larger, and rigged as barques. Brig "Roald Amundsen." RTHiele. Published under GNU Free Documentation License.

The ships themselves could have originated from anywhere in the world. In the registry records of the 1860s you find that the 628-ton *Alliance*, jointly owned by Syed Ahmad bin Abdulrahman Alsagoff and Syed Allie bin Omar Aljunied (both described as "merchants"), had been built in Quebec in 1854.[2] The 513-ton *Augusta*, jointly owned by Syed Ahmad and Syed Mohamed Alsagoff, was built in New Hampshire, USA, in 1849. And the name of Syed Abdullah bin Omar Aljunied appears as the owner of a 1,202 ton three-masted ship, *Cama Family*, again built in the United States of America. One advantage of a barque rigging was in needing fewer crew members than in a fully rigged ship.

A preserved three-masted barque. Barques may have three or more masts but the aftmost, "mizzen," mast of a barque is rigged with sails "fore-and-aft." On the other masts the sails are square-rigged. Barques were popular as they required a smaller crew than a full-rigged ship – ie, one with all masts square-rigged. US Revenue Cutter "Salmon P Chase." Image in the Public Domain.

And if there were no wind?

After the Second World War the average voyage time for a "steamship" from Singapore to Jeddah was reckoned to be about 14 days. Before that war, advertisements gave 17 days as the journey time, and in the days of sailing ships in the nineteenth century 50 days was the expected time. But that did not allow for a wide range of variables.

For a start there is the simple but very significant difference between sail and "steam." It's obvious but still worth saying that a mechanically powered vessel can travel in a straight line. A sailing vessel is completely dependent on the wind. You cannot sail directly into a headwind – a wind that is coming straight towards you – you must tack and tack again. If the wind is behind you then you must jibe and jibe again. And if there is no wind then you stand still, or drift.

An advertisement for Blue Funnel sailings in 1937, from the magazine, "Genuine Islam." Image courtesy of Ibrahim Tahir.

A hajj ship becalmed

On 12 August 1870 The Straits Times Overland Journal ran a brief report that a French troopship, the *Sarthe*, on its way from Toulon to Saigon, had come across a sailing ship, becalmed:

> The *"Sarthe"* reports that on the 14th July, close to Ras-tchek on the African coast, she met the ship *"Henry Harbeck"* of Singapore, with 450 pilgrims and a crew of 50 men, in all 500. The ship was 45 days out from Jeddah, and had been 18 days becalmed; was very short of water and provisions. The *"Sarthe"* gave her supplies, and took her in tow until they met the monsoon breeze in the offing of Cape Gardofuy.

The *Sarthe* arrived in Singapore on 31 July. The *Henry Harbeck* would not finally arrive until 20 September.

If the *Henry Harbeck* had already been 45 days out from Jeddah when the French ship came across her, that means she would have started out on her journey around 30 May. The culmination of the hajj – the 9th day of Dhu'l-Hijjah in the Islamic calendar – was around 12th March 1870, around two months earlier. By way of comparison four other sailing ships were in the harbour at Singapore when she arrived. Though we don't know exactly when they left Jeddah it is likely that all would have left at a similar time after the hajj. Yet the *Fathool Carrim* had arrived on 16 July; the *Almanawar* had arrived on 7 July; the *Fathool Wadood* on 18 June; and the *Fathool Kayah* on 10 June.

How many of the 450 returning pilgrims on the *Henry Harbeck* made it back to Penang or Singapore is another question that cannot be answered, but it points to one more measure of just what the hajj cost each pilgrim in terms of difficulty and personal test. There are many other, similar reports of ships that lost their way or that disappeared, presumed sunk.

This account from 1859 is of a vessel that had strayed well off course:

> The ship *Calliope* from the Mauritius, reports that on the 13th ultimo, she fell in with the ship *Toodul Odoor*, of Singapore, and bound there in the greatest distress, having been six months out from Jeddah with 500 Coolies, or Pilgrims, on board, all famishing, 100 were already dead. They had lost their reckoning entirely. The *Calliope* supplied them with an officer to take the ship to land, also with rice, dholl, water and other stores. The *Toodul Odoor* was very leaky.[3]

Dangers – vessels not fit for the sea

And even before they headed to sea there were dangers. The seaworthiness of many vessels was questioned, despite the fact that in each port under British control there was a Master Attendant with the responsibility to judge on seaworthiness and to determine the carrying capacity of vessels from their port. That at least was the role, but we can read in the 1850s and '60s of vessels sailing in a distinctly unseaworthy condition and newspapers commenting that if those reports were true, "some of the officers whose duty it is to survey such vessels, have been guilty of very great carelessness."[4]

> The *Flavius* sailed for the Coromandel Coast a day or two ago. She carried 45 or 50 passengers, without the slightest provision being made for them. The *Palembang* sailed for Jeddah a few days ago with passengers. Twelve months ago she was, by two Marine Surveyors, condemned as unfit for service out of the Straits. Since then she has undergone no repairs to her hull, and yet strange to say, the Government Surveyor passed her as fit to carry passengers—this same Government Surveyor being one of the two Marine Surveyors who had condemned her a year ago. Does this gentleman imagine that a human life is less valuable than a bale of Cotton? Or does he imagine that the Indian Ocean is less dangerous to a rotten ship commanded by a Native, than the China Sea to the same vessel when commanded by a European?[5]

Dangerous cargoes

Cargoes were carried that could be dangerous when not properly taken care of. In 1838 the ship *Abgarris* was destroyed by fire whilst carrying a number of pilgrims returning from Mecca. The cause: probably from cotton "which formed the chief part of the vessel's cargo" and which had been in a damp state when packed in the hold.[6]

Overcrowding and Overloading

A more constant, and larger danger came from overcrowding and overloading. The overcrowding would be from simply carrying too many people, sometimes far in excess of the Master Attendant's prescribed number. This was something that plagued much of the shipping for poorer people.

In Singapore, newspaper reports published accounts of seriously overcrowded ships from China carrying "coolie" labourers: "a junk of about four hundred tons burthen, having arrived from a port in China with upwards of one thousand persons on board." Across the world it seems to have been a common thing for ships carrying poorer people as "deck" passengers. Immigrants travelling to America to work as servants in the eighteenth century were packed into ships and,

> ... if the weather was bad, and the trip took too long, they ran out of food. The sloop *Sea-Flower*, leaving Belfast in 1741, was at sea for sixteen weeks, and when it arrived in Boston, forty-six of its 106 passengers were dead of starvation.[7]

The best that could be said was that overcrowding would make the voyage extremely uncomfortable. It was made much worse when a ship's master tried to load with cargo as well, or when bad weather intervened. The hajj pilgrim in the nineteenth century would simply have to accept whatever conditions they were given and these conditions would sometimes beggar belief. And whatever regulations were put in place by the Master Attendant or the colonial authorities, they often became irrelevant once a ship had left ports under British control. Regulations are only as strong as the ability to enforce them.

With no control over journey time and conditions on board – 1868, the case of the *Day Dream*

Perhaps the best-recorded example of a violation of standards comes with the account of the ship *Day Dream* that left Singapore in November 1868. The report was written by the ship's mate, Thomas Connell, on 29 January 1869 when he met the Master Attendant at Cochin in India:[8]

> I shipped as Chief Officer of the barque *Day Dream* under British colors [sic] at Singapore in November 1868. The vessel left that port on the 13th of the same month for Jeddah, with about 150 pilgrims on board. She was surveyed at Singapore and licensed to carry 216 passengers. After leaving Singapore, we touched at Malacca, and took in there 23 passengers more. We remained there for about three days and then proceeded to Penang. The vessel was reported at the Master Attendant's Office, and after the vessel was cleared and inspected by the Master Attendant, we received above 50 pilgrims at Penang, which circumstance was not reported to the authorities. The vessel left Penang and anchored on the Pedier Coast two days afterwards, 8 miles west of Diamond Point, between Courtey and Passier. At this place we

again received 154 pilgrims, and then proceeded on and anchored at Toolo Samwoi. After leaving that port, we touched at Passangan where we took 63 more, and then proceeded to Jonkow and took in there 91 passengers. The vessel next touched at Pedier and shipped 35 pilgrims and some cargo consisting of rice. From Pedier we came to Acheen and received about 50 passengers and a cargo of some sugar, oil, and rice. The total number of pilgrims we took in at the ports amounted to above 600. At Pedier, we saw the barque *Fatel Medjeed*, of about 400 to 500 tons under Arab colors, at anchor, which vessel also carried more than 600 pilgrims from Singapore, Penang, and the Pedier Coast. We left Acheen and proceeded on our voyage, and on the 18th January 1869, we anchored at Alleppey for water and firewood. The barque *Fatel Medjeed* had arrived there before us, and I heard from the Commander of the *Day Dream* that several of her passengers had died before arrival at Alleppey. As our ship was in a most unhealthy and dangerous state, and crowded with human beings to such a degree that the space allowed to each man was only a few inches to lie down, and the men were literally huddled together, I thought it proper for my own safety to leave the vessel, and I got my discharge at Alleppey, whence I proceeded to this port. When the *Day Dream* was surveyed at Singapore, she was passed as seaworthy, but in my opinion she is unseaworthy. We had only two boats, one of which was an old jolly boat, and the other a kind of gig. With regard to the space allowed to the passengers, the hold was full, and the cabins were also full, and a small temporary house, a little better than a box, was put on board, wherein nearly 40 women were stowed. This box was about 10 feet in length and 10 in breadth and 3 to 4 feet high. In the round-house, there were about 24 women with their husbands. The squares of all the hatches, which ought to have been left free for ventilation, were all lumbered up with jars of oil, and the pilgrims could but hardly creep out of the between decks. The horrible state of the vessel was indescribable, and the stench arising from the hold was insufferable. There was no opportunity from the crowdedness of the vessel and the luggage being thrown over all the decks, to keep her clean, and she was consequently in the most filthy and dangerous condition.

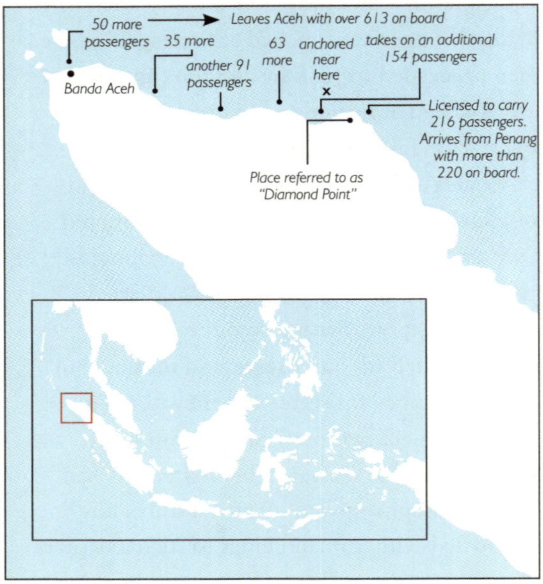

The stopping places of the "Day Dream" on the Aceh Coast. Sketch map by Anthony Green – adapted from a 2003 map by East-West Center (www.eastwestcenter.org).

Cochin was the first "British port" that Connell had been in since leaving the Sumatran coast. He said that his motive in making the report was to show the British Authorities "how unhumanly these pilgrim ships are crowded after leaving the British settlements in the Straits," so he wanted to bring these circumstances to the notice of the authorities.

The dimensions of the "small temporary house" seem barely credible. Ten feet equals three metres, and four feet equals 1.22 metres. To place 40 women in this space seems astonishing. But if all the details of the journey time are correct this ship took two months just to get from Singapore to Southern India. When it arrived it had, crammed on board, nearly three times as many passengers as it was permitted.

Captain Daniel Moreland of the preserved barque *Picton Castle* has given some responses to the questions of how the ship would have handled and what life would have been like on board:

> It is difficult to say exactly how the Barque *Day Dream* would have handled. Clearly she was grossly overloaded in terms of passenger

safety but it is not clear to me if she was overloaded for weight. Weight and how the weight is distributed would be the determining factors in how the vessel handled under sail.

600 people aboard a 400 ton barque would be miserable – such a vessel is only somewhat larger than *Picton Castle* ... but the weight of 600 people is not that much and easily within her range including a good sized cargo in addition. At 150 pounds per person we are only looking at 45 tons and if we figure 200 pounds per person, we still only get 60 tons. This in a ship that could easily carry 500 tons. So while this passage in the heat and with limited water, food etc would be a hellish voyage, it would not necessarily be a dangerous voyage from a point of view considering stability alone. In other words she might not handle badly at all, which is the question you have asked. Other factors could well add to the risk however: trim and how these people are all carried and "downflood" – with this many people aboard it is difficult for me to see them all being on deck at once, nor could the hatches be battened down with the passengers all below as that would be the height of cruelty. With the hatches opened up the ship is more vulnerable to "downflood," ie; seas coming aboard and flooding the ship. That said, if the *Day Dream* was following the monsoons then there would be little threat of this.[9]

Dangers well known, and seemingly ignored

The story of the *Day Dream* in 1868 should not have surprised anyone. Fourteen years earlier, a report in the Singapore Free Press had said:

> The accommodation on board these vessels is in general very wretched and the passengers have to submit to many discomforts and even hardships. The objectionable manner in which the pilgrims are often crowded together in such vessels has repeatedly attracted public attention, but, as far as we are aware, no measures have ever been adopted by the Straits authorities for checking this, either in the case of such vessels sailing from the Straits Settlements or arriving here with pilgrims. It is a subject, nevertheless, which well deserves grave consideration on the part of government...

"Grave consideration" was a long time in coming. Even with the 1880 case of the steamship, *S.S. Jeddah*, which is discussed in chapter 8, overcrowding persisted. The one issue that was more likely to provoke a measure of alarm and to lead to international discussion on issues of sanitation and quarantine was the potential for contagious disease.

But for the pilgrim passengers it was the condition in which many ships' masters allowed their vessels to leave and "the cupidity of the owners" that was likely to have the most direct impact. That same *Singapore Free Press* report that spoke of "wretched conditions" stressed that there often seemed to be very little concern with safety:

> An Arab vessel recently sailed from Singapore for Juddah, having upwards of one thousand persons on board. In addition to her large human freight the decks were lumbered up to the height of several feet with planks, water casks &c. so that, what with the animate and inanimate cargo on deck, the crew had great difficulty in moving about in the performance of their duties. The cargo on board was chiefly wood, and apparently most recklessly stowed, so that the vessel was in wretched trim. When near the Karimons they experienced some smart breezes, which caused the ill-balanced vessel to go over on her beam ends. The passengers were alarmed at this and requested that the vessel should put back, but this the charterer refused and it was only at last after very urgent entreaties and receiving from the passengers a written promise that they would make no complaint, that he consented to return to Singapore. Here a part of the wood was landed and other heavier articles shipped so as to give sufficient dead weight and the vessel again sailed. Some of the passengers who could afford it left the vessel, prepared to forfeit their passage-money, but the greater number, having probably exhausted their whole means in paying for their conveyance by this vessel, were obliged from necessity again to proceed in her. Such an excessive crowding is calculated to generate disease, and should it once break out it must under the circumstances assume the most aggravated form and run with fatal rapidity. In the case of shipwreck, also, experience has taught that in these crowded pilgrim ships the greater part of the passengers are

doomed to death, since the boats belonging to such vessels can only convey a very small part of the unfortunate beings whom the cupidity of the owners of the freighters have crammed into their vessels.[10]

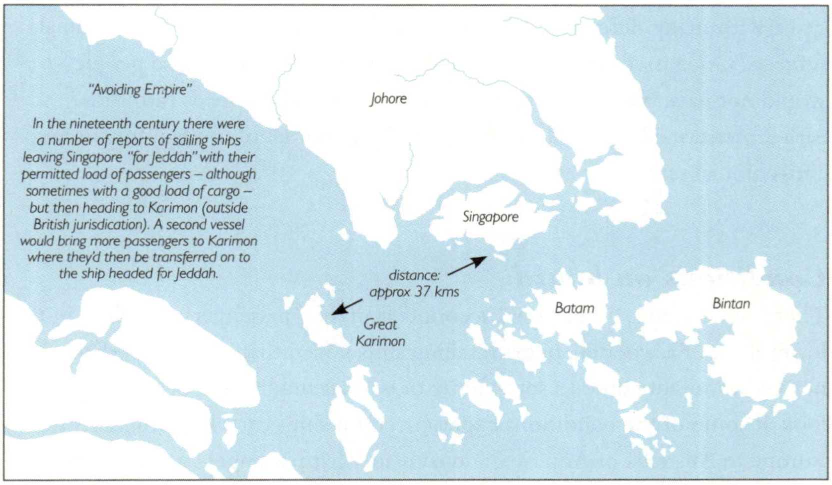

Sketch map by Anthony Green.

The Karimons – the group of islands south-west of Singapore and outside the territorial reach of the British – were a favourite place for ships' captains to attempt to avoid "the reach of empire." A ship might leave port apparently respecting its proper loading of passengers. Arrangements would then be made to send more passengers out separately to the Karimons where they would join the first ship and continue to Jeddah; something that resulted in a kind of "cat and mouse" game with the authorities.

The kapal haji as a meeting place

Leaving aside the fact that the voyage must have been difficult and seriously unpleasant it also provides another example of how an interaction between pilgrims was brought about.

Acheh – traditionally referred to as *Serambi Makkah*, the Verandah of Mecca, – was the last port of call in the Archipelago and for a long time Acheh resisted Dutch control. It's impossible to know where the different passengers for a ship like the *Day Dream* had originated. Malay would be the lingua franca amongst them but the places of embarkation – Singapore, Malacca, Penang, and that list of small towns or settlements up to Acheh in the north of Sumatra – suggest a diverse range of individuals brought tightly together into one small space with many different stories of life and of their experiences as colonial subjects. Once more, those stories can never be known but these people would not have travelled in silence. But this, once again, feeds into those, earlier mentioned, colonial suspicions of the potential of the hajj for stirring anti-colonial sentiment.

Conditions on board

There are, it seems, no personal accounts from hajj passengers travelling in the lower deck of a wooden, pilgrim sailing ship. Given that absence, perhaps the nearest we might come to some sense of what it might have been like is to look at some of the conditions experienced on ships carrying emigrants from Europe to Australia or America, and to read what passengers wrote about, since there are many diaries in existence from emigrants, even working class folk with limited education.

Conditions on board hajj ships would likely have been much less comfortable. They would have been much more crowded and all the evidence suggests that there was less effective legislation to control them. Added to this they were sailing in the heat of the tropics. But the comparison may still be of value.

The paths of the emigrant ships to Australia took them down the west coast of Africa and then through the Southern Ocean at 60° South where the seas might be called "short seas."[11] Conditions at that latitude would be quite different from the northern part of the Indian Ocean but like all oceans, the Indian had its moods. And for people who had never been to sea before, there would have been many issues that could cause fear, and fears can be common to other passengers on different voyages. The spellings in these examples are unchanged from the originals.[12]

• • • • • • • • • • •

Comparing conditions on board: emigrant ships in the nineteenth Century

Smells, crowding, darkness, sickness

A man named Edwin Francis, travelling in 1852 was in the foc'sle – the forward part of the ship, under the crew's quarters:

> The water broke in through the port hole ... my bed and bed Clothe and trowsers & shirt in fact everything was wet through ...
> [my berth mate] was the cause of the sea coming through the port hole, He would have the port open said it was to hot with it closed. One of the oldest of our young men said you must go on deck you will die if you stay here.
> Very Hot Lightening & thunder at night Captain had every Port Hole and Sky light closed.

From Eliza Whicker, travelling in 1854:

> ... during the night the ship rolled heavily, everything rolled about, the rain poured in torrents ... in the afternoon the wind increased to a gale. The sails close reefed, the sea tremendous; the night was awfully rough, the sea washing over the ship & falling through the hatch-ways, washing between the decks over the shoe. [the socket for the mast]

> ... at about ten o'clock a wedge fell from the rigging on the head of a woman, she fell senseless in the arms of a man, her head was cut severely

Toilets and privacy

On board emigrant ships there were few toilet cubicles "and what there were emptied directly over the ship's side, with evident discomforts in a storm." Elizabeth Allbon, travelling to Australia in 1879 commented on how women felt about the lack of privacy:

> [Our] bunks are all fitted up between decks not private at all & just a curtain hung in front.

Daniel Moreland used the word "hellish" in his estimation of the hajj journey of the *Day Dream*. The issue of the almost complete lack of privacy must have been very real and would especially have been felt by women passengers.

The sounds of the sea – a source of fear?

One emigrant spoke of a "dreadful rough in the night":

> ... this is the first time my wife expressed fear she thought the ship struck against a rock but it was A tremendous sea came against the side of the ship ... two people had severe falls.

This fear from unknown noises was another matter to be considered. Wooden structures and wooden ships shift and creak. At sea there would be passengers who found this unnerving.

James Horsburgh, the Scottish hydrographer, charted sea routes, detailed shoals and rocks and landmarks, and noted winds and currents, and produced, in two volumes, his extremely detailed "India Directory."

Many of those who travelled on hajj ships remembered being cautioned that the sea can be rougher once you pass out of the Malacca Straits. The turning point at the northern end of the Straits into the Indian Ocean would be at Pulau Weh, a small island off the north of Sumatra, but in Horsburgh's "sailing directions" he also commented on how the noises of the sea could be "alarming" and of the "great violence" of the water against the hull:

> In the entrance of Malacca Strait . . . there are often very strong ripplings, particularly in the S.W. monsoon; these are alarming to persons unacquainted, for the broken water makes a great noise when a ship is passing through the ripplings at night. In most places, ripplings are thought to be produced by strong currents, but *here* they are frequently seen when there is no perceptible current. Although

> there is often no perceptible current experienced, so as to produce an error in the course and distance sailed, yet the surface of the water is impelled forward by some undiscovered cause. The ripplings are seen in calm weather approaching from a distance, and in the night their noise is heard a considerable time before they come near. They beat against the sides of a ship with great violence and pass on, the spray sometimes coming on deck.[13]

Horsburgh adds the recommendation that ships pass through here by night, "for steady breezes often prevail during the absence of the sun, when calms and faint airs are experienced in the day." The darkness of the night has the potential to exacerbate fears.

Deaths on board

Fifteen-year-old Maria Steley, travelling to Brisbane in 1863:

> A child died to day it is a very serous thing they sowe the body up in a rug then they get a plank and let the body go down the Shool master reed the furnell service.

William Shennan, a 24-year-old blacksmith, travelling to Melbourne in 1870, on watching a child being buried at sea:

> ... the little Childs body was lowered into the deep at Seven School Master read the service the body was rapped in canvice two bricks in it to make it sink the placed on a board which rested on the side of the ship after the Service was read then lifted up the end and the body slided down I was near to the place but as soon as the body reached the water it was out of sight.

Deaths on hajj pilgrimage ships

Death was a constant on pilgrim ships. The causes were varied: sickness and disease; the age of the pilgrims and their weakness at the end of the exertions of the hajj; the miserable conditions on the vessel; and other strains from the voyage. Exhaustion, hunger, and thirst came together and sometimes the numbers of deaths on a voyage could be considerable.

Hunger and thirst

In almost all the emigrant ships that sailed, the common complaint of deck (steerage) passengers was of hunger and the poor diet. The diet "might be an annoyance for a healthy adult," but it was "fatally deficient in the provision for children and infants."

For pilgrim passengers in the Indian Ocean there would be the food they carried with them, supplemented by occasional flying fish landing on the deck and the likelihood of trying to catch fish if the weather were suitable. On a ship as overcrowded as the *Day Dream*, though, it would not be possible for all passengers to be on the open deck. Instead it would be dark and stuffy below.

Emigrant ships carried live animals as food for those passengers in cabins. Whether sail-powered pilgrim ships (in Malay, *kapal layar*) carried live animals on board for food is not clear but, as is discussed later, on the ship, *Jeddah*, with the move from sail to steam there was provision for this.

Water

> Water, water, everywhere,
> And all the boards did shrink;
> Water, water, everywhere,
> Nor any drop to drink.
>
> Samuel Taylor Coleridge, *The Rime of the Ancient Mariner*

• • • • • • • • • • •

One big issue at sea in times past was water. At home in tropical Southeast Asia where the rain can come down like a wall, water is seldom seen as scarce.

Stepping onto an overcrowded hajj ship in the nineteenth century would be like stepping into another world, with its challenge of supplying enough water for the numbers on board and with the duration of the voyage being uncertain.

When water is too low or kept too long

In sailing ship times, given the examples of seriously overcrowded ships like the *Day Dream*, or ships becalmed or drifting, lost, for days, even weeks like the *Henry Harbeck* and the *Toodul Odoor* cited earlier, it would have been extremely difficult to guarantee sufficient water. And the effects of any shortage would have been made worse by being in the heat of the tropics.

In the eighteenth century, on board ships of the VOC – the Dutch East India Company – the water supply was sufficient for four months and stored in large barrels with a capacity of 600 litres. How that water tasted was another question.

> ... the tropical temperatures en route frequently made the water practically undrinkable. The seamen advised holding the tankard in one hand, while pinching shut one's nose with the other, and then sucking the water carefully through clenched teeth to keep from swallowing the teeming worms infesting the water. If a sailor had lost his teeth because of scurvy then, obviously, this advice was not very helpful.[14]

And even in the 1960s, when ships could carry much greater loads and, in a time when journey times could be published with a high degree of reliability, water was rationed.

• • • • • • • • • • •

Disease

There is one more, very significant issue that needs to be included in any reckoning of these journeys, and that is disease: "The one issue that was more likely to provoke a measure of alarm and to lead to international discussion." Throughout the time of the hajj ships there were many cases of communicable diseases on board. Smallpox was one, but far more significant in terms of the numbers of deaths caused was cholera.

Five major epidemics of cholera "devastated the [Indian Ocean] area between 1817 and 1893," with trading ports like Bombay, Jeddah and Zanzibar as "important centres of dissemination,"[15] so returning hajj pilgrims became carriers of the disease. Ships are confined spaces. If onboard facilities and sanitation are poor; if, in particular, sufficient clean water is lacking, and if the vessel is then overcrowded with exhausted people, the risks of contagion are magnified. This report comes from October 1846:

> The Pilgrim ships, the *Friends* and *Sawoodbun*, which came in at the beginning of the week crowded with passengers, report that the cholera was committing great ravages at Jedda, [sic] carrying off from sixty to seventy persons daily—indeed so fatal was the disease that considerable difficulty was experienced in giving internment to the dead with the usual ceremonies. About forty of the passengers by the above vessels are said to have died of this complaint on the voyage down, and, since the ships came into Harbour, there have been several burials, from one or other of the vessels, of persons who are believed to have died of cholera since their arrival here. It would be advisable to require all Pilgrim ships that come into the Harbour to moor at a considerable distance from the rest of the shipping, the crowded and very filthy condition of these vessels generally are sufficient causes to generate fevers and other diseases of the most fatal kind on board, which might spread to vessels anchored near to them.[16]

Quarantine stations were instituted, international legislation enacted, and matters would improve. It would take time.

• • • • • • • • • •

[1] From The Daily Times, 10 September 1880, published in *Newspaper accounts of the Jeddah Affair*, Joseph Conrad Society, compiled by Moore, Gene M. Universiteit van Amsterdam.

[2] All details of ships here come from the Ship Registries at the National Archives of Singapore.

[3] ST. 19 March 1859, p. 4.

[4] SFPMA. 28 September 1865.

[5] ST. 2 February 1861.

[6] SFPMA. 15 November 1838.

[7] Zinn, Howard (1995). *A People's History of the United States: 1492–present* (2nd ed.). New York: HarperCollins. Ch. 3.

[8] Connell introduced his report with the description, "Chief Officer of the barque *Day Dream* under British colors [sic], belonging to Singapore, of 416 tons or thereabouts, Captain W. Wheatley."

[9] Personal email communication with Anthony Green, October 2013.

[10] SFPMA. 3 January 1854, p.1.

[11] This distinction was suggested by Darrell Daish who served on the kapal haji, *Kuala Lumpur*. "Short seas" in this sense would mean, "seas in which the waves are short, broken and irregular, so as to produce a tumbling or jerking motion."

[12] Hassam, Andrew. 1995. *No Privacy for Writing – Shipboard Diaries 1852 – 1879*. Carlton South, Victoria: Melbourne University Press.

[13] Horsburgh, James. *The India Directory, or Directions for Sailing to and from the East Indies, China, New Holland, Cape of Good Hope, and the interjacent Ports, compiled chiefly from original Journals and Observations made during 21 years' experience in navigating those Seas.* Vol 2, p. 68.

[14] Jacobs, Els M. 1991. *In Pursuit of Pepper and Tea" – the story of the Dutch East India Company*, Amsterdam: Netherlands Maritime Museum, p. 41.

[15] Issa, Amina A. 2006. "Dhows and Epidemics in the Indian Ocean Ports." *In Ziff Journal. No 3, 2006.* Accessed online (2017) at https://pdfs.semanticscholar.org/781a/f9762befe7122720fe9c64ed7a09b9ef7bef.pdf.

[16] ST. 31 October 1846, p. 3.

A sense of

Scale and Space

1.

Double-deck bus

Length = 12 metres; approx.

80 - 85 seated passengers (max journey time: approx. one hour)

2.

A three-masted barque

Typical length 140 ft – 170 ft = 43m – 52m

Roughly ***4x*** *the length of a bus*

Most hajj vessels were around 600 tons, the largest used being around 1,200 tons. Ships frequently carried far more than their registered numbers. Normal journey time approx. 50 days but often much longer. In 1868 the ship *Day Dream,* licensed for 216 passengers, carried 616 and took two months just to get from Singapore to Southern India

3.

M.V. Anking / M.V. Anshun

Length 418 ft 4ins = 127.5m

Roughly ***10.5x*** *the length of a bus*

M.V. Anking (built 1950); sister ship *M.V.Anshun* (built 1951 for China Navigation Co, Hong Kong), operated on the hajj from 1953 to the 1960s. "Deck class" passengers slept in bunks, generally two-high; carried in excess of 1,100 passengers including a small number of 1st class; journey time from Singapore to Jeddah about 14 days

4.

S.S. Tyndareus

Length 507 ft = 154.5m

Roughly ***13x*** *the length of a bus*

S.S. Tyndareus (Blue Funnel); built 1916 as a cargo vessel, served exclusively on the Hajj from 1950 to 1960, when she was scrapped. Normally carried about 1,800 passengers; licensed at one stage for about 2,500. In the 1950s they slept on mattresses on the 'tween deck floor; later using camp-beds; journey time about 14-15 days from Singapore to Jeddah.

Graphic © Umar Green

7

The ships they sailed in:

Suez and steam

The ships that had no sails

That first appearance in Singapore and Malaya of a vessel powered by steam was the arrival in August 1845 of the P&O ship, *Lady Mary Wood*, on its way from Ceylon (modern day Sri Lanka) to Hong Kong.

But this was a small paddle steamer – and though it was a good deal faster than a sailing ship, within twenty years larger, faster vessels were being built, intended for longer, non-stop voyages. In Liverpool on 16 January 1866 the mechanical and civil engineer, Alfred Holt, published a circular on a voyage he planned with a ship that he had designed, to travel "non-stop to Mauritius, then on to Penang, Singapore, Hong Kong and Shanghai":

> I beg to inform you that I am about to establish a line of Screw Steamers from Liverpool to China . . . All the steamers have been built on the Clyde; they are full of power, and they will steam the whole passage both out and home . . . My hope is to establish a reliable line of Steamers which will carry cargo at moderate rates of freight, both safely and at tolerable speed.[1]

Others were unconvinced, saying that steamers might go to the Mediterranean, perhaps even to South America, but "China at least is safe for the sailing ships."

Holt thought there was no future in sailing ships. He was successful in his first stated aim and proven even more correct in the longer term but it was the

An example of a "sidewheel" or paddle steamer: the USS Susquehanna arrived in Singapore in the 1850s to join Commodore Perry's expedition to force Japan to open its ports to American trade. Public Domain. {PD-US}

Suez Canal that opened up the route for a model of business that would completely change the calculations. It had its critics.

The Suez Canal – "a dismal but profitable ditch"

The writer Joseph Conrad was scathing about the change that the Canal would bring. The sea, he felt, was something to love and to fear: "It cast a spell, it gave joy, it lulled gently into boundless faith; then with a quick and causeless anger it killed."

Towards the end of the nineteenth century, in *An Outcast of the Islands*, Conrad wrote of "the old sea, the sea of many years ago, whose servants . . . went from youth to age or to a sudden grave without needing to open the book of life, because they could look at eternity reflected on the element that gave the life and dealt the death." And he set this against what the Suez Canal brought:

> That was the sea before the time when the French mind set the Egyptian muscle in motion and produced a dismal but profitable ditch... in order that greedy and faithless landlubbers might pocket dividends ... [and become] a calculating crowd of cold and exacting masters.[2]

Conrad's view might be seen as a kind of romanticising but his perspective on the elemental nature of the sea hints at something of the fears and sense of awe that must surely have been experienced by land-dwelling hajj pilgrims travelling on this voyage through the unknown.

Conrad's voice, though, was somehow solitary.

Who benefits?

The competition for carrying pilgrims on the hajj was building rapidly against men like Syed Mohammed Alsagoff and the other Arab ship owners, and that competition was not just in the numbers of ships or the size and range of companies that would sail through the Red Sea – it was also in the design and build of those ships.

For the early steamships, reliability was a real issue so they were built with masts and were rigged to use sails if engines failed or another source of power were needed. Success would come from those who could ensure reliability and efficiency.

Alfred Holt, founder of the Blue Funnel line, has been described as "that fastidious owner"[3] and as an engineer who "insisted on the highest possible efficiency in every detail of a Ship's Construction."[4] Speaking of the Suez Canal Holt proclaimed that, "We shall benefit by it more than all the nations of the earth put together."[5]

Alfred Holt, engineer and ship owner.

In his designs he displayed a mixture of conservatism and originality, but if his ships were to "steam the whole passage both out and home" he kept the machinery space to a minimum in order to carry enough coal for them to reach suitable bunkering ports, and in order not to cut down on cargo space. He built ships with "dimensions which were then deemed too large for the China trade." And despite the fact that marine engines were in something of an infancy, in 1866 Holt's ships travelled from London to Mauritius with "quite remarkable" coal consumption figures and at a speed "until then considered impossible."[6]

• • • • • • • • • • •

From sail to steam

Sailing ships did not suddenly disappear with the opening of the Canal. As we noted in the previous chapter, in the "Shipping in the Harbour" lists in newspapers in the 1880s there were still many ships in Southeast Asian ports from places like New York, Mauritius, Boston, Hamburg, Liverpool and London that had owed their journey to the wind alone. One real change for hajj pilgrims was in the steady number of ships to and from Europe that now came down through the Red Sea. This led to something of a "free-for-all" and, if you had money enough, it led to increased choice.

The Suez Canal took days off the journey from Europe to Southeast Asia and a Red Sea port like Jeddah now became yet another cargo opportunity, so pilgrims returning to Southeast Asia could find themselves travelling on any kind of vessel, even one that was brand new. By way of example, early in 1878 the *Newchwang* stopped in Jeddah on its delivery journey from Scotts shipyard in Glasgow, to pick up pilgrims. This was a "beancaker," built for the Swire Group in Hong Kong to transport soya bean, bean oil and soya compressed into huge cakes – "beancakes" – from rivers in Manchuria down to Swatow and Amoy in South China as part of the lucrative China coast trade.

Since this ship was destined for a company in the Swire group and the consignee for it was the Singapore company W. Mansfield & Co., it provided passage from Jeddah to Singapore for a fortunate group of returning pilgrims to help allay the cost of the delivery journey.

The effect of the Suez Canal was rapid. Two years after its opening a newspaper account described the great increase in the number of "steamers" and the reduction in the cost of steam navigation as contributing "greatly to the benefit of the pilgrims from these parts to the shrine of Mahomet." Now those who had the money could take a passage "as far as Suez in either the Messageries or homeward bound trading steamers," then connect with a ship to Jeddah. These were ships of the French company, Messageries Maritimes, travelling between France, "Indo-China" and China, and "homeward bound" meant ships headed for Europe.

By this time a network of steamships was developing:

> ... for more than a month past Chinese-owned steamers have been plying between Singapore and the various Dutch ports, bringing pilgrims hither, and two steamers in the China coasting trade, —the *Fusi Yama* and *Venus*—will carry them hence direct to Jeddah, waiting, we presume, to bring them back after completing their pilgrimage.[7]

As an example of the mix of ships in the "free-for-all," in 1917 – the year of the October Revolution – the *Ekaterinaslav*, a ship of the Imperial Russian Navy Volunteer Reserve, would make one journey carrying pilgrims, with the Borneo Company as agents. They had previously carried pilgrims from Odessa in the Black Sea,[8] although this appearance of "Soviets" caused concern in Britain and many ships of the Volunteer Reserve were seized by the British during the war.

Something more established: Blue Funnel and China Navigation

But the longest-serving shipping line to operate on the hajj would be the Blue Funnel Line – a company under the Ocean Steamship Company of Alfred Holt. Holt's own interest in Muslim pilgrims has been described as dating,

> ... from the earliest days when the company's steamers began using the Suez Canal. The passage past Jeddah on the Saudi Arabian coast made the opportunistic carriage of these pilgrims to Mecca an obvious and profitable one, and soon became a regular feature of Blue Funnel services.[9]

The funnel colours of China Navigation Co. ships were black. Postcard kindly donated by Mdm Esah Bee.

Blue Funnel carried pilgrims from their first years of arriving in Southeast Asia right up to 1953 when they handed over to the company they were closely associated with – the China Navigation Company, run by Swire in Hong Kong. Blue Funnel then took responsibility for services from Indonesia while CNCo operated the ships that ran from Singapore and Malaysia.

... but the funnels were initially re-painted in Blue Funnel colours in keeping with the sentiments of hajj pilgrims and their sense of association with the "serombong biru."
Postcard kindly donated by Mdm Esah Bee.

Such had been the familiarity of the "*kapal hadji serombong biru*" – the kapal haji ships with their blue funnels – that when CNCo first introduced their sister-ships, *Anshun* and *Anking*, they re-painted their black funnels in the blue of their predecessors in order to allay any suspicions and to satisfy the sentiments of the local population.

During the 1920s two other shipping lines made attempts to operate hajj services from the Straits Settlements.

One was the Straits-Hedjaz Shipping Company and another was set up by Hadjee M. H. Nemazee (or Nemazie) of Hong Kong. Both began with prominent announcements that spoke of the standard of fittings promised in their vessels but neither of them survived for any length of time.

The difference that steamships brought

The first difference that steamships brought was speed. The journey time to Jeddah would be cut in half. Then, when engines (and propeller shafts) became stronger, there would be predictability: it would be easier to publish times for voyages because the wind did not hold you at its mercy. There would be setbacks, and the incident described in the next chapter is a powerful example of that. Overcrowding would continue for some time but eventually the provision of water, and even food, would reach satisfactory levels. Comfort, though, was another matter.

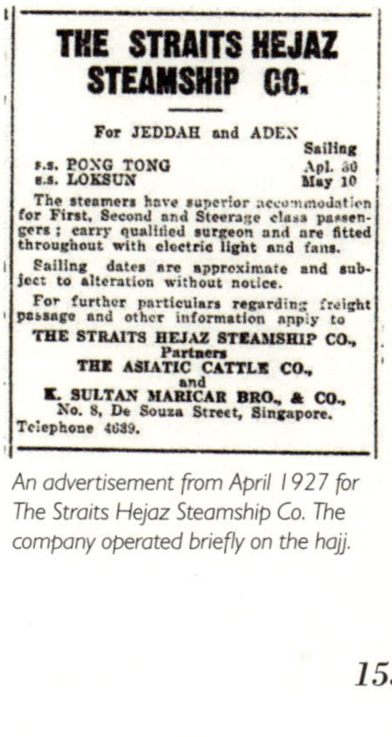
THE STRAITS HEJAZ STEAMSHIP CO.

For JEDDAH and ADEN

	Sailing
s.s. PONG TONG	Apl. 30
s.s. LOKSUN	May 10

The steamers have superior accommodation for First, Second and Steerage class passengers; carry qualified surgeon and are fitted throughout with electric light and fans.

Sailing dates are approximate and subject to alteration without notice.

For further particulars regarding freight passage and other information apply to
THE STRAITS HEJAZ STEAMSHIP CO.,
Partners
THE ASIATIC CATTLE CO.,
and
K. SULTAN MARICAR BRO., & CO.,
No. 8, De Souza Street, Singapore.
Telephone 4639.

An advertisement from April 1927 for The Straits Hejaz Steamship Co. The company operated briefly on the hajj.

Water

From the middle of the twentieth century there'd be water enough on ships – albeit at set times – though for many Southeast Asian pilgrims accustomed to using a *gayong* to scoop water from a *kolam*, or small well, to splash wash themselves, the ship might be their introduction to western style showers and toilets, and staff on the ships would have to do some explaining.

In 1968 an announcement in the Straits Times was headed "All the water they need." The announcement came from Dato Haji Ali Rouse, Controller of Pilgrimage, based in Penang. "There will be no water rationing for Malaysian pilgrims during their trip to Mecca next year," it said. "For the first time, pilgrim ships bound for Jeddah will stop at Colombo to replenish their supplies of fresh water."[10]

On the ship *Kuala Lumpur* in the 1960s, Darrell Daish said:

> You had restrictions on water use – a set time when the water was on for showers; hours when people couldn't use it. We'd start at Singapore and make sure we were full of water, go up to Port Klang and take on more hajjis there and fill with water. At Penang the same; then across to Colombo. Then into Aden for bunkers and water; then on to Jeddah.[11]

David Walker, who also served on *Kuala Lumpur*, adds:

> Fresh Water both drinking and washing was... a scarce commodity that was rationed. We had problems educating the pilgrims in not having unlimited supply. They had to be convinced that a bucket full of water that had been standing for some time was perfectly useable. The temptation to throw it away and refill the bucket as they were used to at home was not an option on a ship with no water generators (they were extremely rare in those days; reverse osmosis had not been perfected) and limited tankage and daily consumption was a constant worry for the Chief Officer. The only time that the taps were turned

> on was as we were on our way up the Red sea and close to Jeddah and disembarkation, when all the pilgrims would wash themselves and dress in the white robes [ihram] in readiness for the Pilgrimage.[12]

By 1910, the Merchant Shipping Ordinance dealing with pilgrim ships[13] leaving from Singapore and Malaya had got to the point of covering every conceivable aspect of life and conditions on a pilgrim ship, from the checking and listing of pilgrim numbers, the recording of deaths and their causes, the proper provision of lifeboats and the carriage or otherwise of dynamite.

And the Ordinance specified a range of requirements related to the quantity and quality of daily rations of food and water to be given to pilgrims, including the supply of "pure water." Fines "not exceeding ten dollars for every pilgrim who has sustained detriment by the omission" were to be liable on any offending ship's master.

Quality, though, can be a subjective issue.

Water... with a taste of oil

When the Blue Funnel ship *Ajax* was used for a run with 1,200 hajj passengers in 1948 it had just completed a cargo journey from Fremantle to Singapore. To prepare for the hajj the now-empty fuel oil tanks were flushed out and filled with fresh water for drinking. But oil has an unpleasant tendency to linger, and Ian Jackson, who was Third Officer, wrote that,

> We all hoped that the water that was in these tanks, which was slightly yellow looking, and which if left standing soon developed a skim of fuel oil, would be reserved for the pilgrims. In the event, we were all using it before we arrived at Jeddah. It wasn't very nice![14]

However unpleasant the taste, fresh water lines were fitted with standpipes with locks on them to restrict usage. Having said that, pilgrims themselves seem to have been made of sterner stuff in times past. Modern day pilgrims prize the water they are able to bring back from the well of Zam-Zam that has flowed for centuries at Mecca. It is all now hygienically-sealed. This was not a luxury that their predecessors on this journey enjoyed. In his recollections of the previously mentioned voyage of the *Priam* in 1926, Captain Brown described some of the things homeward-bound pilgrims carried on board in Jeddah. There were bundles of clothing, basins, buckets, and parcels of food and, in a far cry from the "hygienically-sealed" water that the modern pilgrim brings back, he adds, "not to forget the kerosene tins of Holy Water from Mecca."

And food, a good deal fresher

In a report from 1936 one crew member recalled how,

> Meat was provided by a flock of sheep and goats that were carried in a pen on the deck, and which were slaughtered as required. The animal's head was pointed towards Mecca and its throat was cut. When dead, a small incision was made in the back leg to which the butcher applied his mouth and blew hard. By this means the skin was separated from the flesh. When the carcass was cut up it was used almost immediately. The diet was supplemented by rice and vegetables cooked in steam-heated vessels, and all cooking was done on the open deck.[15]

This practice of slaughtering animals on board continued for some time, although it seemed to be carried on longer on ships from Indonesia. When the *Anking* and *Anshun* began sailing from Singapore and Malaya in 1953 live sheep from Western Australia were loaded on board.[16] And on a vessel like an old steamship, other creative solutions for food might appear. Derek Walker was Second Radio Officer on the ship *Tyndareus* in 1954:

> We carried around 2,000 pilgrims, who were housed in the 11 hatches; it must have been stifling in there in the Red Sea, and most of them sat and slept on the main deck. *Tyndareus* was a steamship and the Hajis used to buy fish from the bumboats in Aden and fry them on the hot steampipes that ran the length of the ship's deck either side.[17]

In the final period of the kapal haji – from the 1950s to the 1970s – food was finally provided from refrigerated supplies and cooked in kitchens designed for the purpose.

Levels of comfort

Throughout this book it's been emphasised that almost all the hajj ships that ran from Singapore and the Malaysian ports had no special sleeping arrangements for pilgrims. A small, fortunate number travelled in cabins but most slept on the decks. There was no air-conditioning and the air that came in was from large "wind socks" or "wind chutes" that can be seen in the pictures of the ship *Tyndareus* on page 179.

The 1950s and '60s

It was from the 1950s, late in the story of the kapal haji, that pilgrims could travel in ships that offered something far closer to a proper provision for sleeping, although even then, for the ordinary class of pilgrims, that was still in simple bunks. That was the case in *Anshun* and *Anking* – the two sister ships, whose names older residents of Singapore and Malaysia remember well. It would also be the case in the last ship to be operated by the China Navigation Company on the hajj, the converted troopship, *Dilwara* and in the very last of the kapal haji in the 1970s.

"Kuala Lumpur"

In 1959 Harvey Lade of Mansfields had been closely involved in the decision by China Navigation to buy the *Dilwara* "for the upgrading" of the pilgrim trade, and he visited Malayan Prime Minister Tunku Abdul Rahman "to give him a choice of the names *Langkawi* or *Medina*" for the new ship.

> Although he was obviously very pleased to have been consulted in this matter he politely declined both these names and expressed a preference for the name *Kuala Lumpur* so the pilgrims arriving at Jeddah from other Muslim countries could see for themselves that newly-independent Malaya had come of age in more ways than one.[18]

Accommodation on Kapal Haji "Kuala Lumpur"

Picture by permission of the late Hj Othman Wok

Then Minister for Social Services, Othman Wok, speaks to two elderly pilgrims beside their bunks on the shelter deck of the ship. The diagram points to the location of the bunks where the photograph was taken on the ships.

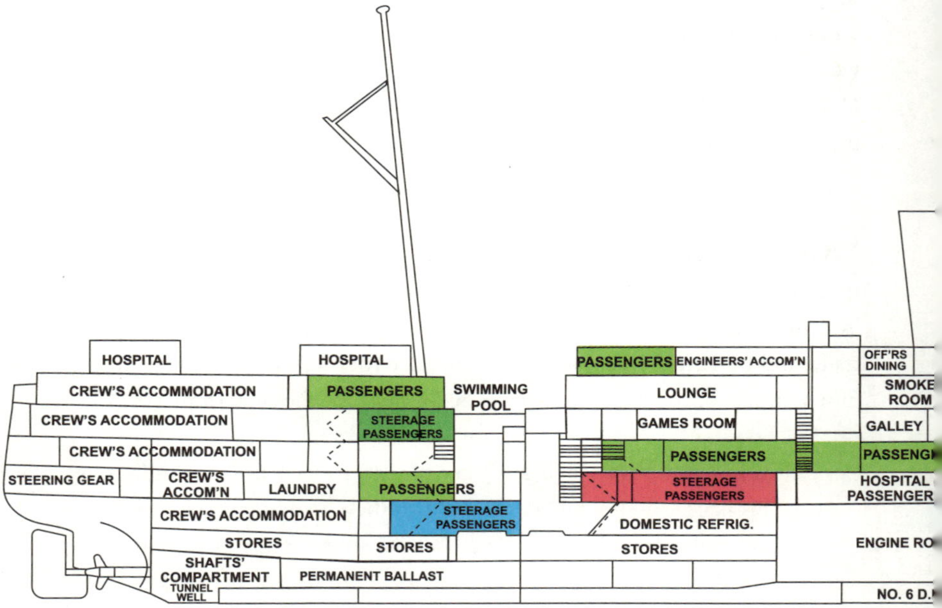

Exploded diagrams of ship supplied by Darrell Daish; original source http://wikiswire.com/wiki/Kuala_Lumpur.

Forward shelter deck (245 passengers)

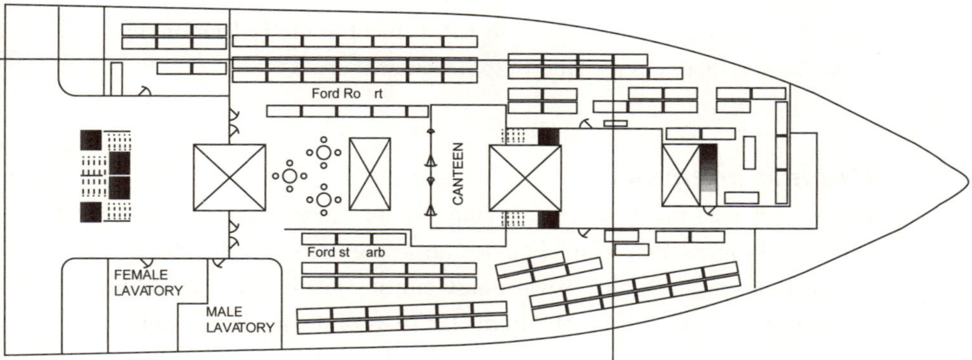

Originally built as the troopship *Dilwara*, then bought by China Navigation Co. in Hong Kong. The name *Kuala Lumpur* was chosen for the ship by Malaysian Prime Minister Tunku Abdul Rahman.

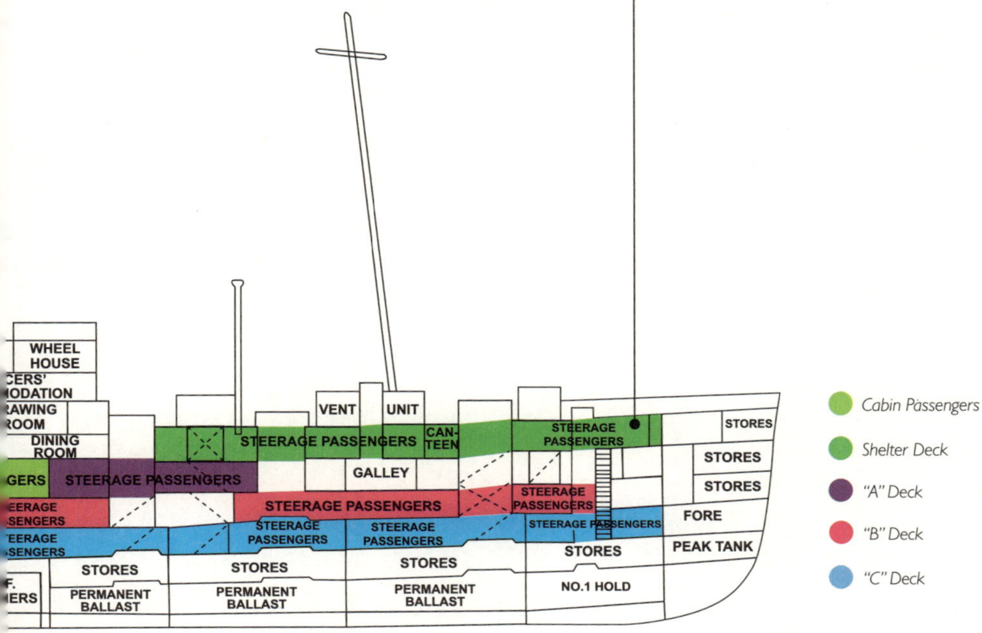

The Federation of Malaya got its independence in 1957 but in August, 1959 came elections for members of the first Parliament of the Federation. The *Kuala Lumpur* then, was a matter of some national pride.

The last company

Those companies that had been carrying pilgrims were progressively pulling out of the business. Blue Funnel carried on sailing from Indonesia until around 1960 and the China Navigation Company finally pulled out of hajj shipping at the end of the 1960s. In the last years of the sea-borne hajj their place was taken by the Great Malaysia Line – the company introduced in the first chapter of this book. Their involvement in this story of the kapal haji was short-lived and this will be commented on later. In the following chapter the focus is on one dramatic incident from 1880.

[1] http://www.red-duster.co.uk/BLUEFUN.htm; Accessed Feb 2018.

[2] Conrad, Joseph. 2002. *An Outcast of the Islands*, Oxford: Oxford University Press, p. 15

[3] Greenway, Ambrose. 2009. The Cargo Liners, Barnsley: Seaforth.

[4] Hyde, Prof. Francis E. "Blue Funnel: The Fleet, 1865-1914." In *The Ocean Nestorian Newsletter No 3*, March 2006, p. 15.

[5] Falkus, Malcolm. 1990. The Blue Funnel Legend. Basingstoke: Macmillan.

[6] Hyde. 2006. p. 15.

[7] STOJ. 7 October 1871, p. 1.

[8] Longhurst, Henry. 1956. *The Borneo Story.* London: Newman Neame Ltd. p. 84.

[9] Falkus. 1990, p. 37.

[10] ST. 11 Sept 1968.

[11] Interview with Darrell Daish, Christchurch, New Zealand, May 2018. Darrell Daish served with China Navigation Co. from January 1962 to February 1974.

[12] Personal communication from David Walker to Anthony Green.

[13] Pat IV ("Pilgrim Ships") of the Merchant Shipping Ordinance No. 125 of 1910.

[14] Jackson, Ian. *Pilgrims*, article – source unknown.

[15] Written report supplied to Anthony Green by Mr Jimmy Main of Fraserburgh, Aberdeenshire. The name of the original writer – now deceased – was removed by Jimmy Main because permission to publish had not been explicitly given and the writer was terminally ill at the time, but Mr Main vouched for the report's accuracy.

[16] Lade, Harvey. This detail is shown in a short film he made, entitled, *"The Singapore Pilgrimage 1953."*

[17] Written communication with Anthony Green.

[18] Lade, Harvey. From the "liner notes" written by him on the cover of the short film mentioned in note 16.

8

The S.S. Jeddah and the Alsagoff connection

Syed Mohamed Alsagoff (1836-1906). Picture courtesy of Syed Mohdar Alsagoff.

8 August 1880 was a Sunday. As he prayed the *fajr*, or dawn, prayer that morning we might wonder what thoughts would have gone through the mind of Syed Mohammad bin Ahmed Alsagoff. A spice trader and ship owner, he was a wealthy man. His ships sailed throughout the Indonesian archipelago, and he had larger vessels – both ones he owned and ones he had leased – taking pilgrims for the hajj. About three weeks earlier it's likely he would have watched one of his ships – the steamship, *S.S. Jeddah* – as it left Singapore and headed for the port from which it got its name. If departures are moments when prayers or supplications are made for a safe journey for those on board, then departures for the hajj take on their own significance, in this case perhaps more especially as Syed Mohammad's nephew, Syed Omar, was one of those departing on that morning.

But in that Singapore dawn of 8 August what he couldn't know was just what was happening to his ship. Over 5,600 kilometres away in the darkness around midnight, the *Jeddah* was drifting without power, and taking in water near Socotra, off the north-east African coast. And what he could never anticipate was that his ship – particularly its captain – would be the centre of an episode in local maritime history that many felt to be shameful.

The *Jeddah* was not an old ship. It had been ordered just nine years earlier from William Denny & Brothers on the River Leven near Glasgow. A letter had come to them from a Mr T. Small of Glasgow to say that "his friends in the East" required a two-deck steamer: a "plain but substantial job." Some second-class cabins were at the stern – there would be no 1st class accommodation – but most of the space was for "portable accommodation for 3rd class emigrants." That meant that, as the ship's plans show on pages 162 and 163, the hajj pilgrims would be in the 'tween decks on "folding up sleeping berths."

The *Jeddah*'s captain, Joseph Lucas Clark, had worked for Alsagoff for over eight years, his name appearing regularly as the Ship's Master in the lists of arrivals and departures. Clark's then "beloved wife, Emma Maria," had sailed with her husband and, five years earlier, in September 1875 she had died while the *Jeddah* was in the Red Sea. Her body would presumably have been consigned to the deep, as was the practice, and the image of a man at sea accompanied by his wife might suggest some degree of responsibility, perhaps of thinking of the safety of his wife. Yet just one month later, in October 1875, a case came up to the Legislative Council that the *Jeddah* had been carrying far more passengers than was permitted. Licensed to carry 662, the ship actually had 1,236 on board. And on this journey in 1880 those limits would again be ignored. The Master Attendant in Singapore would later report that the ship "left . . . with all the requirements of the law observed" but after a stop in Penang there would have been over 950 pilgrim passengers. How that could happen is an open question because the ship should have been checked before departure in both Singapore and Penang, each of which had its own Master Attendant's office. Whether it was a case of old habits of overcrowding seeming to die hard, or a kind of casual inattention or lack of vigilance, we do not know and the question, though noted by the relevant authorities,[1] did not seem to have been actively pursued.

Here, though, in 1880, real danger was a more pressing issue than overcrowding. The weather seems to have been heavy for most of the voyage. But on the 3rd August "the wind increased almost to hurricane, with high breaking sea." The boilers started to move from their fastenings and were secured with wedges, but these later broke away. Three more days of this and the ship started "to leak considerably." One boiler was put out of action and the *Jeddah* limped along.

The ship was rolling and water was coming into the cabins. The weather cleared briefly then a gale built up and "two native water closets and all moveables" on deck were washed away. Hajj ships often carried live animals to be slaughtered on board for food and the ship's plan for the Jeddah shows a structure for "fowls and sheep" on the main deck. If there were chickens and sheep on board, did they too get swept overboard?

Perhaps not surprisingly, details like this are not the kinds of things that concern Courts of Enquiry and the report of the subsequent Court makes no mention of this, but in the noise of the storm live creatures far from their natural environment should not be expected to go quietly to a watery grave.

For three days the crew and passengers worked, pumping and baling, to try to remove the water but at about 9.30pm on the 6th the vessel had to stop for repairs. With the ship rolling the temporary wedges to the boilers broke free. Seven or eight feet of water (over two metres) were inside the vessel and the water put out the boiler fires. Sails were set but then some of those sails were blown away. And even though the pilgrim passengers "appear to have given willing assistance" and to have carried on pumping until around midnight on the 7th, Captain Clark gave the order for the lifeboats to be got ready and swung out over the side. Ships of that time were unlikely to carry enough lifeboats for all deck passengers, and it is clear from the plans of the ship that the Jeddah indeed did not.Despite that the abandonment went ahead, with the First officer, Augustine Podmore Williams, playing a big part in urging this course of action. It was Williams who was judged by the Court of Enquiry to have given "officious ill-advice" and shown "unseamanlike conduct."

Apparently convinced that the *Jeddah* would go down, Clark, together with his new wife and the chief engineer, took what is generally regarded as unthinkable action by a ship's master and climbed into the lifeboat, leaving his passengers behind. Clark took with him Syed Omar and as the boat was lowered "the pilgrims commenced to throw boxes, pots and pans, and anything they could lay their hands on," into it.

Captain Clark got away. Rescued by another steamship, the British India Line, *S.S. Scindia*, he made no attempt to request that his rescuers search for his supposed lost ship. Instead, he and his group were taken to Aden. Once there, Syed Omar left for Mecca and it was from Aden that Clark sent his telegram:

> To Alsagoff, Singapore
>
> Aden, 10th August, 8.20pm. Jeddah foundered. Self, wife, Syed Omar, 18 others saved. CLARK

The news would shock the Straits Settlements. The Straits Times reported:

> A telegram was received here yesterday from Aden by the Agent of the Singapore Steam Ship Company, announcing the total loss by foundering of the Company's steamer, Jeddah, which left here with planks and about 950 pilgrims for Mecca on the 9th July... The telegram was short ... It merely stated that the steamer had foundered ... and from this there was too much reason to fear that a terrible calamity had taken place, and all the other passengers, numbering over 900 if not more must have gone down with the wreck.[2]

Reactions, attitudes, labels and perceptions

The *Jeddah* incident threw up a range of responses. When the news broke – in the Straits Settlements and in Britain – perceptions, preconceptions and past experiences came together in letters to the press from ships' masters who had carried pilgrims.

Truth was an early casualty.

The *Times of India* printed a story from their Aden correspondent claiming that,

> The pilgrims murdered the second officer and second engineer, and did their best to kill the Europeans who have been saved, by throwing boxes and other heavy articles into the boat as she was being launched

The 1872 shipbuilder's drawings and rigging plans for the Alsagoff ship S.S. Jeddah.

Built by William Denny & Brothers, Glasgow.

With engines in the early steamship lacking reliability, they carried masts and sails, which they resorted to when necessary.

Captain's room

Engine room where the boilers broke loose

"Native galley" with "steam kettles"

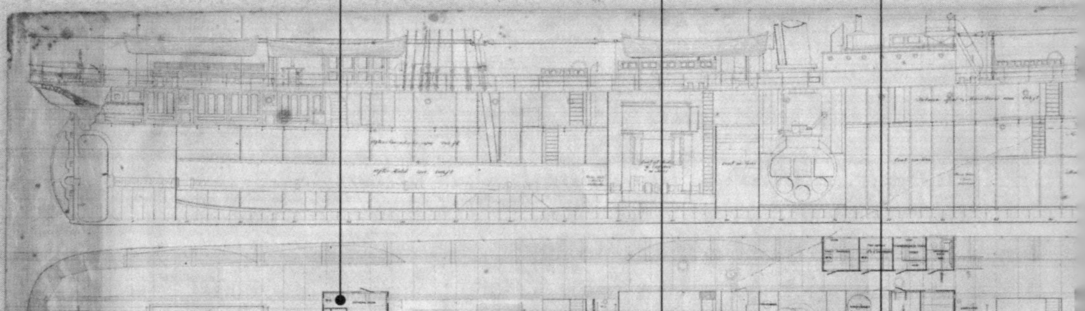

2nd class, twin berth cabins at the stern of the ship. Syed Mohammad's nephew, Syed Omar would likely have slept here.

The accommodation area with "folding up sleeping berths" for the 950 pilgrims.

Officers' accommodation.

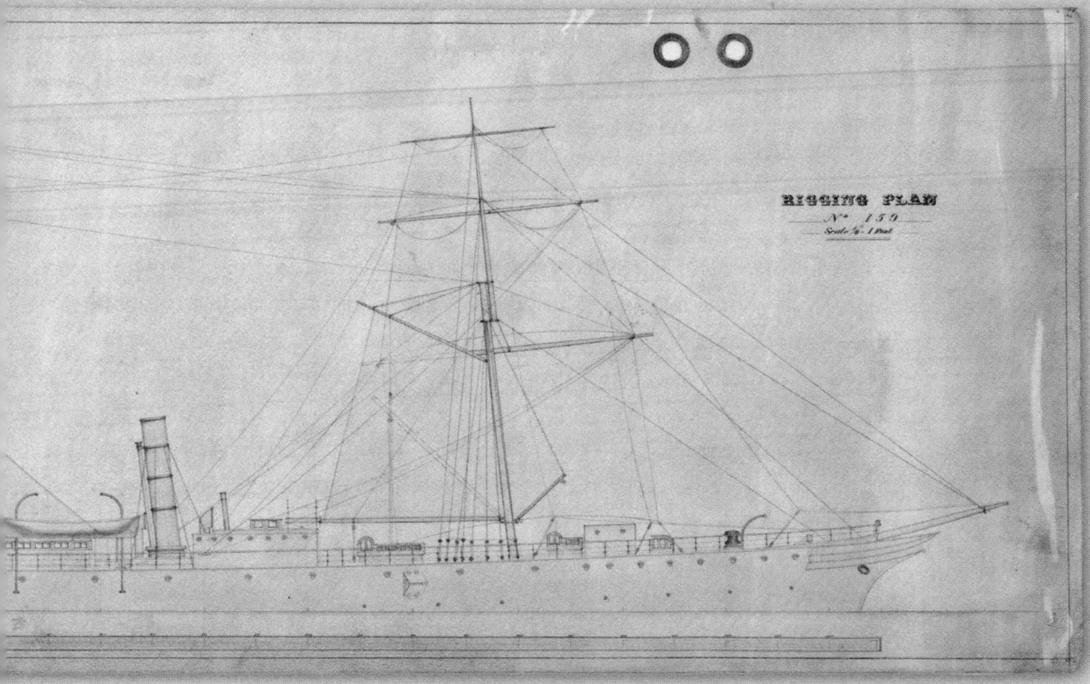

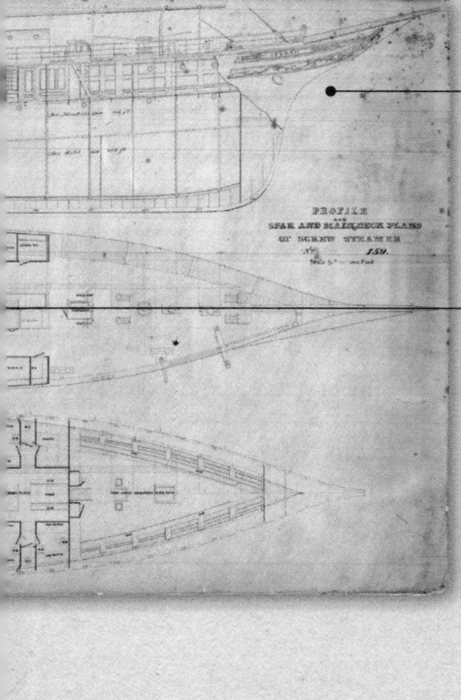

A "clipper bow" – many of the first generations of steamships were often designed very much along the lines and the thinking of the sailing ships they were replacing, although the "Blue Funnel" ships they would be competing against were generally of a newer, "more modern" design.

Box or pen for "fowls and sheep".

Ship Plans © National Maritime Museum, Greenwich, London

> ...When the boat shoved off the *Jeddah* was sinking fast. I am told that it was an awful business.

In London, *The Times* published a letter that had been written by a Captain Henry Carter some months earlier. He spoke of pilgrims as "these wretched fanatics"; of horrors on board their ships "which no Christian has ever dreamt of . . . wickedness worse, by far, than was ever found on board a slaver."

The two signal flags – N (upper) and C (lower) together send the message "I am in distress and require immediate assistance"

The ship that Carter had been on had not sailed from Southeast Asia and that fact prompted a response to The Times from someone signed "A Singapore Merchant":

> Sir, – It may interest your readers to know that no such horrors as those depicted by Captain Carter have been known in the pilgrim trade between Singapore and Jeddah, at any rate for many years past.[3]

But the ship had not "foundered." At about 4.30pm on the day the *Jeddah* had been abandoned, another hajj ship, the Blue Funnel vessel *Antenor*, responded to the distress signals that had been hoisted. Once he'd boarded the *Jeddah*, the Chief Officer, Randolph Campbell found "everything on board was in confusion, and all persons on board were panic stricken" but after a short discussion with his own captain they decided the ship might be towed into Aden. In Campbell's words,

The signal flags D (upper) and X (lower) together send the urgent message "I am sinking".

> I called the headmen amongst the pilgrims together and organised gangs amongst the pilgrims to pump and bale the vessel. This was done, the men constantly relieving one another . . .

The rescue was in marked contrast to the abandonment but it was still a tricky business. The *Antenor* was already fully loaded with passengers and cargo but without its full complement of officers. Matthew Nelson, the third officer, had contracted smallpox and been left in Singapore so the captain, John Bragg, and the second officer kept alternate watches. Together with Randolph Campbell they agreed on signals to be sent between the two ships in case the *Jeddah* started to go down and they kept up regular communication between them with cheers from the crew of the *Antenor* when they saw a signal that the water level inside the vessel had lowered.

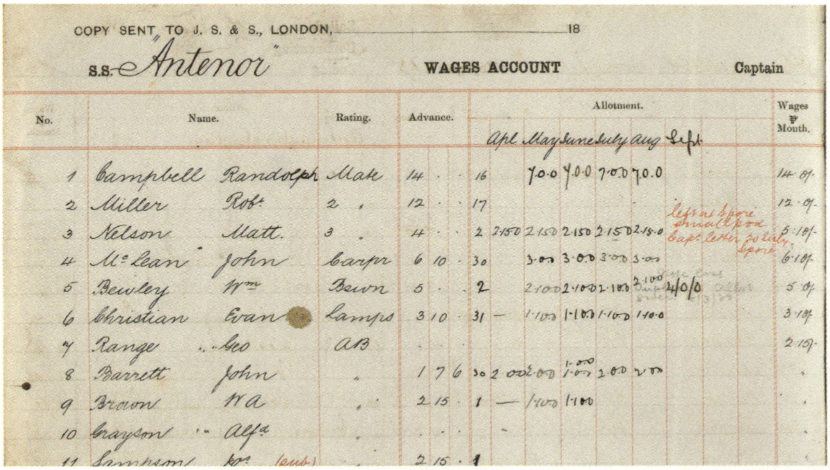

COPY SENT TO J. S. & S., LONDON, 18

S.S. "Antenor" WAGES ACCOUNT Captain

No.	Name.		Rating.	Advance.	Allotment. Apl	May	June	July	Aug	Sept	Wages ₱ Month.
1	Campbell	Randolph	Mate	14 · · 16		7.0.0	7.0.0	7.0.0	7.0.0		14 · 0/-
2	Miller	Robt	2 „	12 · · 17							12 · 0/-
3	Nelson	Matt.	3 „	4 · · 2	2.15.0	2.15.0	2.15.0	2.15.0	2.15.0	left at Spore smallpox Capt. letter to Ealr. Spore	5 · 10/-
4	McLean	John	Carpr	6 10 · 30		3.0.0	3.0.0	3.0.0	3.0.0		6 · 10/-
5	Bewley	Wm	Bosn	5 · · 2		2.10.0	2.10.0	2.10.0	2.10.0	2/0/0	5 · 0/-
6	Christian	Evan	Lamps	3 10 · 31	—	1.10.0	1.10.0	1.10.0	1.10.0		3 · 10/-
7	Range	Geo	AB								2 · 15/-
8	Barrett	John	„	1 7 6 30	2.0.0	2.0.0	1.0.0	2.0.0	2.0.0		„
9	Brown	W A	„	2 15 · 1	—	1.10.0	1.10.0				„
10	Grayson	Alfd	„								„
11	Sampson	Jos (sub)	„	2 15 · 1							

The entry in red in the Antenor wages list shows "Matt Nelson: left at Singapore, smallpox." The top of the page shows that a copy would be sent to J. S. & S., London (John Swire and Sons). It suggests how closely the two companies – Holts and John Swire – worked together. Image courtesy of Deutsche Post AG (Ocean Archive at National Museums Liverpool, Merseyside Maritime Museum).

"Experienced nautical men" gave their opinions that the *Jeddah* was in great danger and that the *Antenor* ran considerable risk to pass a towrope on board, a risk enhanced by the strong currents, by the strong breezes at the height of the monsoon, and by the approaching darkness.

The S.S. Antenor – the Blue Funnel ship that towed the Jeddah into Aden. Picture sourced from Blue Funnel and Glen Line Bulletin; reproduced courtesy of John Swire & Sons Limited.

Yet an anonymous note in the Blue Funnel Archives in the Liverpool Maritime Museum points to the Company's "Ships Journal No, 3 (1878 – 1880)" which sums up the incident with the cryptic reference:

> 7-0 P.M. 8th. Aug. took in tow S.S. 'Jeddah' abandoned at C. Guardafui. Towed into Aden.

It's common for the conversation of people engaged in similar work to be in terms of their shared experiences. In Singapore at that time, Charlie Emmerson's tiffin rooms near the Cavenagh Bridge was one of those places where seafaring men met to exchange information. News spreads through such places and when this full story broke in Singapore, "public excitement" was said by the newspapers to have "risen to fever heat." The writer Joseph Conrad worked on ships owned by Syed Massim (or Mohsen) Aljoofree around Southeast Asia and it was at Charlie Emmerson's where he was believed to have heard the story of the *Jeddah*.

The port of Aden, around 1891. Image in the Public Domain.

The port of Aden in the 1880s was not large and the arrival at 5.15 in the evening of a battered *Jeddah* under tow must have caused a stir, especially for a ship's captain who was sure he'd seen the last of it. And so, the day after he'd sent his first telegram, Captain Clark had to send this, no doubt surprising, message to Singapore.

```
Aden, 11th August, 9.15pm Antenor towed down
here Jeddah full of water. All life saved,
now in charge Government Telegraph further
particulars tomorrow. Omar gone Jeddah
last night.
```

A natural violence – "even for Europeans"

The emergence of the full story led to that Court of Enquiry, and this in turn to a string of newspaper features, and motions being urged in the Straits Settlements Legislative Council. The Court found that,

. . . the captain entirely forgot his first duty as a shipmaster; that until he got into the lifeboat "no violence or show of force had been made by the pilgrims to anyone on board"; "that it was only when the boat was being lowered" and they found themselves being deserted by the one man who should protect them that this roused the pilgrims to violence [such as] "might naturally have been expected from any body of human beings, even Europeans, situated as the pilgrims were."

Their summary was that he had failed completely in his duties; that the chief engineer was very much to blame for not taking proper measures to secure the boilers; and that the first mate, Augustine Williams, was greatly to blame for working on the fears of the master.

Clark had claimed that he feared the pilgrims intended to kill him and his wife. Yet there was no evidence for this and the Assessor's Report identified that the captain's wife got from the captain's cabin to the lifeboat – a distance of 40ft (about 12m) – unmolested.

Newspapers in London contrasted the values that were expected of the British mercantile, and of an "Englishman":

From *The Times*:

> There is something very unpleasant in the facts thus stated; for, to honour of sailors, nothing is more rare than that, in a disaster at sea, the captain and the principal officers of the vessel should be the chief or sole survivors.

From *The Daily Chronicle*:

> It is to be feared that pilgrim ships are sometimes officered by unprincipled and cowardly men who disgrace the traditions of seamanship. We sincerely trust that no Englishman was among the boatload of cowards who left the *Jeddah* and her thousand passengers to shift for themselves.

This was "a slur or stain upon the whole British mercantile service" and the Legislative Council, meeting in Singapore on 14th September, heard members urge that "the Government is bound to protect the pilgrim traffic from these ports and to show these devotees . . . that such unprincipled conduct as Clark's does not pass unheeded."

The feeling was that the Enquiry erred on the side of leniency in suspending Clark's Master Certificate for just three years. It was suggested that, "if those 900 passengers had been English, he would not have been so leniently treated," and the question posed, "whether any of us in the same situation would not have shot Captain Lucas Clark like a dog for his dastardly attempt to desert his vessel."

Captain Clark returned to Singapore to sort out his affairs and then, it appears, he left the colony "to return to England."

Footnote

Augustine Podmore Williams – the Mate of the *Jeddah*, and the one who had urged she be abandoned – also returned to Singapore but in his case he worked quietly to reinstate himself in some way. He died in 1916 and was buried in the old Christian cemetery at Bidadari.[4] The writer Gavin Young has cited his obituary from the Singapore Free Press, 17 April 1916. It has an almost disparaging quality in its reference to the *Jeddah* incident.

> Many wreaths were sent to the funeral having reference to his nautical career, besides many others from private friends. The late Mr Williams was chief officer of the Singapore Steamship Co's Jeddah, a pilgrim ship which met with an accident in the Red Sea and was abandoned with about 1,000 coolies aboard.[5]

And the pilgrims themselves?

In all of this closely documented episode, what of the passengers, the pilgrims – the ones labelled here as "coolies"? Where were they throughout the experience and what might they have been feeling or have called out?

Their numbers have been given as 778 men, 147 women and 67 children. For the vast majority of them this would have been their one and only hajj voyage, and almost certainly their first time at sea. The ship's master and the first mate – experienced sailors – were in such fear of their lives that they abandoned the ship. The storms were so violent that, as earlier noted, "two native water closets and all moveables" on deck were washed away. And since those storms continued for a number of days, it seems unlikely that many could have stayed on deck, exposed to the elements. From the ship's plans the question is just what would they have held on to?

If they – presumably women and children – were huddled below while the men helped to work pumps to bale water, what fears were there? But when you listen for their voices all that you hear is a silence in the midst of the storm.

Throughout the history of the hajj in colonial times there was a current of confusion and misunderstanding about the hajj, and the speculation that, because many who travelled were simple folk, they could not have understood a great deal of what the hajj meant.

We cannot know who amongst them could explain the teachings of their faith but some pointers can be suggested. There are verses in the Qur'an (2: 155 –157) that teach Muslims that they will be tested "with something of fear and hunger and a loss of wealth and lives and fruits." Whether those on the *Jeddah* could have recited this, or put it into words, the notion of a test, or fear, would likely have been present.

Whether in a village surau or a mosque those who set out on the hajj would have turned their face regularly in a certain direction – the *qiblah* towards Mecca. How much they knew of the teachings of their faith would vary but a kind of fatalism would have shaped and coloured their lives. Each individual would accept that life had a term; that death was to be accepted when it came because the truth was that no-one knew when or in what place they would die.

The reactions of each of these individuals on the *Jeddah* will remain forever beyond our knowledge but with the question posed by some scholars as to what the hajj meant to those who made it, and with this *"Jeddah"* experience behind them, their private feelings as they finally arrived in Mecca would likely have been very moving and a degree far past simple relief.

Identity and attitudes

Looking back, the priorities or sense of values of the account in The Straits Times might seem odd: the *Jeddah*'s cargo of "planks" – i.e., wood – was listed first, and then "950 pilgrims." A small detail but quite telling.

The *Jeddah* incident revealed a strain of dismissive, even disdainful, attitudes and perceptions about the pilgrims as people, about just what the pilgrimage entailed and what the intentions were of those pilgrims. They were, "Wretched fellows, who do not care if they die because they are convinced they will go to heaven."

The idea was frequently expressed that the object of the pilgrimage was to visit the tomb of the Prophet Muhammad:

> The tendency of the members of most religious persuasions to attach peculiar interest to certain spots supposed to possess especial sanctity is well known. Among none is this sentiment more strongly developed than with those professing the Mahomedan faith. With a very pious Mussulman, to visit the holy places at Mecca and Medina is the dream of a lifetime. From his earliest youth it is the one object of his ambition, and to gratify it he will put by, year after year, every piastre that he may be able to scrape together, and not absolutely required for the wants of himself and family. Nor is this surprising. He is taught by his religion that by visiting the places sacred to the memory of

> the Great Prophet he will expiate his past sins – and those who know him will admit that these are neither few in number nor limited in character – and will also do much to secure his eventual entry into Paradise.[6]

It was true that making *ziyarah* – visiting tombs – was something that people took the opportunity to do when they went on the hajj, but it was not part of the rituals of the pilgrimage. And after the 1920s most of those tombs that would have been visited were systematically removed when the forces of Ibn Saud took control of Mecca, and actively discouraged the practice.

Together with an inadequate understanding of what the hajj entailed, what was being expressed or denigrated in this example and in many other places was the character of the pilgrims as people who were somehow those whose "past sins" were "neither few in number nor limited in character."

The Alsagoff family and steamships – an unfortunate involvement

Amongst the Arab shipowners the only family with steamships capable of making the voyage to Jeddah seem to have been the Alsagoff family and their Singapore Steamship Company, but the period of time when they operated these ships was brief. One other Hadhrami owner, Syed Masim Al-Joofrie, had a steamship called the *Vidor* that Joseph Conrad served on but this was smaller and used just for short distance work around the region.

In an earlier chapter we mentioned some of the setbacks experienced by Syed Mohammed Alsagoff with his ships. The incident with the 1,100 ton steamship *Medina* six years before this was costly. She'd been purchased in February 1874, the newspapers reporting that she was,

> ... a noble vessel of high class, and will probably be employed in the Hadjee trade. She is able to carry a large cargo, and burns few coals — which now-a-days seems to be the essential point in steam-ships.[7]

Built just one year earlier in County Durham in England, the shipping registers show that the company's mortgage on the ship was for $80,000 "with interest at eight per cent payable by monthly instalments at $2,200 per month or more" to "Charles Dunlop of Singapore, Merchant."

In May 1874 the *Medina* returned to Singapore from Jeddah, via Penang and Malacca. This meant she made just one trip carrying returning pilgrims about three months after the completion of the hajj. Between the hajj voyages, Alsagoff's ships were also used around Southeast Asia and up to China but the grounding and the loss of the *Medina* in October 1875 meant that after just over eighteen months in their service, the ship had to be scrapped. Ten years later, in February 1885, the certificate of registry for the *Jeddah* was also cancelled and the registry closed. The involvement of the Alsagoffs with steamships lasted for less than fifteen years. With arguments in court it could not have been profitable for them.

• • • • • • • • • •

1 Report of Legislative Council, 17 October 1875.

2 ST. 14 August 1880, p. 6.

3 The Times. 17 August 1880, p. 8

4 The cemetery no longer exists and all remains have been exhumed.

5 Young, Gavin. 1996. Introduction to the Folio edition of Conrad's *Lord Jim*. London: The Folio Society.

6 Moore. Op cit.

7 Straits Times Overland Journal (hereinafter STOJ). 19 November 1873, p. 7.

Age

Throughout this book the age of the pilgrims has been a recurring theme. Young children travelled and babies were born and the photographs in chapter 3 from Snouck Hurgronje include faces both young and old. But for the vast majority of the pilgrims the hajj journey would only be possible after a lifetime of saving and perhaps the sale of land or valuable possessions. By way of example, in April 1963 Sulong bin Bakar, from Kampong Perapak in Terengganu, Malaysia, journeyed with his wife on the *Kuala Lumpur*. The cost was from all their savings, augmented by the sale of eight buffaloes. He was 95 years old. She was 90.

The story of the kapal haji is full of examples such as this, so that boarding the ship and setting out was itself a kind of realisation of all that they had striven for. Returning was not a concern. There are many photographs of old, seemingly frail, men and women beginning their journey. It seems unnecessary to present a collection of such images. One may suffice. Here, in May 1953, one elderly man is helped to the ship at Tanjong Pagar, Singapore by Red Cross nurses.

May, 1953. An old man is helped to the ship.
Ministry of Information and the Arts Collection, courtesy of National Archives of Singapore.

9

Tyndareus: Photo essay

The pictures on the following pages were taken in 1960 on the last journeys of the Blue Funnel ship *Tyndareus* from Lombok and Java in Indonesia to Jeddah but they give a good idea of pilgrim accommodation in the period before the mid-1950s, except that before this time pilgrims would likely have slept on mattresses on the bare deck and not on the "camp beds" that are shown here.

Built in 1916, *Tyndareus* was used on the hajj from Singapore and Penang in the early 1950s, normally carrying around 1,800 pilgrims, but sometimes well in excess of 2,000, before the China Navigation Co ships *Anking* and *Anshun* took over this service. *Tyndareus* was then used exclusively on hajj journeys from Indonesia before being scrapped in 1960. In between the hajj it would be laid up in Singapore and repaired in dry-dock there. These images and the accompanying comments are from the 2nd Mate, John Spain.

Nb All images in this "photo-essay" by permission of John Spain

"It was steam up-and-down, reciprocating – so it was the most beautifully quiet ship because there was virtually no vibration apart from right aft, from the propellers. And we were the only ship on the haj run – although I think, *Gunung Djati* – who didn't ration water, because we carried so much. We carried the big side bunkers full of water."

"The 'barang-barang' came aboard in rope slings and then they pulled the edge and let it go. A motley collection of cases, wicker containers and things, all belonging to individuals, then the men came on board and sorted out their things. All sorted out and disappeared eventually."

"That person there . . . we called him Joseph [probably Yusuf?] and he was the last, I think, of the original, Arab 'mobile travel agents.' He had with him his drum, and his mat and his umbrella. And his worldly possessions, most likely. They used to go round Java or any of the islands, beating on the drum and virtually selling the pilgrimage service. I think that was his last voyage and that the Indonesian government stepped in to the extent that so many of these villagers fulfilling their pillars of Islam did sell up everything they had purely and simply to make the pilgrimage – which is not quite what the pillar says.

"He was a great raconteur – he would sit on the hatches and talk with them . . . It would be lovely to find Joseph now, but he went back to Saudi and you can see by his age and his greying beard, that he's most likely no longer with us. But he had a reasonable command of English and obviously was fluent in Indonesian.

"We had to learn Indonesian as apprentices. We had instruction here in England and had to do a certain amount of homework. You did a four-year apprenticeship and during that time you were supposed to learn Indonesian, because that was our main trading area. The main instructions for loading cargo, which is what we were employed to do."

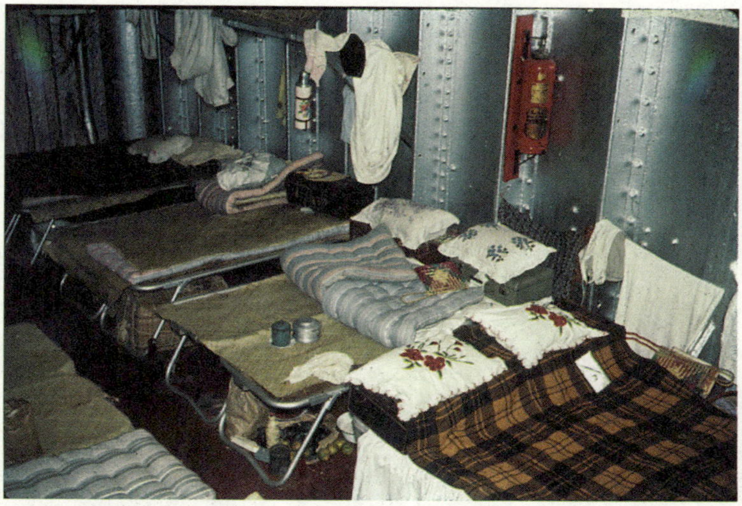

"This was how the accommodation was. These were taken in the morning and in the late afternoon because they had times when we cleaned out the decks so we had a whole lot of what we called 'sweepers' that used to go around and sweep out all the accommodations. They'd turn the mattresses back. So each pilgrim had a bunk, which was a portable bed with springs and a mattress which we supplied and then that was theirs – obviously you couldn't put someone else on it in the next voyage. There's one of the sweepers in the background there. And that's the ladder up from the 'tween deck to the main deck. There were upper and lower 'tween decks. And then also in the side bunkers."

"The third mate in the chart room. Holts laid down certain standards as far as routing was concerned. And on the charts – and this was laughed at by lots of other companies' people – they thought that all our charts had red lines and we steered along the red lines. There were only a certain amount but they were on the main routes from, for example, Aden south to Minicoy Island, to the Acheen Head in Sumatra. There were various routes and those were the ones that we followed. Obviously, once you went into the Singapore Straits and up through the Indonesian islands there were just ordinary ones. But there were always certain details laid down as to what was a safe distance off a head. Whereas people like P&O, with passengers on board, used to cruise quite close along the coast purely and simply to show passengers things."

"At sea, we used to rig awnings over all the hatches, and the big, canvas wind chutes, to gather air down to the 'tween decks, and the big ventilators, back to the wind, to take the air out of the hold. But it was the north-east monsoon haj, so obviously the Indian Ocean was a fine, smooth crossing. It would be infinitely different in the south-west monsoon. Everyone was down below.

"If you saw a rain shower ahead you'd go around it, as long as you didn't go zig-zagging in between rain showers. But rather than call out the bo'sun and take all the wind socks or wind chutes down, you'd just alter course a few degrees and go round it and keep the ventilation. If you saw a storm ahead you'd have time to go around it. Obviously there were times when you had an extensive rain squall and you'd have to call out the bo'sun and drop all the wind chutes, which would take half an hour at the most. But it meant of course closing up the hatches because you had to lift the wind chute out of the hatch. You pulled a corner of the hatch back to drop the big wind chutes. They were quite broad. And of course you had to pull the hatches back into place and cover them over with a tarpaulin. "

"Because I was second mate I was always on the 12 to 4 watch, and they used to bake the bread at about 4 o'clock in the morning, and make all these rolls for the pilgrims. The bakers were Indonesians. Lovely bread! By the time I'd finished my rounds I used to go down there."

"This was in Aden, bringing the goats on board. They were all killed on deck. We managed with our own refrigeration meat up until Aden and then topped up with live goats. They were kept in a pen on deck."*

* *Goats were often referred to as 'Welsh Fusiliers' because goats were used as the mascot of the Welsh regiment.*

"Queuing to come back on board in Jeddah. So patient – there's no pushing or shoving."

"Many of these people were farmers, villagers who had a little shop – a different type of people altogether. Far more rural. They were just gentle, nice people. They really were. But I'm afraid that the majority of the words we used, for loading cargo, were known by the port-workers in English. And you find that they want to practice their English."

The Keppel Dry Dock where Blue Funnel ships would be cleaned or repaired when they were not on hajj duty.

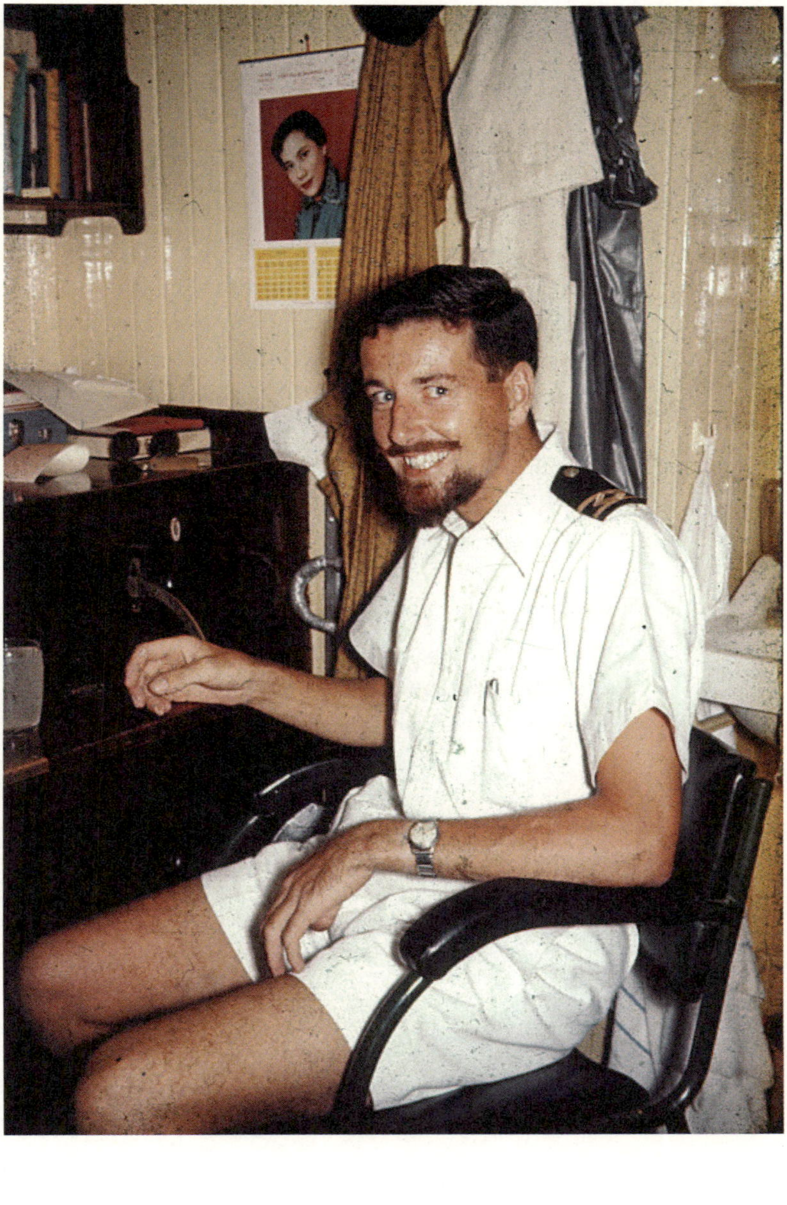

Seen here in 1960, John Spain, 2nd Mate of the Tyndareus, supplied the photographs and the extract from the ship's log shown in chapter 12.

10

At sea

Partings now are not as they were. Families bidding farewell at an airport can have their final hugs and tears and then the one who is leaving steps away from them, often through a glass doorway and into a secured space. Sometimes you can watch the formalities, from a distance or through that glass, as their passport is stamped, then a few more steps, a look back for a last wave and they turn and pass out of sight into airport anonymity. The visible connections are broken.

In the time of travel by sea it was different. The decks lined with passengers; the ship often "dressed" overall with signal flags; and large crowds of friends and families on the dock to bid their farewells...

4

NOTICE.

THE Undersigned begs to notify to his Friends, both well and evil-disposed towards him, that he intends, please God, to leave this Settlement within *Twenty Days* from this date; and that any Person or Persons having Claims against him of any description soever, will be pleased to inform him of the same or make their claims before that time.

SHAIK SALLIM BIN OMAR BASHARAHILL.

Singapore, 9th July, 1855.

DOMESTIC OCCURRENCES.

MARRIAGE.

In England, on the 10th May, Francis Augustus Brett, Esqre., 43rd M. N. I., to Julia Henrietta, youngest daughter of the late S. Matthews, Esq., of Plymouth.

DEATH.

At Sea, on the 22nd Jan., on his passage from Manila to London, Captain Arthur Smith, H.C S., second surviving son of the late David Smith, Esq., of Arbroath.

Straits Times.

SINGAPORE: TUESDAY, JULY 10TH, 1855.

Before parting, a common wish is to settle all debts. This 1855 newspaper classified advertisement captures something of the strength of that intention. 'Shaik' Sallim owned two ships that operated to Jeddah – the "Persia" and the "Ruby" – and seems to have been back in Singapore in the 1860s when his ships were sailing.

For a reflective person, every separation or parting must be realised to be possibly the last, and a parting for the hajj has, and always has had, extra layers of significance. These are not casual send-offs and in the time of the kapal haji, in a real sense, no one left alone. Departures were shared things. You left accompanied by the prayers and presence of your family and community. In Singapore a "godown" – a warehouse – at the Tanjong Pagar dock would be set aside to be turned into a kind of vast, communal, final gathering place. The hajj was, and is, a journey that embodies many features of what have been described as transformative *rites de passage* – rites of passage – because the pilgrim sets out "as if he [or she] were leaving this world."[1]

As a 20-year-old, Fatmah Mohamed Salim accompanied her parents who were leaving for hajj in February 1967. She remembers the atmosphere in that godown as being like,

> ... a very big festival for all those people going to the hajj with their families... we brought our mats to sit on, and all that, and a little food until the time for them to leave for their pilgrimage.[2]

In the godown at Tanjong Pagar Cik Siti Aishah bte Shaikh Osman sits surrounded by family and friends before boarding the "Kuala Lumpur." Picture courtesy of Fatmah Mohamed Salim.

The gathering for a "kenduri" at home, before departure. Picture courtesy of Fatmah Mohamed Salim.

The kenduri – feast and prayers before parting

Even before the departure there would be a *kenduri* – a kind of a gathering together to eat, and as an occasion for prayer and *dua*: supplications. Her family then were living in a house at Lorong Marzuki in Kembangan and her father was active in Masjid Abdul Razak nearby, so the kenduri brought together relatives, brothers and sisters, neighbours, colleagues from the mosque and the work place for a kind of farewell for, as she put it,

> a safe journey, for good health; for those who go and also for those who are at home. To say a lot of prayers for those going for the hajj.

Whether in Singapore, at Port Klang (then called Port Swettenham) or in Penang, all of the pictures of hajj sailings from the 1950s to the 1970s convey a powerful sense of the presence of a community. In Singapore in the time leading up to the ship sailings the streets of Kampong Glam would be packed with the would-be pilgrims, a great many of whom would have been staying there in the preceding weeks, in the houses that were turned into temporary sleeping spaces. Prayers first in Masjid Sultan then out into the accompanying crowds and onto trucks to head to the dock.

In February 1963, the oldest person on board the ship *Kuala Lumpur* was a lady named Salinah binte Awang, from Kampong Melayu in Singapore. She was 93. The newspaper reports said that, "two bus loads of relatives and neighbours from Kampong Melayu... were at the barricade to see her off."

> "This has been my life's ambition," she said. "I saved since I was a young girl for this trip. Now I shall be able to die happy."[3]

A crowded Bussorah St in Kampong Glam – hajj departure time in January 1972. © Singapore Press Holdings Ltd.

Boarding

David Walker was Second Mate on the *Kuala Lumpur* in December 1967:

> Once the vessel was ready to embark pilgrims we would berth alongside in Singapore and two enormous gangways would be rigged at the main deck to the quay. Pilgrims with families and well-wishers were then allowed to board with their belongings and to take up their berth allocation in the troop decks. Each berth was numbered and each compartment named by deck and number. In addition each compartment had its own sign such as sun, star, moon, or donkey, cat, or dog as there were a number of pilgrims who were unable to read or write, thus making it easier for them to follow directions to their allocated bunk.
>
> There would be a period of viewing and a carnival atmosphere, all supervised by the Malay Staff under the supervision of the Staff Captain and Chief Officer, who was also concerned with topping up with capacity fresh water assisted by the ship's carpenters. Then, prior to sailing, all visitors and pilgrims were returned to the Quay godowns whilst the ship was thoroughly searched for stowaways.
>
> Once this had been done pilgrims were embarked in single file up the two gangways with a shore representative of The Malay Moslem Commission (The Ships Charterer) at the foot of each of the

gangways. At the top would be a Malay Purser checking tickets and documentation along with a Ship's Officer whose sole responsibility was a head count. The head count would be compared by the ship and the Moslem Commission before the ship sailed. Woe betide if there was a discrepancy. There were at times compartment differences which meant that pursers and officers would have to go to that particular compartment and do a head count. The disembarkation of a whole ship full of Pilgrims and re-boarding with tally doesn't bear thinking about.

Emotions would be running high, as can be imagined when this was a life's ambition: to become a Haji, having saved all one's life to do so. It was not uncommon for pilgrims to fall upon their knees and kiss the deck of "Kapal Haji Kuala Lumpur" on boarding. This would cause a certain amount of delay and congestion and would have to be dealt with in a manner that would not hurt sensibilities, but keep the progress of embarkation from gumming up. It was mostly the older and perhaps less educated that were not as sanguine as the younger pilgrims. There were certainly whole families taking part in the hajj, from grandparents to very young grandchildren, but mostly the more mature pilgrim.[4]

Singapore minister, Othman Wok inspects the ship. Ustazah Maimunah binti Ahmad had commented that when she travelled in 1970 some older ladies removed their shoes when they got on board the ship. Here, two ladies on the right are barefoot. Picture by permission of the late Hj Othman Wok.

(above) A hajj ship departure invites many responses – for the young, a kind of adventure

(top right) Boarding at Port Swettenham (Port Klang)

(right) At Penang the sign says "Tanga Turun Sahaja" – 'Stairs for going down.'

Pictures courtesy of Fatmah Mohamed Salim.

At each port it would take from about 0900hrs at berth to about 1600hrs unberthing, i.e. departure, to embark pilgrims. And at each place – Port Swettenham and Penang – pilgrims were disembarked and re-boarded with a head count in total and a stowaway search in each port before re-embarkation. It might be thought laborious but David Walker stressed that,

> ...it was essential that the pilgrims should be allowed with the minimum of marshalling and hassle to start on what was a very emotional journey, but it was essential that this was done with an eye to stowaways and getting everyone aboard and in the right place. It had to be done firmly but sensitively.

That mention of stowaways is important. Darrell Daish worked on *Kuala Lumpur* on three hajj voyages – the first two as Mate, responsible for the upkeep of the ship and to assist the Staff Master, and the last as the Staff Master. In those journeys he doesn't recall any serious misunderstandings but he tells the story – one that's not exactly a stowaway – of an incident at Port Swettenham when two men tried to bring another who had died onto the ship:

> That fellow had died so they tried to bring him on board. We always had the bosuns and quartermasters and crew at the top, and the Malay pursers counting them and checking them on and making sure they had their tickets. And this fellow, though he was upright, was "being helped" shall we say.[5]

If this sounds far-fetched, it's worth looking back at recommendations that were contained in the 1927 report from Jeddah of the Malay Pilgrimage Officer, Hj Abdul Majid Zainuddin:

> In order to prevent the present practice of allowing hopelessly invalid and often dying persons, together with women about to give birth, on board pilgrim ships, I would propose that the Port Health Officer, or a European deputy, be present in person to examine all pilgrims before boarding, and that he reject any such as are in his opinion unfit to undertake the journey.

Vernon Elliott, who sailed on the Blue Funnel ship *Rhesus* in 1948 and 1949, recalled that the ship's Surgeon had the last word about the acceptance of the boarders on health grounds, "and I remember the anguish when he refused certain people."[6]

The possibility of death on the journey itself was an understanding, and as part of their luggage many carried with them their *kain kafan* – the sheets of white cloth in which a deceased Muslim is wrapped for burial. In fact, to be able to "die happy" in Mecca or Medina was, for many, like a quiet hope.

Hj Ahmad Abdullah remembered the family gathering around his brother-in-law as he described where he wanted his possessions to go if he did not return – "his motorcycle to go to his son"[7] and so on...

There should be no surprise in this. While young people did travel and many times women gave birth on pilgrim ships and in the Hejaz, the majority who travelled were older. It was noted in an earlier chapter just how old some of the oldest pilgrims were. Omar Baobed worked with the harbour police at the time when pilgrim ships were leaving, and the way he recalls the scene is echoed by most people who witnessed the departure of a kapal haji:

> It was very sad; very, very moving to see. All the pilgrims lined up on the deck and so many of them old people. With their age you knew that many might not return. And when the azan was called almost everyone had tears in their eyes.[8]

In Singapore at the time of the ship's sailing the call of the *azan* – the call to prayer – was made by a religious figure from Johore or Singapore. But ships pull away slowly and all the ingredients are in place for the emotions to be tugged: the sight, the sounds, the people, the occasion, and the significances; the long, "last look."

Fatmah Mohd Salim holds a clear memory of her feelings as her parents left:

> The *azan* seemed to go on forever, as if it were hanging on the water.

Retired teacher Mohd Fadzil bin Hj Anwar Bashir lived in Kampong Glam during the time when the presence of pilgrims was part of the calendar of the community. His father, Hj Anwar, was a registered pilgrim broker in the 1960s when they lived at 61, Bussorah Street and Cikgu Mohd Fadzil saw the departure of the *Anshun* and heard the adhan as the ropes were let go. He described the feeling as being "very *sepi*, very *sayu*," the two Malay words coming together to connote that melancholic sense that mixes quiet longing, sadness, and aloneness.

Long looking, long desiring, long loving
– these win at last into the inmost being of a thing.
–Walter de la Mare[9]

If the majority of those leaving were old then this represented a kind of culmination – the one journey they wanted to make; had saved hard to make.

Lamah Hj Omar

Hjh Lamah bte Hj Omar. Picture taken from her 'Pas Haji' (see pages 222-223). We acknowledge the kindness of Mdm Faridah bte Mohd Kassim and Mdm Najad bte Abdul Rahim, of the family of Hjh Lamah Hj Omar, in permitting the photographing of her Hajj Pass.

That would certainly have been the case for 55 year-old Lamah bte Hj Omar. She'd worked for many years as a nurse at Singapore's Kandang Kerbau Hospital, and as a midwife bringing babies into the world, travelling across Singapore, in a sampan to the island of Pulau Bukom, to the south of Singapore, and across the Causeway to Batu Pahat and Ayer Hitam in Johore in Malaysia. Small sums saved and saved from this work for one purpose. The commitment in such savings is enhanced when we factor in that not every birth might have led to payment. These were the times when families might not have money, so the stories are recalled of how a midwife might receive batiks or rice or a chicken in lieu of cash, and even then some time after the birth when the new mother's family could afford it.[10]

She's remembered by her family as "a very strict and disciplined woman, and very fierce"; someone who kept herself in a state of *wudhu*, of ritual cleanliness ready for prayer. Her determination was to make the hajj and her stated wish was to pass away there.[11]

For most of the twentieth century hajj pilgrims would expect to be away for about three months so they took food and cooking implements and clothing. That meant – *beras* – rice and, in the case of Fatmah's parents, many items for relatives in Jeddah: *kecap*, black soya sauce; Indonesian *emping*, the crisps known in Malay as *keropok Belinjau*,[12] and *belacan* [shrimp paste] for cooking Southeast Asian food. Amongst the items Lamah bte Hj Omar took with her was her old *batu lesong* – her pestle and mortar. That alone weighed 10kgs.

Going beyond food one brief, yet detailed account from 1908 described the scene below decks, a scene that included one family's odd and most unusual "personal treasure": when they were allowed on board.

> Sixteen cubic feet is allowed per man...Those desirous of greater privacy had curtains hung up, peeping behind which, one saw, snugly ensconced in his wooden cage, even the family blackbird, who will be petted, taken to Mecca and brought home again.[13]

Food and fire

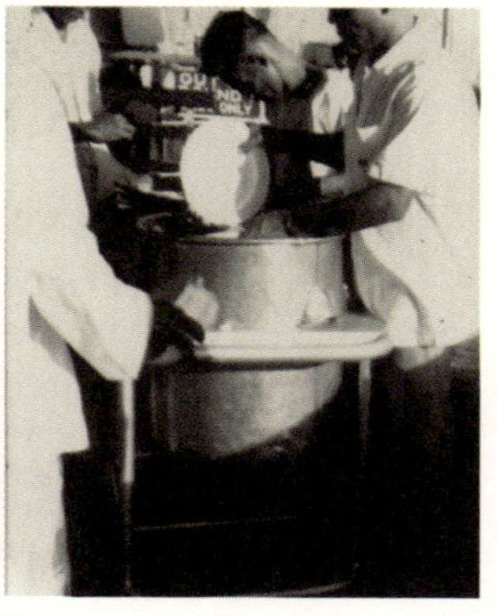

On deck, on board "Kuala Lumpur" in 1967 – cutting meat and cooking rice. Pictures courtesy of Fatmah Mohamed Salim.

Food was provided by the ship. This was a vast improvement over the time before the Second World War. In 1926 when Captain J.H. Brown was Mate of the Blue Funnel ship *Priam*, "from Jeddah to Batavia via Sabang and Padang," the ship was still only providing firewood and fresh water, "the latter being rationed."[14] But whether because they preferred their own food or were unaware of what would be provided, many came prepared and expecting to cook on board. Darrell Daish again:

> Another main danger you had to keep a look out for was fire because they were great ones for bringing on board a little primus stove. You would allow to a certain extent on deck but not below deck. You had to make sure that if they did that it was drummed into them and if you found it you'd confiscate it and make sure it didn't happen again.

On deck it was wood; below it was steel and lino but if any bedding caught fire . . . ! But you can't tell people who are coming straight out of a village where that's how they cook that they were going on a big ship and food would be cooked for them. You can't explain that when they hadn't experienced it. So, among the few possessions that they'd brought on board they would have stuff, thinking, "I'm going to have to feed myself!"

The late Syed Hussein Aljunied. Photograph by Anthony Green.

Syed Hussein Aljunied's "shop on the ship"

It would not just be food and cooking arrangements that would surprise. Aisha Angullia described how an on-board community developed as strangers came together. For people who had never been to sea those two weeks on the ship would reveal many issues for which they'd be unprepared.

Whilst this was a voyage with a spiritual purpose, people have everyday needs so it was also an opportunity for industry and within the on-board community there'd be those who could provide some solutions. The late Syed Hussein Aljunied understood this.

Born in 1933 of a Hadhrami family he went to Mecca for the first time as a young man in 1950:

> I went alone. My father gave me one gold coin to exchange there in Jeddah. One gold coin. He said you can exchange in Jeddah. When I went there I exchanged. There's no such paper note at that time. Gold coins and silver.[15]

His father joined him there in 1963 for the hajj. Arriving back in Singapore the small issue of citizenship arose, since the world had moved on and there'd been significant changes in the status of Singapore:

> My passport was difficult when I reached here. My passport said, "Citizen of United Kingdom!" When I reached here the immigration stopped me from going down. "You don't belong to Singapore."

These things seemed to be resolved with no great stress. But that journey suggested opportunities and the next time he travelled he took with him "all the things which a pilgrim can forget." Such as?

> Such as rope. Because on the ship everything you have to take out. Then you have to rope it again. Then the announcement: "We're going to reach Jeddah tomorrow. Everything must be packed." "Alamak!" Thousands of pieces of rope I can sell easily. And slippers.

Why slippers?

> We pray. There is a mosque there. These people; sometimes they don't put marks on their slippers. So he does not want to take the slippers that belong to others. It's *haram*! [Forbidden!] So even though it belongs to him he don't know. Come morning, along comes the cleaner. *Buang laut*! [Throw into the sea]. Then tomorrow they buy from me. Beautiful! Japanese slippers, rubber slippers.
>
> And they use small towels – thin Chinese ones. They hang sometimes. Then *angin laut* [the winds while at sea]. Singlets – fantastic! Mostly they hang and they blow away. Paper, envelope, ball pen, every day! Sometimes they don't think. They've never been on board before.

He recalled how the older ladies used to sit outside "because they cannot *tahan* [couldn't tolerate] below." It was just too hot!

> But to me, ok. I work. What's my job? Every morning, wake up, go to pray. I made the call to prayer. Then I sell breakfast. They cannot go up on deck. They're *sakit* [feeling sick]! They eat *nasi lemak* – *mabuk*! So many were downstairs. So there's a cook and I take commission from them. *Mee goreng, epok-epok, pisang goreng.*[16] I go downstairs very fast, get my commission, have a coffee, a cigarette, then rest. Then I start to open my shop.

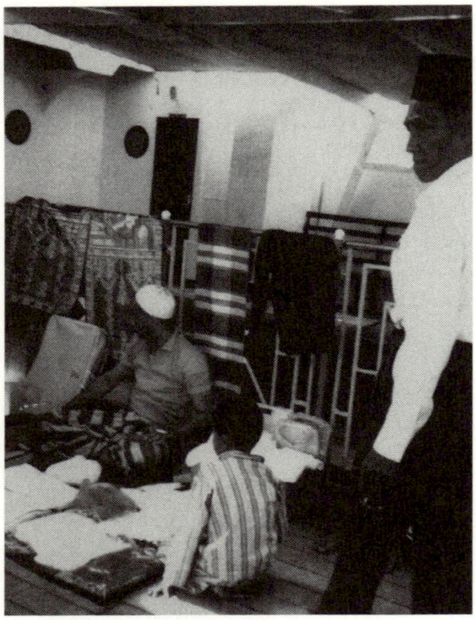

Syed Hussein Aljunied with his wares for sale – on board the "Kuala Lumpur" in 1967. Picture courtesy of Fatmah Mohamed Salim.

And on the return, the business was the same but the goods were different. "Going is one item; coming back is another." This time the concentration was on souvenirs that they'd forgotten to get. He described the pilgrims calculating how many relatives they needed to give gifts to and realising that they needed 25 sets of prayer beads but they'd only bought 15. And sarongs and good quality Indonesian batiks which, at the time, were very expensive in Malaysia, he'd ship up the coast from Singapore.

And there was the unusual fruit solution. Any large waves once they reached the Indian Ocean would lead to seasickness for many pilgrims. Syed Hussein was already used to it so it was no problem but he stumbled across a solution. In Jeddah, friends asked why he didn't bring something – perhaps a fruit – that they didn't have there. He thought there was no fruit that could keep for two weeks until somebody told him that, "*buah kedondong*[17] can do it!" Its sour taste seemed to work well for seasickness and he would take five sacks of the fruit into his cabin with him.

Buah kedondong – Latin name 'spondias dulcis' – ('buah' is the Malay word for fruit)

Monsoon seas

The monsoons in the Indian Ocean affected sea conditions in different ways. The writer Ian Cook described the Ocean as being:

> ...calm in the northeast monsoon season... In the southwest monsoon from May to September we had a lot of rain ...vicious squalls would strike with such force that a fog would develop about two feet off the ground. At sea such a downpour would flatten a choppy sea.[18]

Organisation, Representation, Questioning

On the hajj ships a number of elders would be appointed to represent the pilgrims and their needs, and they would meet and liaise with the Staff Captain and the Chief Officer on a daily basis to iron out any problems. The Navigator's duty was "to send down daily to the Purser a diagram with the ship's head on it and the times of alteration of course and another direction relative to the ship's head indicating the direction of Mecca."[19] Hajj ships had a *mussolah* – a prayer room – with a metal pointer to indicate the *qiblah* – the direction to pray. On the *Kuala Lumpur* this was in the form of the Malaysian flag. Ships have to change direction and these matters can give rise to doubts, something that David Walker comments on:

> One had to be careful during prayer times not to alter the ship's course. This could present some problems in traffic if one had to alter course and one tried not to do it but ship's safety and that of passengers always came first, and rarely had to be explained away.
>
> There was one occasion when we had with the Pilgrim Committee a delegation to the Bridge where I had to explain the direction of the ship versus the direction of Mecca. One pilgrim had got a bee in his bonnet that we were not giving them the true direction of Mecca relative to the ship's head. He wasn't a particularly well-educated man but no fool. It took a certain amount of patient persuasion to convince him, and not before he discovered the discrepancy between the magnetic compass and the Gyro Compass, one being magnetic and the other being True North. By patient explanation he grudgingly accepted that we

Time to talk on the ship – three men: Encik Madon, Bidin, and Cikgu Shamsuri sit together. From the slippers left by the door this may be outside the prayer room Picture courtesy of Fatmah Mohamed Salim.

> weren't misleading him. A testy diplomatic problem that had a lot of importance to a faithful pilgrim and could have caused rumblings amongst the pilgrims in general.[20]

Outside of the hajj time, the space used for the mussolah – the prayer space – was the ship's ballroom and passenger lounge bar, combined via folding doors, all carpeted in a rich green carpet. For the hajj the contents of the bar were removed and boarded up.

Any doubts and disagreements over direction would surely disappear once the ship reached the Bab el-Mandeb – the "Gate of Tears" – the strait, about 25kms wide between Yemen and Djibouti, where the ship's course turned more northerly, towards Jeddah.

One more delay: Kamaran Island and quarantine

For many years, however, there would be one more delay before reaching Jeddah. This was the quarantine island of Kamaran. A quarantine station had been built by the Turks in the second half of the nineteenth century to handle pilgrims arriving from eastwards and Dr. F.W. Hogarth recalled how, in August 1910, he had "personally paid Turkish officers in gold sovereigns for fumigating pilgrims and ship."[21] The British occupied the island in 1915 and continued its use as a place of quarantine. The 1927 "Report on the Pilgrimage" from the British consul in Jeddah, though, repeated earlier complaints of the avoidable inconvenience of the enforced stop at Kamaran, something that Dutch colonial authorities seem to have handled better than the British:

> Quarantine regulations at Kamaran caused a good deal of discontent, especially among the Malays, who envied the Javanese their exemption from the irksome formalities. All pilgrims from the Netherlands East Indies are vaccinated and inoculated against cholera before embarkation. Dutch ships can therefore, on presentation of a clean

> bill of health, hope that two hours will see the formalities at Kamaran completed, whereas ships sailing from Indian ports or from Singapore are often delayed twenty-four hours and, on occasion, even forty-eight hours, while pilgrims are disembarked and disinfected.
>
> Several of the leading Indians complained that the constitutions of the more aged pilgrims were unable to resist the cold bath at Kamaran, and that many who went on shore quite fit came back suffering from chills. Moreover, the benefits accruing from disinfection of the bodies and clothes of the pilgrims were largely discounted by the fact that the bulk of the pilgrims' baggage remains on board.

The report urged that regulations be introduced to enforce compulsory vaccination and inoculation of all pilgrims, something that would avoid the need to land at Kamaran, protect against infection, minimise the risk of infection in the Hejaz and benefit the schedules of the shipping companies. The 1927 hajj was declared "clean" – i.e., free from outbreaks of disease so, on this occasion, ships on the return journey did not need to stop there. Throughout the nineteenth and early twentieth centuries perhaps the two major diseases of concern were smallpox, which tended to be more prevalent in the summer, and cholera, with water quality, sanitary conditions and overcrowding being major concerns.

• • • • • • • • • • •

What then might hajj pilgrims encounter once they landed in the Hejaz? And what were the attitudes and the roles of the colonial authorities in the Straits Settlements, Malaya and Singapore? What was their interest and involvement in the journey of the pilgrims once they were on land? Modern accounts of the hajj are streamed live through visual media so the "outsider" can see what takes place, but what might pilgrims have witnessed and experienced in days long past?

1 Quoting from Al-Qalyubi (d. 1004/1596), mentioned in Roff, William R. 2009B. *Sociological Interpretations of Religious Practices*, in Studies on Islam and Society in Southeast Asia. NUS Press, Singapore, p. 272.

2 All comments from Fatmah Mohd Salim come from personal interviews with Anthony Green in Singapore, 2017.

3 ST. 27 February 1963, p. 8.

4 Personal communication from David Walker to Anthony Green.

5 All comments from Darrell Daish come from personal interviews with Anthony Green in Christchurch, New Zealand, May 2018.

6 Personal communication with Anthony Green.

7 Green. 2006, p. 25.

8 Ibid. p. 36.

9 de la Mare, Walter. In the Foreword to *Edward Thomas: Collected Poems*, Faber and Faber, London. 1985, p. 10.

10 Observations made to Anthony Green by James Chua in 2017. His mother was a midwife and his aunt was the midwife who delivered the children of the father of Syed Hassan Alatas.

11 Interview with Najad bte Abdul Rahim and her mother, Faridah bte Mohd Kassim.

12 Made from *melinjo* or *belinjo* (*gnetum gnemon*) nuts.

13 ST. *Bound for Mecca: Animated Scenes at Embarkation*. 19 September 1908, p. 7

14 Brown. p. 284.

15 All comments from Syed Hussein come from an interview conducted by Anthony Green in 2009.

16 Local Malay foods: *mee goreng* is fried mee [noodles], *epok-epok* are similar to curry puffs, *pisang goreng* are bananas that are battered and fried.

17 Also known as *buah amra* or *spondias dulcis*.

18 Cook, Ian. 2010. Those in Peril. Christchurch, New Zealand: Wilson Scott Publishing, pp 84 & 175.

19 Walker. op cit.

20 Ibid.

21 Hogarth. pp. 185 – 191.

Haji Hasan bin (?)
Sheikh Hasbullah

Sheikh Zaini Ramu
Mohammed bin Haji Abu
Singapura

Umar bin Ali,
Singapura
Al-Sheikh Jamil
Saraf

Jamiah bin Jamali
Kampong Chambong
Kampong Rabun Mas (?)

Sheikh Maimunah Asmuni
Kampong Samiah
Mekkah

Sapri (Sapre?) Rambu
Negeri Sembilan
(now Malaysia)

14 "P.L.B. Rd" (Paya
Lebar Road) Singapura 7

Departure time, outside Godown 44, Tanjong Pagar docks, May 1953. Many of the items of luggage have their owners' names, places of origin, and sometimes the name of their "sheikh haji" in Mecca, written in Jawi.
Ministry of Information and the Arts Collection, courtesy of National Archives of Singapore .

11 On land in the Hejaz

In this 1909 photograph many of these dhows are flying the Ottoman flag. All hajj pilgrims were transferred between the ship and the shore by dhow, though an unfavourable wind or a large number of hajj ships being present at the same time (in 1897 a maximum of 22 ships was reported) might mean pilgrims having to wait to be transported. Reproduced by kind permission of the Trustees of the Mohamed Ali Foundation and of the University of Durham.

And so to the Hejaz – to Mecca and the rituals of the hajj. The force of faith reaches its destination and the colonial presence continues in different ways.

This book does not focus on the details of the rituals: there are a great many, very valuable accounts of this elsewhere. It deals instead with the sights and day-to-day experiences of these pilgrims from far-away and how they themselves were perceived by others. In particular, what those sights and experiences might have been like as the centuries turned from the nineteenth to the twentieth.

For the greatest period of time, and until the advent of motor transport, travel across the desert would be by camel if you could afford it, or on foot if you could not. Different charges and taxes were levied, men appeared offering services, robberies happened along the way, and a great deal of that was affected by the political forces and dynamics that were at play.

A modern-day pilgrim will likely pay in advance for a hajj trip that packages all the major costs of the journey, the extras being up to the individual. In times past there would be a long list of separate charges published and hen recorded in the annual colonial reports from Jeddah. They went from the cost of unloading baggage from the steamer to the boat, to boat hire – whether from the outer, middle, or inner harbour, to getting the baggage unloaded from the boat to the customs, to porterage – carrying the baggage to the lodging. The fees continued – some fixed and some to be negotiated – for vehicle hire, whether lorry or car, to Mecca; municipality dues for the *shuqduf* – the closed litter carried on the back of a camel; and fees for the *shuqduf* and camel hire to and from Arafat and Mecca.

But, however many costs or difficulties are chronicled, the core remains that for a hajj that is *marbrur*, i.e., that is "successful" in the sense of earning God's pleasure; of serving the Creator, the pilgrim must complete the rites in the right place at the appointed time and with the proper intention.

Readiness

Near a boundary area surrounding Mecca and Medina there are points called the *meeqath*. By the time pilgrims reach these they must have cleansed themselves and put on the garments of *ihram*, the plain white cloth that removes all outer distinctions of position or power or wealth. Inwardly the pilgrim must put away worldly desires and enter the spiritual state for the pilgrimage. On many ships sailing up the Red Sea in past times, pilgrims would change into ihram some way south of Jeddah in readiness for their disembarkation and earlier in the book it was noted that the water taps would be turned on as the ships approached Jeddah so that hajj pilgrims could clean themselves and perform the ritual ablutions before reaching the entry points for the hajj itself. Once again, one can only speculate as to what pilgrims on an overcrowded sailing ship could have done as they made ready, although they almost always arrived many months before the hajj.

Those rites of the pilgrimage – called the *manassik* – and the sites at which each of the rites are performed have been unchanged since they were laid down centuries ago. The black cube of the Kaaba has stayed constant. However, between the early years of the twentieth century and the present day much else has changed in the physical structures that the pilgrims would visit and through which they would travel.

In January 1910 the mosque was described as being capable of holding "about 83,000 persons."[1] The expansion that was begun just over a hundred years later, in 2011, was planned for it to be able to accommodate 2.5 million.

... and the influence of events

One period of considerable change was that time from the First World War through the 1920s and after, so for our pilgrims from Southeast Asia something more was added to the experience, not just of the rites of the hajj, but to the experience of being drawn into a coming together of far-flung communities in a time of some turmoil and conflict. At the start of the twentieth century political trends within and beyond the Hejaz were shifting and would impact on the experience of hajj pilgrims. In Russia the rise of Bolshevism; in Turkey the waning and eventual end of the Ottoman Empire; in Europe that odd mix of alliances and powers that would build to the blind carnage of the First World War; and in the Hejaz the gathering of competing forces seeking control over the Holy Places.

At the start of hostilities in Europe in 1914, a tired and drained Ottoman Empire, realising the inevitability that it would have to choose a side and left with little choice, formed its alliance with Germany. The British saw an opportunity and T.E. Lawrence – the man known as

Taken around 1909, the exact location of this photograph is unknown. The transport taken by pilgrims depended on what they could afford. The journey from Jeddah to Mecca by camel was spread over two stages with a stop at Wadi Fatma where water was supplied from open wells dug into the sandy bottom of the wadi. Richer pilgrims took a camel with a shugduf – a covered platform; the poorer, with perhaps one camel between four, would take it in turns to walk and ride. (In listing costs and charges for the pilgrimage, the reports from the British Consul in Jeddah sometimes referred to the cost of hiring of a "half camel" – presumably one shared by two people). Those with no funds would walk the whole distance. Camel caravans could be attacked and the pilgrims robbed. Reproduced by kind permission of the Trustees of the Mohamed Ali Foundation and of the University of Durham.

"Lawrence of Arabia" – was directly involved in the encouragement of an Arab uprising against the Turks. Writing in his memoir of that time he said:

> Some Englishmen, of whom Kitchener was chief, believed that a rebellion of Arabs against Turks would enable England, while fighting Germany, simultaneously to defeat her ally Turkey. Their knowledge of the nature and power and country of the Arabic-speaking peoples made them think that the issue of such a rebellion would be happy: and indicated its character and method. So they allowed it to begin, having obtained formal assurances of help for it from the British Government. Yet none the less the rebellion of the Sherif of Mecca came to most as a surprise, and found the Allies unready. It aroused mixed feelings and made strong friends and enemies, amid whose clashing jealousies its affairs began to miscarry.[2]

That Lawrence should slip easily between "Englishmen" believing in the rebellion and "the British government" giving formal assurances suggests unconscious assumptions about identity within Britain: England is not Britain. That, though, is a side-issue with regard to the hajj. Of more importance is that the promise of British support led Hussein ibn Ali al-Hashimi, the Sherif of Mecca, to proclaim the uprising against the Ottomans, and with the abolition of the Ottoman Caliphate in March 1924 he declared himself Caliph. His claim to the Caliphate was short-lived and widely decried. In October, he was defeated by the forces of Ibn Saud and a new order, and sense of order, came to the Hejaz. In describing that time, the January 1926 British report from Jeddah said that events:

> ... have succeeded each other with kaleidoscopic rapidity... On the afternoon and evening of the 28th of November the whole of the forces defending Jeddah decided to combine and loot the town the following morning.

Ibn Saud entered Jeddah on the morning of 23rd December, and "a reception for foreign representatives and notables was held." This new order was one that would come to disagree with some of what had been practised by pilgrims in the Hejaz; in particular the attitude towards graves and historical sites. These held a significance for many Muslims in the practice of *ziyara* – the visiting of the tombs of major figures in Islamic history – and the late 1920s saw the demolition of many such places. There were loud protests, in particular from Muslims in India, at this perceived attack on their understanding of the faith but the demolitions went ahead.

First, though, what might pilgrims have seen or visited?

The Hejaz before the 1920s – "Eve's Tomb" and other places

In 1910 F.W. Hogarth was surgeon on the Blue Funnel ship *Cyclops* when it arrived in Jeddah. As a non-Muslim he could not travel to Mecca but he wrote in his diary of a brief trip into the desert beyond the port city:

The tomb of Khadijah, the first wife of the Prophet, taken in 1910. The tomb was subsequently destroyed. Courtesy of the Farjam Foundation.

> March 15th. A small guard of Turkish soldiers, with a lieutenant, took us out into the desert, and I had a good look at Eve's Tomb, and was not permitted either a camera or to stay very long.
>
> This proved to be a very ancient building about ninety yards long, and twelve to fifteen feet wide, with no roof, but considerable architectural features. The bulge in the centre

Congregational prayer at Masjid Haram in Mecca, taken in 1910. Courtesy of the Farjam Foundation.

> – hardly cross-shape – had a large meteoric stone of more or less globular shape. This seemed to be the main feature, and how the meteor of this size had reached the spot without burying itself deep underground, no one had any idea. It was at least six or eight feet in diameter. Unfortunately no one I enquired from had any idea about why Eve came to be there.[3]

Eve's tomb was destroyed in 1928 and subsequently sealed with concrete in 1975.

The so-called "Eve's tomb" was not part of the hajj but Snouck Hurgronje noted that some pilgrims visited the place. If so, perhaps they left it no wiser than when they arrived. A far more significant site of interest to many hajj pilgrims from Southeast Asia and other places would likely have been the grave of the lady Khadijah bint Khuwaylid, the first wife of the Prophet and the one known to Muslims as "the Mother of the Believers." Her mausoleum was demolished in 1925. Graves such as these and the graves of family members and companions of the Prophet were all in turn demolished in the light of the belief that such places encouraged practices unacceptable in Islam.

Snouck Hurgronje listed many of those "holy places" to which visitors might want to go, obtaining admittance only by a gift to the owner or caretaker:

> The dwelling house of Abu Bakr, the birth houses of the Prophet, of Ali, and of Abu Bakr ...in the graveyard of al-Maalâ, the domed tomb of Khadijah and Aminah; near that graveyard the prayer-house... where the seventy-second chapter of the Qur'an was revealed: and countless other less generally visited buildings of historic interest.[4]

The Egyptian Mahmal

Aside from the visiting of sites, in the days before 1925 one more experience for Southeast Asian Muslims would have been witnessing the arrival, and loud spectacle, of the annual Egyptian Mahmal procession, flanked by armed soldiers on horseback and musicians. This was a procession of covered litters carried by camels and in that procession was the *kiswa* – the covering for the

The arrival of the Egyptian Mahmal procession in 1910. Courtesy of the Farjam Foundation.

Kaaba. This was part of what was sent from Egypt to Mecca:

> Work on the *kiswa*, which was heavily brocaded in gold and silver and adorned with precious jewels, began six months before the pilgrimage season and was periodically inspected by the Ottoman governor of Egypt. Upon completion, it would generally contain 17 *qintars* (approximately 765 kilogrammes) of silk and three qintars (approximately 135 kilogrammes) of pure silver. Then there was the grain dole Egypt sent annually to feed the residents of Mecca and Medina. The grain was sent by sea from Suez to Jeddah, along with the cash gifts for the nobles of the holy places. The man in charge of protecting the pilgrimage caravan and the transportation of the *kiswa* was a senior military figure who was granted the title Amir Al-Hajj, one of the highest positions of the state. He was the central figure of the grand procession of the *mahmal* which was marked by massive popular celebrations.[5]

This, too, came to an end around 1927, partly due to attacks on the mahmal procession and partly because of the view in the Hejaz that it was a procession of pomp and show that had no place in the pilgrimage, though the procession and what it carried was a significant cost to the Egyptian economy. Again, the questions arise: what impressions would be taken back home by a pilgrim from a far-away village in Southeast Asia? And how much would these experiences have affected the individual pilgrim's sense of identity and belonging?

Coming ashore

From the ship to the shore was by Arab dhow, or *sambouk* – "solidly built and safe sea boats." Charges for this were fixed by the government of Ibn Saud, though the picture painted by Snouck Hurgronje of the world before Ibn Saud took over is full of "taxes" and charges being levied on pilgrims:

> The Grand Sherif asks for "free contributions" [effectively taxes] for such things as "the maintenance of the Mekkan aqueduct."[6]

> . . . at the Customs, where all sorts of presents are demanded from them and fines levied. Thus they must pay for a "Turkish passport," give a dollar as a voluntary contribution to the waterworks of the Holy City and of its harbour, they must pay boatmen and porters...[7]

In discussing the 1881 case involving indebted returned pilgrims, the Singapore newspaper commented that the "new rule" at Jeddah demanded that people would not be allowed to land if they had not enough money to pay for their maintenance and enough money lodged at the consulate to pay for their return passage but that many of these people were "fleeced, according to all accounts, on all hands in the most merciless manner" so that they had to mortgage their labour for years to pay for their debts. What happened in the Hejaz had consequences back to the Straits Settlements and the Netherlands East Indies.

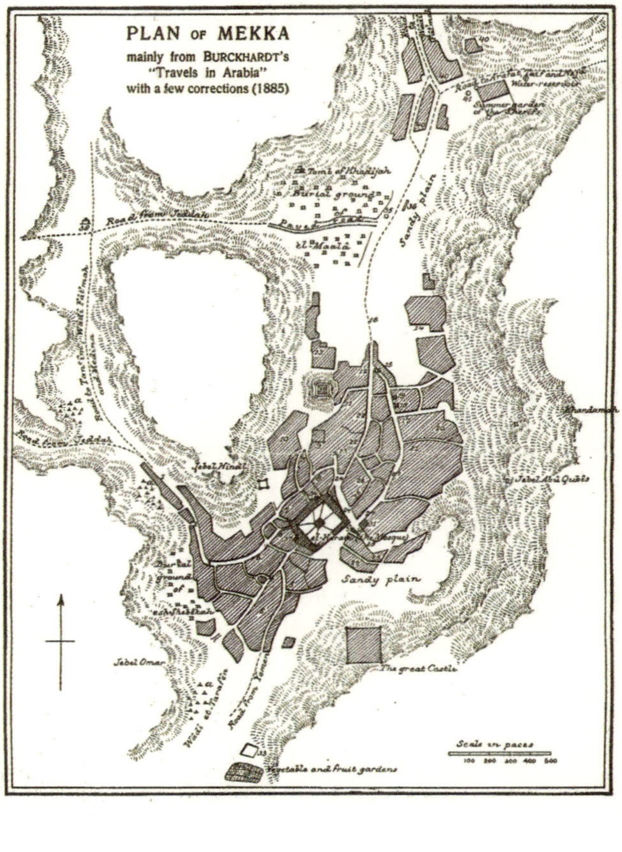

Plan of Mecca in 1885. From Snouck Hurgronje: Makka in the Latter Part of the Nineteenth Century: Daily Life, Customs and Learning. Courtesy of Brill Publishers.

Perceptions

Hurgronje wrote about how the pilgrims from Southeast Asia seem to have been perceived; that an Egyptian engineer-officer had published a report on his experiences, and that in 1886 he spoke of the merchants in Mecca who,

> ... exploit the pilgrims as much as possible, particularly the Jâwah because these are foreigners and well-to-do.[9]

It was not just to do with being seen as having money; it was also a certain lack of forcefulness. A 1920 article in the Singapore Free Press was written, it would seem, by a sympathetic-sounding non-Muslim lady who had travelled with the pilgrims to Jeddah. In it she reported the perspective of "a capable and very kindly Indian Intelligence Officer" – the "Friend of the Pilgrims" – who was traveling back to India in her ship with his small family. This was, in all probability, Dr Abdul Razzack, the man mentioned in an earlier chapter.

> After three years of incessant work the Hakim was to have a month's holiday in his old home, and then return to the increased work of shepherding the wanderers. He spoke much of the great docility of the Malay, in fact said they were too docile in Mecca, for when their Mutawifs, Pilgrim Guides ordered them about remorselessly, they at once obeyed. "Reh [sic], stop here until I return," it might be a spot in the blazing sun, and it might be for hours, but it was a command therefore inexorable. Often a Malay or Javanese has not got a Mussulman name, then it may be changed. For this, the Pilgrim Guides have been known to charge the equivalent of one gold sovereign: in reality payment is unnecessary.[10]

Changing Times

The consequences of that period of events succeeding each other "with kaleidoscopic rapidity" revealed themselves from the end of Ottoman control of the Hejaz to the overthrow of Sherif – or "Caliph" – Hussein by Ibn Saud. The loss of Turkish control had some monetary impact, as explained by Geoff Wade:

> ... [previously] the Bedouins on the route were subsidised by Government, and made responsible for the peace and control of the route and for the provision of escorts for the pilgrim parties. Nowadays there was no subsidy, with the result that the Bedouins had instituted what the Malay-speaking Sheikhs term "chukai padang," [field tax] and each pilgrim pays to the chief of his party 50 cents a day to meet this levy. Parties were liable to be held up at any time and pay ransom according to the whim of the particular Bedouin chief. Pilgrims were also said to suffer a certain amount of pillage and robbery at the hands of the Bedouins.[11]

In late 1922 *Oetosean Hindia*, the official journal of the Sarikat Islam movement in the Netherlands Indies, reported on a host of issues that pilgrims should take precautions against and concluded that,

> The Netherlands East Indies Government is therefore again forced to warn would-be pilgrims against (1) extortionate Hejjaz taxation (2) actual peril on the Medina Road (3) water shortage at Jiddah.[12]

It was perhaps no wonder that Ibn Saud was keen to send his telegraph in February 1926 to stress that some calm and order prevailed.

The Colonial perspective

Over much of the time of Empire, the British government felt itself to have a special position in the world because of the number of Muslims it ruled over in a "wide-ranging imperial engagement,"[13] from Africa, through the Middle East and the Indian sub-continent, to Southeast Asia. It resulted in a kind of "inner Muslim empire" existing within the larger Empire. In consequence, at different times in the early twentieth century, The British Empire was described with phrases like, "the greatest Muhammadan Empire in the world."[14]

There were two aspects to the reports sent from the Jeddah consulate to London, India, the Straits Settlements and elsewhere: one focused on detailed concerns over conditions and practical arrangements for pilgrims; another was on political considerations. Those practical concerns included a comprehensive range of issues such as the need for passports or special passes, concerns for the destitute and those who arrived each year with insufficient funds, the facilitation of arrangements for arrivals and departures, and the basics of water and sanitation. The sanitary conditions that existed in the mid- to late-1920s seem to have been very poor and the 1927 Jeddah report has a quietly graphic description:

> Sanitary conditions at Mecca leave much to be desired. Latrines were lacking and the streets were foul with animal and human excreta. Houses were dirty and sanitary arrangements therein defective. Though most of the blame for this state of affairs naturally falls on the Hejaz Sanitary Administration, not a little attaches to the pilgrims themselves, who, however near a latrine may be, relieve nature when and where nature calls. The precincts of the agency bear fragrant witness to this habit.

While both the Dutch and the representatives of British India maintained consulates in Jeddah to provide services for the pilgrims, and reports flowed back to London and Amsterdam, the representatives of "British Malaya" seemed to leave looking after political matters to others, so the impression according to William Roff, was of:

> ... a relative lack of interest [on the part of the Straits authorities] in the supposed political implications of the pilgrimage – a matter of considerable concern to British India and not significantly less to the Netherlands East Indies. Though in point of fact neither of the latter governments seems ever to have obtained much political information of consequence through their establishments in Jeddah.[15]

The Malayan Bulletin of Political Intelligence

Based in Singapore, the Malayan Bureau of Political Intelligence was in operation from 1922 to 1930. As part of its work it looked at the hajj and the conditions under which the pilgrims travelled. It investigated "the question of Pilgrim Brokers and Pilgrim Lodging House Keepers, who it was alleged were not dealing fairly with the pilgrims, and was also enquiring whether it would be possible for the shipping companies to supply food to the pilgrims for an all-inclusive ticket price."[16]

Intelligence reports from Jeddah, and the continuing unrest there, would lead the Straits Government to caution on the extreme unlikeliness that the 1926 Pilgrimage would take place, so that intending pilgrims should be warned to "defer their intention of proceeding on the Haj for another year."

But events in the Hejaz were just a part of the issues that interested the intelligence agencies in the Straits. They paid attention to the movements of particular individuals in territories of interest to the British. The 1926 Bulletin of the Bureau listed a meeting of "The International Union of the Oppressed Peoples of the East" in Canton [Guangzhou]; Communist propaganda among troops; the movements of Raden Darsono – "one of the most influential leaders of the communist party in Java"; and the activities of a "Communist Centre in Singapore," mentioning the presence of the significant figure, Tan Malaka, and the use of a house in North Bridge Road as an address for "letters for Communists." The house was the premises of a pilgrim broker and it said that the "missives [were to be enclosed] in an outer envelope" addressed to the pilgrim broker. The North Bridge Road address was an apparent change since "the local communists" had become suspicious of another address and of "the safety" of an address in Onan Road.[17]

At different times the colonial powers saw the hajj from Southeast Asia as a possible breeding ground for pan-Islamic or anti-colonial sentiments to ferment, but also as a place for Communist feelings to be spread. A letter sent to the Colonial Office from the British Consul in Jeddah in June 1927 was filed under "Bolshevik Propaganda by Javanese amongst pilgrims." A detailed examination of these criss-crossing issues is beyond the scope of this book. The aim here is to paint a picture of what the hajj might mean to those who undertook it; to look at how it was organised and developed; at the companies and systems that were involved, and at the challenges and difficulties of the journey itself.

A great mix of nationalities

In discussing the feast at the end of Ramadan, Hurgronje noted that, "though in a mosque of the size of the Haram not more than one hundredth part of the congregation can understand a syllable of the Friday sermon, here there is no lack of 'reverential stillness.'"[18]

The mix and variety of people alone would take Southeast Asian pilgrims into a different world. The 1920 Singapore Free Press article described initial fears:

> Some of the pilgrims looked furtively at a Bedouin man and woman of ferocious aspect, until they discovered they were beggars of importunate type. Too importunate, we had difficulty with them ourselves. Then down the principal street where . . . a bronze covered minaret caught the rays of the sun, swaggered two Bedouin soldiers their belts full of cartridges. The Malay women shivered, and drew their sarongs closer.[19]

With the war in the Hejaz declared over the 1927 Hajj Report prepared by the office in Jeddah reported that the gathering of 29,604 "British Malayan" pilgrims present and 39,157 from the "Dutch East Indies" was "the largest since the [1914-1918] War." But in the list of those who came by sea, broken down by nationality there were Zanzibaris, Afghans, "Sarawakis," Somalis, Palestinians, Turks, Nigerians, Senegalese and more. The vast majority of those were carried there by ships labelled as being under the British flag. The Appendix shows the breakdown of these figures of pilgrims by sea in 1926/27 and their means of transport.

Practicalities for the pilgrims

Another of the challenges was that of weather: the highest temperature that year was recorded as 124°F (51°C) and the resulting number of 1492 deaths – (roughly 12% of the pilgrims) – was said to be "considerably higher than in 1926 but slightly lower than in 1924."

But the timing of the hajj, fixed by the hijri calendar, "shifts" forward each year according to the Gregorian so there are times of cold and even storms. In January 1910 reports had come from Constantinople (modern-day Istanbul) of "heavy rains in the Hedjaz and severe floods at Mecca." Eight persons were drowned and one killed by the collapse of a house."[20]

When Ustazah Maimunah Binti Ahmad travelled as a young woman with her family in 1969 / 1970 she was not prepared for the cold. No one had talked to them about the conditions they might face and tropical clothing – sarongs and Malay bajus – proved to be inadequate:

> We were so cold we ground black pepper with our batu lesong and rubbed the pepper into our clothes to see if we could get any warmth from it. The sheikh haji gave us three meals on our first day and then we were on our own. We had to find our own food, so we bought cheap fish and fried it so that we could eat half one day and keep the rest for the next.[21]

The experience and the leaving

In the introduction we observed that each of "those who make the hajj go as the 'dhuyyuf,' the guests of God," and that, as guests on this particular journey, you accept whatever comes to you. Whatever difficulties or tests arose these were not what people took away with them.[22]

Maamor bin Sutan Nordin, the man who had worked on Malayan Railways, had spoken of how he performed the hajj one year after he felt he "belum ada seruan" – did not yet have the calling. He also spoke of how he felt the hajj had affected him; that the lack of patience that had annoyed others had changed. And he described how, in the course of circling the Kaaba, he had tried two or three times to kiss "the black stone." It is not a requirement of the hajj but he tried again in the middle of the night, yet each time he had felt as if he was being pulled back; and then that finally he went with a friend and was successful. And that, one month after he left Mecca to return home, he still felt that he was in Mecca; that the experience takes much time to forget.

[1] ST. 11 January 1910, p. 7.

[2] Lawrence, T.E. 1935. *Seven Pillars of Wisdom*. London: Jonathan Cape, p. 7.

[3] Hogarth, Dr. F. W. "A Voyage Worth Remembering." In Ocean – *The Journal of the Ocean Steamship Group*, January 1969, pp. 185 – 191.

[4] Hurgronje, Snouck. 1931. *Makka in the Latter Part of the Nineteenth Century: Daily Life, Customs and Learning*. Leiden, Holland: Brill Publishers, p. 23.

[5] http://weekly.ahram.org.eg/Archive/2001/540/chrncls.htm. Accessed 15 May 2018.

[6] Hurgronje. p. 78.

[7] Ibid. p. 226.

[8] STOJ. 28 July 1881.

[9] Hurgronje. p. 215.

[10] SFPMA. 8 July 1920, p.1

[11] Wade, Geoff. *The Malayan political intelligence bureau and its middle eastern Concerns in the 1920s*. Singapore: Nalanda-Sriwijaya Centre, ISEAS. p. 12.

[12] Wade. p. 10.

[13] Slight, John. 2015. *The British Empire and the Hajj – 1865-1956*. Cambridge, Massachusetts: Harvard University Press, p. 26.

[14] Ibid. p. 202.

[15] Roff. 2009A. p. 311.

[16] Wade. p. 12.

[17] National Archives, UK. *Malayan Bulletin of Political Intelligence*, Issue No. 36, February 1926. CO 273/534/6.

[18] Hurgronje. p. 73.

[19] SFPMA. 8 July 1920, p. 1

[20] ST. 11 January 1910, p. 7.

[21] Green. p. 38.

[22] For some reactions to Mecca from a number of "western" travellers to Mecca, see Paul Lunde: *The Lure of Mecca*, in Saudi Aramco Nov/Dec 1974, published on their website http://archive.aramcoworld.com/issue/197406/the.lure.of.mecca.htm Accessed 20 November 2018.

The route home, as described by John Spain:

from Aden...

south to Minicoy Island

round the southern tip of Sri Lanka (Ceylon)

... to the Acheen Head (Pulau Weh) in Sumatra

The route taken, as described by John Spain. 1853 map, from the collection of Anthony Green.

12

Returning: A changed person

And so the hajj is completed and the pilgrims turn for home, at least those who have the money or a ticket.

Before dedicated passenger vessels, a trip carrying hajj pilgrims might form just part of a ship's overall voyage. It will likely have gone to a number of other places before the hajj trip and carried a range of cargoes. In 1926, Captain J. H. Brown's ship, *Priam*, had carried coal from Birkenhead, near Liverpool, to Port Said. Cleaning up and getting rid of the coal dust in the places where the pilgrims would sleep was the task between Port Said and Jeddah, though the dust and smell of coal would be difficult to remove. A midshipman in 1947 wrote,

> The 'tween decks, where they will live, are all cleaned out and disinfected . . . pilgrim ladders are shipped and bolted into place, lifejacket racks are put in position and filled, extra fire extinguishers are put in place . . . windsails are hoisted, galleys erected, latrines and showers tested, ration cards prepared, and 50-gallon drums cement washed, ready for issuing fresh water.[1]

In the 1920s and 1930s pilgrim ships would be anchored off-shore at Jeddah, sometimes five kilometres out, and the hajj pilgrims would be transported in Arab dhows, "each carrying about 25 persons,"[2] just as they had been on arrival.

But the wind is blowing onshore all day and the dhows can make very little progress against it. That means, of course, that we stand around all day waiting for them and when knocking off time comes so does the offshore breeze and the dhows all arrive at the same time, causing a great deal of pandemonium. However, we get them all stowed away and then wait for the morning for the rest of them to come aboard.[3]

This report from 1936:

> When the pilgrims came aboard they were allocated spaces, and they then rigged up screens of mats or curtains for their own privacy. They spread mats and rugs on the steel deck. No bedding was provided, so they made their own sleeping arrangements and some had simple collapsible camp beds. They were mostly in family groups, and any single men were segregated.[4]
>
> One old woman comes aboard on a stretcher, a horrible sight with her face covered in flies and her unable to do anything about it and probably not noticing it anyway. She is taken straight aft to the hospital but she dies before she gets there and is taken ashore again, for the last time.[5]

Becoming a brief note in history

In this woman's case she is taken to be buried on land. Once the ship has got underway it would be different. John Spain's log of the ship Tyndareus in 1960 records in bare details the end of the lives of two pilgrims who'd come originally from somewhere in Indonesia. Who they were, where exactly they were from, we do not know.

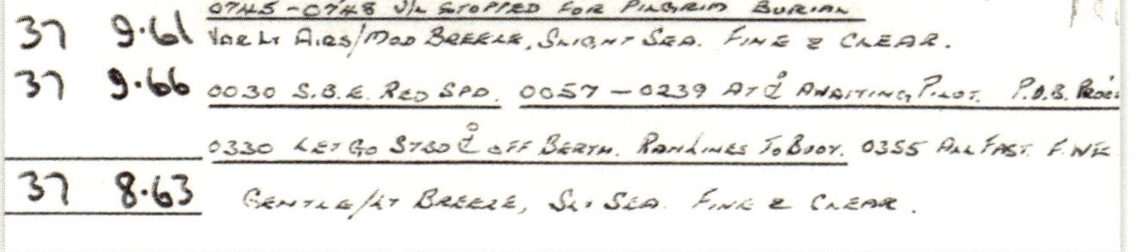
1625 S.B.E. COM HEIGH ⚓. 1636 ⚓ AWEIGH. V.M.O. 1645 F.S.A.
0930 – 0933 V/L STOPPED FOR PILGRIM BURIAL.
37 7·09 VAR LT AIRS, SLIGHT SEA. FINE & CLEAR. SLIGHT SAND HAZE.
0745 – 0748 V/L STOPPED FOR PILGRIM BURIAL
37 9·61 VAR LT AIRS/MOD BREEZE, SLIGHT SEA. FINE & CLEAR.
37 9·66 0030 S.B.E. RED SPD. 0057 – 0239 AT ⚓ AWAITING PILOT. P.O.B.
0330 LET GO STBD ⚓ OFF BERTH. RANLINES TO BOOY. 0355 ALL FAST. F.W.E.
37 8·63 GENTLE/LT BREEZE, SL. SEA. FINE & CLEAR.

The Mate's log from the last voyage of Tyndareus – leaving Jeddah with returning hajj pilgrims for Indonesia, 23 July 1960, equivalent to 28 Muharram, 1380 in the Islamic Hijri calendar. Log courtesy of John Spain.

The culmination of the hajj would have been eighteen days earlier. At 4.25pm the orders are to "stand by engines" and start weighing the anchor. At 4.36 the vessel moves out and at 4.45pm it's full speed ahead.

And somewhere on the ship that evening, having completed the hajj, one pilgrim is dying. The religious duties of the pilgrimage may be over but for the community on the ship other duties must continue. The person's body is washed in the required *ghusl* washing and wrapped in the white *kain kaffan* cloth. Prayers will be said and the next morning the pilgrims will assemble together at the stern of the ship for the *jenazah* (funeral) prayer. At 9.30 the ship is stopped. The wind is light. It's a fine, clear day with a slight sand haze and a "slight sea." The weighted body is slid down into the water and, after just three minutes, *Tyndareus* gets under way again.

The next morning, at 7.45am, there will be another pause for three minutes and one more pilgrim will be buried at sea.

Communication

In times past, once a hajj ship left for Jeddah there would be no real opportunity to communicate with those who had departed and in the time of sailing ships, there could only be minimal communication between vessels once they'd left port. If two vessels passed at sea then brief messages could be sent by semaphore flags and the one reporting the message would say they "spoke" the other vessel. So snippets like these would appear in the English language press:

> The British bark, *Henry Darling*, Captain Reid, from Macau reports having spoken the Danish brig *Clarissa*, dismasted, bound to Singapore. The *Clarissa* had nine feet of water in her hold.[6]

> CAPTAIN White, of the *S.S. Celestial*, reports that he passed, yesterday, at noon, the British barque, *Glance*, in the Rio Straits. She wishes to be reported here, all well.[7]

At times in the twentieth Century telegrams might be sent from the ship but it was not always easy for them to get through. Derek Walker was 2nd Radio Officer on the *Tyndareus* from Java and from Palembang in Sumatra in 1954:

> My main memory as R/O was of the pilgrims queuing up to send telegrams back to Indonesia when we were about to reach Jeddah. They could only go via Djakarta Radio, (call sign PKI), which was difficult to raise at the best of times; in the Red Sea it was hopeless. Even if you managed to contact PKI, as soon as the operator there heard my call sign (GMKX)[8] he would immediately lose interest and become deaf, as he knew I would have a batch of 40 or 50 telegrams to send. It was sometimes days before I could clear all the traffic.[9]

The silences while pilgrims were away meant that a family might go to the dock to meet the ship on which their loved one was due with no way of knowing how that person was, or whether they would even be on the ship. When the *Kuala Lumpur* returned to Singapore in 1966 for example, it was met by the family of Hajah Lamah. They were handed the pestle and mortar – the *batu lesong* – that she had carried with her, and her sarong, together with her *"Pas Haji"* – her hajj passport. She had not returned. In the *"Pas"* the Malay translation says that she had died in Mecca but the stamp in Arabic over her picture, together with the detail, says that she had passed away in Medina. Medina and Mecca are both holy sites for Muslims and she had died, perhaps as she would have wished, in the Holy Land.

Such scenes were not uncommon.

The "batu lesong" – pestle and mortar – and the "kain" (sarong) of Hjh Lamah, handed to her family after the ship returned from Jeddah. Photograph by Anthony Green.

The "Pas Haji" for Lamah bte Haji Omar (1966)

It was only when her family went to meet the ship she was booked to return on that they learned that she had passed away while on the hajj. There was no news before that. They were handed this document, her *"batu lesong"* (pestle and mortar) and a sarong.

Stamp says: "Office of Affairs of the Deceased in Medinah al-Munawwarah, issuance of kafan given the deceased lady's financial need" (The kaffan is the burial cloth used in Muslim burials).

Handwritten endorsement to say that Hj Lamah passed away in the hospital in Medinah; The date was 13 Muharam 1386 in the Islamic (Hijri) calendar; approximately equal to 4 May 1966.

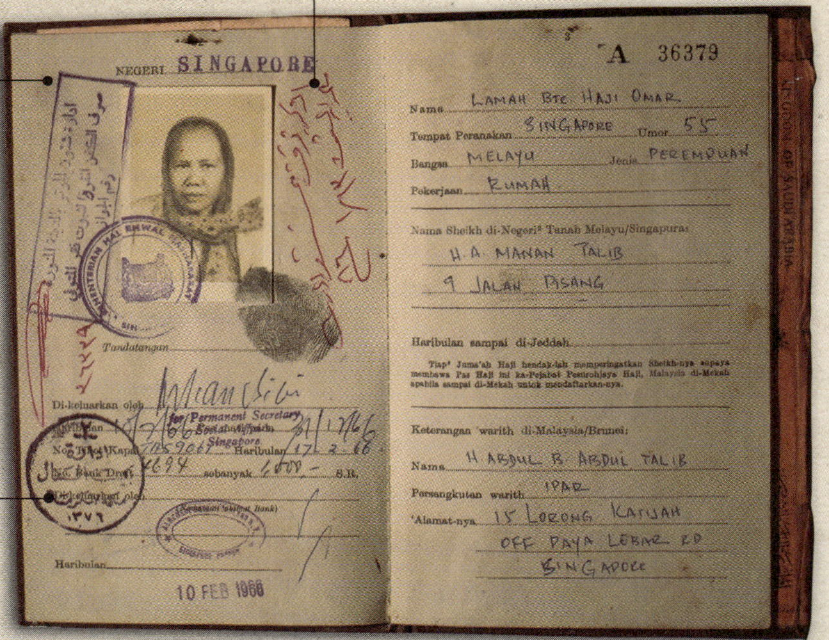

The stamp for the Saudi Office of the Baitul Mal (the Islamic treasury).

We acknowledge the kindness of Mdm Faridah bte Mohd Kassim and Mdm Najad bte Abdul Rahim, of the family of Hjh Lamah Hj Omar, in permitting the photographing of her Hajj Pass.

The "Chatetan Rasmi" (notes) pages of the "Pas".

This endorses the "Pas" holder to sail on the 'pelayaran ka-tiga' (the third sailing) of the ship Kuala Lumpur. It's signed by Haji Sidek Siraj, as the "Malaysian" Pilgrim Officer in Singapore, even though Singapore was no longer part of Malaysia. The person in charge of deciding the number of sailings required was Hj Ali Rouse, the Pilgrimage Control Officer, based in Penang.

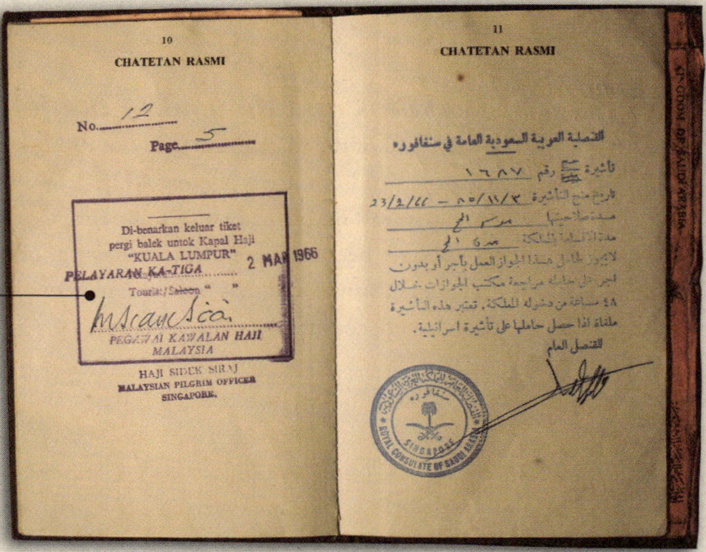

The inside back cover of the "Pas". It is customary to say to those travelling on hajj "Hajj Mabrur," meaning that the hajj is accepted by God and the hajj pilgrim is made free from sin.

Here this is indicated and translated by the Director General of Passports wishing the prospective pilgrim a "pardonable Hajj".

Weakness and the end of the journey

By the end of the pilgrimage many of those who had taken part were exhausted and in the days before 1929/1930, when it became compulsory to provide meals on board British ships, this was not helped by the food that they would have been eating. In his recollection of the voyage from Jeddah to Java, Capt. J. H. Brown said that once the pilgrims had boarded and firewood had been issued, cooking began:

> The food was rice, dried fish, etc., which had been brought from Java and stored in cellars and godowns in Jeddah while the pilgrimage was underway. By this time it was pretty ripe and smelly; doubtless being the cause of dysentery which nearly always occurred with resultant mortality.[10]

But, he adds that, "in sickness, rarely was the ship's surgeon called upon, not even by the elderly people." In addition to the surgeon, the ships carried "restoratives" for anyone who was weak, though these now seem strange, as they may well have done even then to the pilgrims. For women in confinement before giving birth, "a bottle of Guinness was given to the mother." If they did drink it thinking it was medicine one wonders if they knew it was alcohol. Something more Islamically acceptable but still from a different culture appeared on the *S.S. Tyndareus* in the 1960s. John Spain remembers Marmite:

Marmite: part of the rations of British troops in World War One to combat beri-beri, and used in the 1930s to treat anaemia in mill workers in Bombay, and malnutrition in a malaria epidemic in Sri Lanka; it was fed to homeward-bound hajj pilgrims on the "Tyndareus."

> The doctor was European – quite an old, senior doctor. But the main problem always coming back from the pilgrimage was Beri-beri. They'd just not eaten the right foods, and some of them were in a pretty bad state. But, as he said, two or three days on Marmite, and they regained all the strength they'd ever lost. Just to replace all the vitamin B, which they'd lost. For an old person the hajj was quite an onerous task.[11]

Captain Gwilym Owen had joined Blue Funnel as a deck boy in 1945 and was an Able Seaman on the ship *Atreus* in October 1948:

> These pilgrims had been for several weeks in the intense heat of Saudi Arabia and most of them were elderly people, and therefore very sad to say we had a funeral almost every day. The ship was stopped at noon for the funeral, which was carried out over the stern of the ship. The ship's carpenter had made a wooden base to lay the body on and the bosun had rigged a tackle from a small davit right over the stern of the ship with a rope rigged to one end of the wood base to tilt it so that the body would slide off into the sea after it had been lowered down to the water's edge via the tackle.

Death on board, and burial

But a sense of respect comes through in Captain Owen's account:

> One day I was the 10.00am to noon helmsman on the 08.00 – 12.00 hrs watch. When I was relieved at noon there was a funeral taking place. I left the bridge and proceeded aft to the accommodation and went to wash my hands before having lunch. I could hear some commotion on the deck above where the funeral was taking place and when I lifted my head to look through the porthole directly astern – I could see the corpse swinging around in the moderate breeze with the shroud being blown off the corpse to expose the bare feet and legs. The rope tackle had got twisted with the moderate breeze to cause this ugly incident.
>
> One morning we had to carry a very sick pilgrim up on deck from number three hatch and tried to find a sheltered spot to lay him down on the main deck. This was about 08.30hrs and he died at 15.30 hrs that afternoon.
>
> We carried a ship's doctor and two or three male nurses as extra hands to look after the pilgrims. They all did their very best, but sad to say, many of the pilgrims were very sick when they boarded for their homeward passage. I remember another sad incident when the ship's doctor was pulling large worms from the veins of the legs and feet of a pilgrim on the main deck abreast of number six hatch.[12]

The ship's master was required to register any births or deaths that took place on a voyage. In the case of births, the date, name (if any) of the child and the details of the parents. In the case of deaths, the date of the death, full name, age, occupation, nationality and cause of death. Under "Burial at sea" in the Medical Guide it was stated that the captain should "Record the event in the official log book with the exact time and position of burial." Ralph Kennett was a CNCo master of the hajj ship, *Anshun*. Writing of the years 1966 to 1968 he recalled that,

> ... we had an average of six deaths outward and six deaths home and since two voyages were needed each Hadj season, this added up to 24 burials at sea per Hadj. Death at sea requires the Master to fill in 34 forms and all in all prevention is preferable, and we all worked toward this end.[13]

Births on board

And, too, there were births. And on occasions – J.H. Brown wrote that this was "invariably" – the child might end up with a name unusual in the Malay world with the ship's name included in their own. On the ship *Tyndareus* in 1951,

> There were ten deaths during the 18-days voyage home. But there was an addition to the group, when, 14 days ago, Mohamed Tyndareus was born at sea. He was named after the ship.[14]

And in June 1966, on the *Anshun* 1,127 pilgrims arrived: for Penang, Port Swettenham, Singapore, Kuching, Labuan and Jesselton. That number included a baby. "He was named Abdullah Anshun, after the ship. His parents are from Langgar, Kedah." Dutch ship records indicate that for the "place of birth" the ship's captain would enter the coordinates of latitude and longitude: we all must be born somewhere! Whether those ship names stuck as personal names once these infant pilgrims were home is another interesting question.

Respect

Earlier chapters cited some dismissive, even contemptuous, nineteenth-century references to hajj pilgrims and there were enough people in colonial times who often saw little dignity in the faith of those they ruled over:

> Texts taken from several royal libraries that were taken as trophies of war, from Selangor (1784), Yogyakarta (1812), Bone (1814), and Palembang (1812 and 1821)... failed to convince some Europeans of the commitment of Southeast Asia's Muslims to their faith.[15]

When the Indian Passenger Act 2 of 1860, was passed it was said to be,

> ... with the laudable design of preventing the overcrowding of passenger ships, by emigrant coolies in search of employment, and by *fanatic Hadjees in search of Mahomet's paradise.*[16] [emphasis added]

And when the abandonment of the Alsagoff ship *Jeddah* was first reported the Singapore newspaper identified that it carried "planks and 950 pilgrims," the wood seeming to take priority in importance over the people. But in many twentieth century accounts or recollections of those non-Muslim crew members who interacted with them or at least observed them, a different tone comes across. A report from 1936 was of a young man who had sailed as "an apprentice" – a midshipman. Looking back on that experience he wrote:

> I was young then, and the carriage of pilgrims at certain times of the year was just part of the job I had chosen to do, but with hindsight I realise I was very fortunate to have had the experience of another culture, even though I was only an observer.[17]

Capt. Paddy Gorman was master of the *Kuala Lumpur* in the 1960s. He was recorded as having carried 40,000 Malaysian hajj pilgrims over five years and in the 1969 "Merdeka Honours" he was awarded the Johan Setia Makhota Award (JSM), together with a standing invitation from Malaysia's Prime Minister, Tengku Abdul Rahman, to stay in his Penang house

Paddy Gorman, presented with the Malaysian JSM Award by Tan Sri Jamal Bin Abdul Latiff, then Malaysian High Commissioner to Singapore]. Picture sourced from CNCo Newsletter; reproduced courtesy of John Swire & Sons Limited

"anytime Captain and Mrs. Gorman visit the island." Capt. Gorman's comment was that, "The pilgrims are very gentle people. They have never given the crew any trouble. They spend most of their time praying, or getting to know one another."[18] It's a response well remembered by Darrell Daish. He sailed with Paddy Gorman and recalls him looking at the pilgrims, shaking his head slowly, and saying, "Ah, they're lovely people, Darrell, lovely people."[19]

Quarantine

There were times when that long hajj journey did not end with the return of the passengers to their home port. In late 1949 there was another outbreak of smallpox in Saudi Arabia and in early December of that year, a seven-year-old boy on the *Tyndareus* was found to have the disease. There were 2,012 other passengers on board and, aside from a few fortunate souls who were travelling first class, 868 of them who might have expected to be

Pilgrims disembarking at the Singapore Harbour Board wharves on 23 Dec 1949 from their two weeks' quarantine on St John's Island, ready to board special trains to take them back to "Johore and Northern Malaya." Courtesy of The New Straits Times, Kuala Lumpur.

disembarking at Penang had to continue straight past – one can imagine, within sight of waiting families and friends – down the Straits of Malacca to St John's Island, just off Singapore. Here they were quarantined for two weeks before they could finally board specially chartered trains at Tanjong Pagar Station to travel home. Whatever their inner feelings, the photograph suggests it was a further test of stoic patience and some tiredness.

The International Code Flag "L" or LIMA, meaning "You should stop your vessel instantly." Raising the "L" flag is intended to warn other vessels from approaching the vessel that has an outbreak of disease onboard.

A new title of respect

But those who returned home could now assume the title Haji or Hajjah and the men could wear the white *songkok*, or skull cap, to denote their status, especially at "any other occasion that required [someone] to assume [their] religious persona."[20] In Southeast Asia this was always treated as a special title, "a term that was important [to an individual] and his neighbours," and even if, at times, the returning hajji was not specially versed in the teachings of the faith, they might assume a new role in their village community. Roff's observations in Malay villages were that,

> ... *imams* led prayers in mosques and village *suraus, khatibs* delivered Fridays *khutbahs*, returned *hajjis* gave elementary instruction to children in Qur'an recitation and the elements of the faith, usually in their own homes or the *suraus*.[21]

In these cases it meant the continuation of a pattern of modest learning within a society shaped by respect for traditional, almost feudal structures. It was towards the end of the nineteenth century that many of that increasing number of those who had stayed and studied in the Middle East would bring back reformist ideas of how the faith of Islam should be understood and taught – the kaum muda that we have spoken of. In Indonesia that movement argued against the syncretic nature of the practice of Islam. These arguments were discomforting to established understandings and established societal relationships and order. In the Malay Peninsula – less so in urbanised Singapore – the kaum tua, the older group, might feel threatened by any number of seemingly trivial issues.

> It needed only one *haji* to return from the Middle East fired with reform ideas, one religious teacher to study at a *kaum muda* madrasah in Singapore, Perak, or Penang, to divide a village temporarily into two rival factions . . . Arguments about whether it was permissible for a Muslim to wear trousers and a tie . . . divided people along the same lines as arguments about . . what was the correct interpretation of a verse of the Koran.[22]

To be "kaum muda" came "to espouse modernism in any form and go against tradition; to be "kaum tua" was to be in favour of all that was familiar, unchanging, and secure."[23] Pilgrims would return with a range of responses and William Roff has cited the role of Snouck Hurgronje, in "distinguishing between the general run of pilgrims and the *muqim* – the resident – who stayed longer and became politicized." [24]

Young men returning from Mecca on Tyndareus in 1960. Photograph by permission of John Spain.

A Changed Identity?

It's this "general run of pilgrims" with whom this book is primarily concerned. Earlier, we mentioned David Walker's memory of some hajj pilgrims "falling down upon [their] knees and kissing the deck" when they boarded the ship. As a sign of what the journey meant for many hajj pilgrims, that sight seems to have a quiet power.

For the crews of the ships the hajj voyage was part of the job and up to the 1930s and '40s it ended with a pilgrim bonus. When you were paid off you got one "old" (pre-decimal) penny – 1d. – for every pilgrim on board. The "apprentice" who had sailed in 1936 wrote:

> The numbers carried varied from 500/600 to over 1,000 depending on the size of the ship and the space available. I know that on one

> occasion the number was over 1,000 since I received £4. 10s. 0d. . . . At that time I was paid £6 per year, so it was a very noteworthy occasion that sticks in my memory.[25]

But for the pilgrims the performance of the hajj is seen as the chance to wipe clean past sins, to fulfil a duty of faith, and to journey to a centre and an ordering of the world that made sense of what it means to be a human being.

1 "Report by a young Midshipmite." 1947. http://myweb.tiscali.co.uk/chinaboats/midrpt.html. Accessed 13 Feb. 2011.

2 Brown. p. 285.

3 "Report by a young Midshipmite." Op cit.

4 See note 15, chapter 7.

5 "Report by a young Midshipmite." Op cit.

6 Straits Times and Singapore Journal of Commerce, Saturday December 31st 1864.

7 ST. 27 March 1880.

8 Every ship had a four-letter "call sign" that was used to identify it.

9 Personal, written communication with Anthony Green.

10 Brown. 1966. p. 284.

11 From an interview with John Spain in 2010.

12 Personal, written communication with Anthony Green.

13 Kennett, Ralph. 2003. *All Hands.* Journal of the Warsash Association.

14 ST. 12 November 1951.

15 Laffan. p. 93.

16 ST. 2 February 1861, p. 1.

17 See note 15, chapter 7.

18 CNCo Newsletter. 1 June 1970.

19 See note 11, chapter 7.

20 Roff, Wiliam R. 2009B, p. 270.

21 Roff, Wiliam R. 2009D. "Pondoks, Madrasahs and the Production of 'Ulama' in Malaysia." in *Studies on Islam and Society in Southeast Asia.* Singapore: NUS Press, p. 117.

22 Roff. 1980, p. 86.

23 Ibid. p. 87.

24 Roff, Wiliam R. 2009E. "Sanitation and Security." In *Studies on Islam and Society in Southeast Asia.* Singapore: NUS Press, p. 300.

25 See note 15, chapter 7.

13

Looking back:
The end of the kapal haji

The thirty years from the end of the Second World War in 1945 saw great changes in the way that people journeyed and goods were transported. Economies would take time to recover and in the maritime world many Merchant Shipping fleets had been drastically reduced by wartime losses. In the skies the jet engine would alter completely the face of aviation and the possibilities for long-distance travel. And the retreat from Empire – voluntary or somewhat reluctant – changed the nature and scope of the European presence and involvement in Southeast Asia.

The view of the companies: Blue Funnel

For the companies that provided the ships, the hajj was a part of their business although, in terms of financial returns, never a strong part. Blue Funnel was a principled company, and its founder, Alfred Holt, was a Unitarian Christian. He claimed to build his ships to a higher standard than was generally demanded and did not insure them. Instead the company "self-insured" by bearing any loss. But like any company it needed to make a profit, and between July and November 1948, a series of letters passed within the Ocean Steamship Company (the Blue Funnel Line) in Liverpool and across to their sister companies in Holland. The discussion began with the concerns in a letter, dated 23 July 1948 to Sir John Hobhouse from A. McLellan:

> As far as the Straits Pilgrim trade is concerned I feel in our own interests we must continue to cater for the traffic. The pilgrimage is part of the national and political life of Malaya and if the Blue Funnel Line is to retain the premier position it has held for so many years it must continue to be regarded as a necessary part of the economic and national life of the country.
>
> We should not of course be expected to carry pilgrims at a loss. Increased costs and the demand for better accommodation may well mean that the resultant fare will be beyond the means of the ordinary Malay.[1]

But "premier positions" would not last. For Blue Funnel before the War, almost all of its ships could carry pilgrims, which increased the possibility of ships being available if demand happened to increase, since the numbers of pilgrims were not consistent. Add to this the fact that "outward cargo" – cargo from Britain eastwards – was "markedly less than the homeward." Extra ships run over and above scheduled services offered advantages to the company and they made "a very small profit" out of these extra voyages.[2]

The company recognised that pilgrims would demand better accommodation, which would likely result in higher fares in a time when numbers were uncertain and their own fleet, because of wartime losses, was "much smaller than in 1939." Their "general inclination" was,

> ... towards making no attempt to maintain our present monopoly of the pilgrim traffic and limiting our interest in the trade to what we can carry without loss and without disrupting our services.[3]

That meant no longer accepting pilgrims from The Philippines and China and perhaps just confining the hajj to one ship "of very small residual value such as 'Tyndareus.'" Blue Funnel was edging away from its long involvement in Southeast Asia and the hajj.

China Navigation Company

In 1953 the old *Tyndareus*, built in 1916, took over hajj sailings from Indonesia to Jeddah and that closely aligned company, China Navigation, introduced its two ships, *Anking* and *Anshun*, on the hajj. They had been built for the emigrant trade from China to Southeast Asia; a trade that disappeared in the early 1950s[4] so the Swire Group was another owner needing to find work for its ships. With those two vessels and the *Kuala Lumpur* C.N.Co. carried thousands of hajj pilgrims until 1970 but the seaborne hajj never proved commercially successful for them, and by the end of the 1960s it was no longer able to compete with the pilgrim services operated by the airlines. These were both faster and more cost-efficient, and this fact was reflected in their cheaper fare structures. The hajj was a seasonal business and it was becoming harder and harder to find other uses for vessels outside of that season.

The Great Malaysia Line

The two main ships of the Great Malaysia Line – *Malaysia Kita* and *Malaysia Raya* – had been built for the French company, Messageries Maritimes. The "Messageries" ships had been carrying passengers out to what was known as French Indochina from the nineteenth century and, in those times, bringing "the mails" to welcoming Europeans in Singapore and the Malay Peninsula. But the Vietnamese push for independence after 1945 and the crushing French defeat at Dien Bien Phu marked the closing of French colonial rule in Southeast Asia. Both caught fire – the *'Kita'* off Bedok in Singapore in 1974 and the *'Raya'* off Port Klang in 1976.

Marine Engineer Ronald Pereira described them as full-blown passenger vessels converted to carry "deck passengers" under the SIMLA rules. It was, he said,

> ... a special conference they had, in order to convert a lot of old passenger vessels for the carriage of pilgrims to Mecca ...They made the lower decks into what we call shelter decks ... where they took away all the partitioning bulkheads, the dividing bulkheads, for the passenger cabins and as a result were able to put bunks. They were just frames, with canvas, so everything was inflammable.[5]

In the case of the *Kita*, "they tried to fight this fire, of course . . . put a lot of water into the shelter decks, which, of course, affected the stability of the vessel. And as they towed her out, she keeled over."

Those who have worked on ships speak of certain vessels with fondness. Darrell Daish described *Kuala Lumpur* as a friendly ship. John Spain described *Tyndareus* in the same way. Lives are lived on them, so the ways in which ships end their days brings a kind of sadness to those who have sailed on them, and when the Angullia sisters heard about the ship they had journeyed on to Jeddah their reaction was simple:

> "We sent to see *Malaysia Kita* sinking off Bedok. We started crying."

The ship was on its side; the salvage company went to work; stanchions were welded on the hull, and she was rotated upright and then de-watered and that was the end. As a constructional total loss, she went to the breakers. "Great Malaysia" ran one more ship – the *Eastern Queen* – for a short while until 1976 and the company closed down its business.

One final look – what might have been

In these final days of the kapal haji, one unique, and impressive, Blue Funnel ship sailed for a time from Indonesia. This was *Gunung Djati*, described by Geoffrey Holt, a descendant of old Alfred Holt, as "the finest ship ever to sail on the hajj." This, though, was a deepening twilight for hajj ships. M. Roslan Ja'afar sailed on the *Malaysia Baru* in 1971 and recalled seeing her. "We saw *Gunung Djati*. She came up past us and just drew on ahead and disappeared." Built in Bremerhaven in the 1930s in a time when ocean liners operated, she offered a level of space and comfort that pilgrims of earlier years might have struggled to recognise.

The sea – community, and a different space

To all of the descriptions given of life and conditions on board there is one more observation to add. In Singapore, the late Ustaz Zhulkiflee Hj Ismail once said of the difference between the sea-borne journey and the one by

"Gunung Djati"

First Class Lounge

Musholla or Mosque

Lounge Entrance

With space for 106 1st class and 2000 other class pilgrims, *Gunung Djati* entered service in 1960 to replace *Tyndareus*, operating only from Indonesia. She was sold in 1962 to the Indonesian government and then, in 1979, to the Indonesian Navy. In her time as a hajj ship she offered a very different level of comfort.

Dining Room

Ship photograph by permission of John Spain; interior photographs from Blue Funnel and Glen Line Bulletin; reproduced courtesy of John Swire & Sons Limited.

air, that, "When you travelled by ship and you reached Jeddah, you were a different person." You would eat together and pray together and talk together. But, "When you arrive by air, you're just the same."

When the Angullia sisters took the ship, flights to Saudi Arabia were already becoming more common but, for Aisha, the aeroplane was very expensive. Putting the matter of money aside, she liked the ship "because we can learn more. We can meet people." Haji Maamor also preferred the ship, "because you can meet so many people." Ustazah Maimunah Binti Ahmad spoke of how,

> We had a real kampung feeling. With 14 – 15 days it was a chance to meet different people from other places, from all over Malaysia, and to make many friends; we prayed in Jemaah together with our friends; we had a chance to learn from the guru kapal, and there were the Qur'an reading competitions on board.[6]

Beyond community, this was also a different space. Looking back on his own journey, Ustaz Hj Ali offers his thoughts on that space:

> When you're in the middle of the sea and all you can see is the sea and the sky that, I think, purifies a person's mind and heart. And with that the thinking goes up to the spiritual level. It's not miracles, but something that you can feel. When you're here [in the urban existence] it's being disturbed by many things. Then you see things that you don't see here; especially with the heart; when you can purify the heart and the mind. We can see the creation of Allah when we are in the ship and you see that God's creation is greater.

Ustaz Hj Ali Hj Mohamed. Photograph by Mohd Raman Daud.

> I think there is a vast difference between an aircraft and the ship. The time alone can change a person. But of course, now we don't have that much time, only about one month to and fro. I think, if we have time, maybe people will choose the ship. Although there are many challenges there is a difference and of course when a person is being tested I think they are tested more on the ship, and especially when you see someone pass away so they have to see people being buried

> in the heart of the sea. All that will make a person think more about what is life. Changing a person is not only with *dua* [invocation]; changing a person is with the reality of life, when they see life.[7]

In his voyage from Jeddah to Southeast Asia in 1910 as the ship's doctor, F.W. Hogarth wrote:

> *March 20th.* Off to Penang at 10 knots, the wires vibrating with the rush of sea through them; it sounds like a cotton mill. Wind aft. Smoke going straight up. Red Sea like a lake. Temp, 82° [28°C]. I spent hours right up in the bows looking at porpoises, dolphins and flying fish.
> *March 29th.* Passed Ceylon at midnight. Could smell its lovely spicy odours distinctly, miles out at sea.
> *April 2nd.* Sumatra, in distance, shows the 'Golden Conical Mountain', 5,600 feet. Brilliantly phosphorescent at night.[8]

In a website thread that invited sailors to write of their memories of being at sea, one retired sailor has said that "Shoresiders aren't like seamen; different mind set all together!" And seamen speak of many sights at sea that have brought a sense of awe, from the green flash on the horizon at sunset to whales breeching and stars in millions, far beyond counting. One wrote:

> Seeing the Red Sea off Jeddah on the 12 to 4am so luminous as to lose a ship's lights 15 mile in front of us, in what looked like a 'wall of light.' When we passed through it there were yellow and green and red strips of luminous colours coming off the bow . . . The AB on watch getting nervous, as he was a Muslim and it was Ramadan, and we were close to Mecca. He kept saying, "The will of Allah."
>
> It went on for miles seemed like it went right from coast to coast of the Red sea. The 2nd mate thought the Radar was orientated wrong; he thought the light he was seeing was the land and the lights off Jeddah. So I was called on the bridge to check out the radar. It's a sight I'll always remember.[9]

This may be what Alan Villiers has described as "the extraordinary 'milk sea,'" a phenomenon reported by many ships, in which "the whole sea seems to boil with light and ships to sail upon liquid fire."[10]

Villiers quotes Frank Bullen's description from his round the world voyage:

> It was a lovely night with scarcely any wind, the stars trying to make up for the absence of the moon by shining with intense brightness. The water had been more phosphorescent than usual, so that every little fish left a track of light behind him greatly disproportionate to his size. As the night wore on the sea grew brighter and brighter, until by midnight we seemed to be sailing in a sea of lambent flames. Every little wave that broke against the ship's side sent up a shower of diamondlike spray, wonderfully beautiful to see, while a passing school of porpoises fairly set the sea blazing as they leaped and gambolled in its glowing waters. Looking up from sea to sky, the latter seemed quite black instead of blue . . . In that shining flood the blackness of the ship stood out in startling contrast, and when we looked over the side our faces were strangely lit up by the brilliant glow. For several hours this beautiful appearance persisted, fading away at last as gradually as it came.[11]

Not all who travelled by sea would witness such a thing; perhaps it was very few, because natural phenomena cannot be summoned up by order and in any case, it is not everyone who gazes at the stars or the sky or the sea. In the photograph of *Tyndareus* on page 179 some hajj pilgrims are visible standing on the foredeck looking at the sea but Captain J. H. Brown wrote of his voyage in 1926 that for some of the pilgrims the mustering to be counted "would be the only appearance on deck for the whole passage." Yet to understand the pilgrimage as a shaping experience for an individual then each part of the journey has a role. It begins, as we've said, with intention – with niyah; is there in the travel through busy places and among strangers; is intensified in the clothing of *ihram*, reaches its peak in the high point of the hajj, the *wuquf*, or "standing," at Arafat, and flows on in the return.

This book is, in part, an invitation to reflect on the experience of a journey by sea; on how it might have contributed to the overall experience of undertaking the pilgrimage; and of how that might differ from modern-day travel. The focus has been on people from one part of the world. These are the Muslims from Southeast Asia up to and including the Philippines, and even, at times, including some from China, and the book has offered accounts and anecdotes of the ways in which these people have been seen – as a group – and described by others. Those sentiments have varied greatly over time.

But whilst Muslims have journeyed in large, ship-bound communities to perform the hajj, and whilst the congregation gathered in Mecca has often been vast, the essence of the hajj is singular. As was noted at the end of the previous chapter, the pilgrimage itself is made as a personal duty for which an individual is answerable. And, from every account, that experience is one that has the potential to deepen faith and to speak to an individual's sense of themselves and their place in the world.

The hajj itself, then, is personal and what it means is private within each pilgrim. Some experiences cannot adequately be described to others, so a scholar like William Roff, a man with a long and close relationship to the Muslim community, could write:

> In most respects the hardest task remains – to come closer to understanding what for the pilgrim and the community of pilgrims was the meaning and the effect of the journey.[12]

Over the centuries the hajj has also been private, in a sense, to Muslims because the sites of the hajj are "off-limits" to those who are not of the faith. Yet we live now in a time that is loud with visual images. Anyone with a mobile phone has a camera, and these are days when the events of the hajj can be photographed, even live-streamed, in a way that would have been inconceivable, perhaps bewildering, even intrusive, to those from the past.

In modern times, at airports of departure or transit during the season when hajj pilgrims are travelling, non-Muslim travellers can come across groups dressed already in the white cloth of ihram. There is a kind of brief encounter, a certain curiosity perhaps, then each of them parts to his or her own purposes.

But the hajj journey by sea from Southeast Asia was significant in a number of ways. A ship is a unique space and this was perhaps the longest journey of its kind. In a time before cameras became commonplace – certainly for the pilgrims – travelling communities of Muslims spent a total of a month, sometimes far longer, in a space shared with others; at times in the twentieth century more than 2,000 passengers and crew together. And even if the interactions between crews and pilgrims were limited there was the opportunity for observation. It was as if that part of the pilgrimage took on a public face because the journeying had a kind of "public" quality to it, and the ways in which the pilgrims conducted themselves did not go unnoticed. J.H. Brown noted how, in sickness, "not even the elderly" complained. Gwilym Owen recognised distress and loss of dignity when a breeze disturbed a burial at sea. John Spain's photograph on page 179 came with his comment on the patience that he identified in the Indonesian pilgrims queueing to board in an orderly line, something that he contrasted with a ship tied nearby in Jeddah, whose passengers from a different place of origin "swarmed aboard" once the signal was given, even up to the "monkey island" – the topmost accessible point of the ship – so that the vessel departed from the dock listing to one side. Paddy Gorman's observations of the pilgrims he carried were similarly respectful.

In his book, *The Hadj: An American's Pilgrimage to Mecca*, Michael Wolff describes making his pilgrimage with friends from Morocco. There is a moment in Mecca when they are urged to come outside quickly because someone has encountered a man who has walked all the way there. There is something about distance and difficulty that can stir an added layer of respect; perhaps a thought that the time spent out of the normal, worldly concerns plays its part in shaping a person. The Qur'an itself recognises the effect of distant journeys:

> And proclaim the pilgrimage among men: they will come to Thee on foot and on every kind of camel, lean on account of journeys through deep and distant mountain highways.
> Surah Al-Hajj, 22: 27

Times change and values change, and the numbers of individuals who have experienced the journey both by sea and by air dwindle. There are few now. So it is hard to come to a measure of comparison. But for the Muslims of Southeast Asia the hajj undertaken by sea, conducted the way it was, deserves a degree of special consideration. Travelling by kapal haji, the "highways" were through deep and distant waters, far from urban existence. Their hajj offered both demands and opportunities alien to the comfort of air travel: tests, time, fears perhaps, and the chance of much reflection.

[1] McLellan, letter dated 23 July 948. Blue Funnel Archive. Merseyside Maritime Museum.

[2] "Confidential" Letter from Alfred Holt & Co, Liverpool, dated 11 November 1948.

[3] Ibid.

[4] *Ships of the Hadj.* http://merchantnavyofficers.com/hadj.html. Accessed November 2009.

[5] Interviewed in Singapore by Anthony Green. 2009.

[6] Green. p. 38.

[7] Interviewed in Singapore by Anthony Green. October 2018.

[8] Hogarth. pp. 185 – 191.

[9] Taken from recollections in a thread on the "Ships Nostalgia" website. The 'thread' was started by a member called Kenneth Crosby, who asked the question: "What have you seen, that you know landlubbers, never will?" The writer was a man who signed himself as "Hughesy."

[10] Villiers. p. 8.

[11] Ibid.

[12] Roff, William R. 2009A. "The Conduct of the Hajj from Malaya." In *Studies on Islam and Society in Southeast Asia*. Singapore: NUS Press, p. 332.

Timeline:

Some key events

1858	**Indian Law No 21** regulates "the carriage of natives of Asia from any place within British India to any place in the Red Sea or the Persian Gulf and which is applicable to ships proceeding from Singapore." This stipulates the **amount of space to be allowed for each passenger** and the number of passengers that can be carried relative to the tonnage of cargo.
1866	(August) Report published from the "Conference Sanitaire Internationale" (International Sanitary Conference) – held in "Constantinople" (Istanbul): "Report on measures to be taken in the East to **prevent new invasions of cholera in Europe.**"
1869	(June) Straits Settlements receive reports from the Government of Madras on the **overcrowding of pilgrim ships**, with particular reference to the *Day Dream*. Report mentions the practice of ships calling at ports where they "effectively evade detection, and place themselves beyond the reach of British supervision and penalties." Similar complaints continue throughout the 1870s.
1873	(4 June) Governor-General of "Netherlands India" announces **blockade** of "the ports and landing places, coasts, rivers, bays, and creeks" of "the country of **Acheen**." On this coast pilgrim ships from Singapore and Penang were in the habit of picking up additional passengers well above their permitted number.

1873	(29 Aug) Report from Master Attendant, Singapore on **alleged overcrowding** on pilgrim ships. Of 36 ships that departed for Jeddah seven of them left from Singapore "carrying more passengers than the law allowed."
1875	(October) Alsagoff ship *Medina* stranded on rocks in the Red Sea; hajj passengers transferred to another ship; complaints of theft of their money.
1876	(April) **"The Native Passenger Ships Act"** passed by the Government of India, to specify which ports ships should sail from, what ships' masters should report, conditions on board, penalties, etc.
1880	(August) **The *S. S. Jeddah* incident** that led to Joseph Conrad's story *Lord Jim*.
1897	**Plague in the Hejaz:** "the Ottoman and the international board of health does not impose any quarantine on ships carrying pilgrims to India, Straits Settlements and Java on condition that they should not touch the Ottoman shores again on their voyage after leaving Jeddah." (FO 195/1987)
1897	(June) Letter from British Consul: "the pilgrim caravan for Medina was stopped by Bedouins; these pilgrims mostly Malays and British subjects with some Indians also, are as it were prisoners in Rabuc." (28 July) Pilgrims released but unable to visit Medina; "They protest against their treatment, stating that they have been detained thirty days and forced to procure food, so that they are now naked and starving."
1897	(29 July) **Jeddah declared free from plague.**
1906	Outbreak of **plague at Jeddah**
1919	(9 April) Agreement drawn up between **Syed Omar bin Mohamed Alsagoff** and **W. Mansfield & Co**, whereby all pilgrim tickets will be purchased by pilgrim brokers from Syed Omar.

1922	**Pilgrim Ordinance** – stipulates pilgrim ships must be "at least 5,000 tons"; cannot carry non-pilgrim passengers; that in cargo ships pilgrims must be in decks "above the waterline"; amount of space for each pilgrim; drinking water availability; numbers of bathrooms; stairs to prevent slipping; space for prayers; provision for a hospital on board; a loud-speaker in every hatch to provide a "smooth information service" etc.
1925	British Agency, Jeddah reports on "the estates" of pilgrims dying in the Hejaz: "72 out of 100 Indians, 13 out of 15 Egyptians, and 28 out of 29 Malays left a return ticket only . . . It is . . . incredible that so high a proportion of **pilgrims** who died should have been **penniless at the moment of their death** . . ."
1925	(December) "**Tin and rubber are booming** in the Straits Settlements and in the Federated Malay States" [Letter, National Archives, UK: CO 273/530]
1926	(17 December) **Pilgrim Pass Rules** (1926) in Straits Settlements ("No pilgrim shall travel or attempt to travel in a pilgrim ship, unless he shall have in his possession a pilgrim pass duly issued to him"). (At this stage pilgrim passes from the Straits did not contain a photograph of the pilgrim)
1926	**Paris International Sanitary Convention** – recommendations to ensure that contagious diseases shall not be carried to and from the Hejaz by persons performing the pilgrimage.
1926	(March/April) **Soviet authorities** desire to send Russian pilgrim ships to Jeddah and ask for a copy of quarantine regulations. Colonial Office, London, object that "no steps should be taken which would give the Soviet Government opportunities to introduce agents or literature into the Hejaz."

1926	Pilgrimage Report says, "All pilgrims and visitors to the Hejaz since Ibn Saud has assumed control are loud in their praises of the perfect security of the roads to Mecca and the caravan routes from Mecca, Jeddah, Rabigh, and Yambo to Medina . . . The memory of the caravan robbed at Khaif and the hundreds of pilgrims killed and robbed annually on the Haj by Bedouin robbers during the reign of Ibn Saud's predecessors throws the performance of clearing up the country of these people into brilliant relief . . ."
1926	Report urges that **food be provided in hajj ships**. This will also mean that ships will "become less filthy and odoriferous and liable to foment diseases amongst the pilgrims. The Dutch have adopted this system . . . and there is a great difference between their ships and those carrying pilgrims who are allowed to provide and cook their own food."
1927	(25 July) Dutch consular representative at Jeddah reports to "the Governor-General the Netherlands East Indies" on "two societies formed among our pilgrims at Mecca, with the object of furthering **communist activities** in the Netherlands East Indies"
1927	(17 October) British Consul in Jeddah (F H W Stonehewer-Bird) reports that "the **pilgrimage of 1927** was **the largest** since the [First World] war, "and, indeed, is thought by many to have established the record of all times."
1928	(22 February) S. S. Intaba (Nemazie Steamship Line) calls at **Port Swettenham** (now Port Klang): the **first time pilgrims could join a hajj ship here**.
1929	(February) British Consul in Jeddah writes urging **compulsory vaccination against smallpox**, as was already done in N.E.I. Further, that doctors on board ships be able to vaccinate if the initial vaccination has been unsuccessful.
1929	British Government makes an amendment to the Pilgrim Ships Rules, 1911, to make it **compulsory for pilgrims to be provided with food on board** (starting from the 1929 – 1930 pilgrim season). Advertisements exist of ship sailings from the Netherlands East Indies providing food in back in 1888.

1931	**Total number of overseas pilgrims** estimated at 39,346; less than half that of the previous year (84,821) – according to Report of British Consul in Jeddah.
1931	**"SIMLA Rules"** came into effect, (Relates to ships carrying "large numbers of unberthed passengers in special trades"). CNCo newsletter, August 1967: "They allowed for relaxation from the International Convention for the Safety of Life at Sea with particular reference to the number of lifeboats that needed to be carried." [CNCo decided unilaterally that the Simla Rules were outmoded and unsafe and "decided to improve the standards of lifesaving appliances of our two ships concerned."]
1939	(17 November) **"Pilgrim traffic to be resumed:** Seas declared to be safe" (ST 17 Nov 1939). However, "Six hundred pilgrims who started from Malaya before the outbreak of war have returned without reaching Mecca."
1944	(June) Viceroy of India writes to the British government to **request that the Admiralty provide an escort vessel to accompany hajj ships** from "India" (ie, Karachi to Jeddah) so that the hajj can be resumed – it being "important to Moslem morale" and since "Moslem friendliness is of obvious importance" against Japanese propaganda that the hajj could not be protected. (Letter from India Office, London to Lord Alexander Wavell, 1 June 1944).
1946	(June) Two ships to sail for Jeddah (**first hajj ships for six years**). Fare $360 per head compared to $285 in 1940. Pre-war $800 sufficient for a pilgrim; now at least $1,200. About 600 Malayan pilgrims to make the trip (ST 9 Jun 1946)
1949	**Blue Funnel's ship** *Tyndareus* (built in 1916) allocated to serve on the hajj from Singapore and Penang to Jeddah. The ship never suffered any breakdown in service. Continued to operate from Indonesia until the decision in 1960 to send her for scrap.
1953	**China Navigation Company (Swire Group) takes over the hajj shipping** run from Singapore and Malaya with their ships *Anking* and *Anshun*.

1960	**T.S.M.S.** *Kuala Lumpur* replaces *Anking* and *Anshun* (capacity 1,186 passengers) as the principal ship on the hajj from Singapore and Malaya
1965	T.S.M.S. *Kuala Lumpur* (operating under the 16 sq ft rule – ie each pilgrim must have this amount of space) carries 2,047 passengers from Malaysia to Jeddah. (max capacity 2,011)
1966	(January) **For the first time**, a hajj ship (*Anshun*) picks up **pilgrims from Borneo** at "Jesselton" (now Kota Kinabalu); Labuan; and then at Kuching, 26 miles up the Sarawak River. Here the ship was turned around with just enough water in the river and pilgrims had to be embarked within two hours from launches as the tide was ebbing. (CNCo newsletter, March 1966)
1966	Heavy floods in Kelantan and Terengganu mean large numbers of **cancellations of hajj bookings**.
1970	**CNCo withdraw** from the hajj
1972/74	*Malaysia Kita* of Great Malaysia Line **destroyed by fire** off Singapore (1974) and *Malaysia Raya* destroyed off Port Klang. Replaced by *Eastern Queen*.
1976	Final hajj ship sailing from Singapore and Malaysia.
1977	(April) **Great Malaysia Line stops trading.** Its financiers, Moscow Narodny Bank, sell the *Eastern Queen* to the Bangladesh Shipping Corporation.

Appendix:

Pilgrim numbers from Southeast Asia in 1927

1927 pilgrim numbers: those who came by sea

To give a sense of the Southeast Asian representation on the sea-borne hajj at its high point and the numbers of European (especially British) ships involved, the figures below have been taken from the 1927 Pilgrimage Report from the British Government's office in Jeddah.

nb The terms used for the different nationalities are exactly as written in the report

The number of pilgrims who arrived at Jeddah by sea from various countries:

Country of embarkation	*No of pilgrims*	*Country of embarkation*	*No of pilgrims*
British Malaya	29,604	Egypt	18,876
Dutch East Indies	39,157	Syria	1,977
India	36,089	Tripoli and Tunis	1,855
East Africa	104	Russia	315
Massowa, Mokalla,		Turkey	574
Hodeida and Aden	1,945		
Sudan	1,613	**Total**	**132,109**

Pilgrims included in the list were of the following nationalities:

British Malayans	29,604	Somalis	180
Javanese	39,704	South Africans	100
Indians	29,496	Zanzibaris and Other	
Afghans	3,858	East Africans	104
Bokharans	3,469	Egyptians	15,547
Cingalese [Singhalese?]	18	Syrians	1,511
Sarawakis	102	Palestinians	333
Persians	2,248	Turks	684
Muscatis	117	Russians	315
Iraqis	677	Mograbis (Tunis, Tripoli,	
Kurds	73	Algiers & Morocco)	2,735
Arabs	187	Sudanese	957
"Hajazis"	335	Nigerians	589
Hadramis	669	Senegalese	124
Yemenis	1,334		
Nejdians	39	**Total**	**132,109**

The numbers of pilgrims carried in ships of different nationalities:

Flag	*No of pilgrims*
British	79,272
Dutch	31,353
Italian	18,812
Egyptian	977
Greek	111
Russian	315
Turkish	574

Ships employed on the pilgrimage:

Flag	*No of Ships*
British	102
Dutch	27
Italian	30
Egyptian	1
Greek	1
Russian	1
Turkish	1
Total	**163**

1927 pilgrim numbers: those who came by sea

Report from British Consul, Jeddah, 14 October 1897

"The number of sea borne pilgrims is gradually but surely increasing. For the present sixty thousand may represent the average under normal conditions and a glance at the figures bears this out."

Period	Annual average of sea borne pilgrim arrivals
1867 – 1872	39,704
1872 – 1877	35,999
1877 – 1882	42,710
1882 – 1887	39,965
1887 – 1892	45,374
1892 – 1897	65,493

"It is needless to observe that the increase has come about mainly through the growth of the world's shipping and ease, rapidity and cheapness of sea voyages ...Javanese and Malays have only begun to come in thousands where before there were hundreds since within the last twenty years; their average between 1877 – 87 was 8,600 approximately, whilst 17,000 arrived for last and 13,000 for this year's pilgrimage ...Even at the present time the problem of providing space for receiving at least 15,000 pilgrims at one and the same time should receive attention. In one single day shortly after this year's Haj as many as thirteen steamers were lying in Jeddah roads mostly waiting to embark pilgrims and twenty two has been the maximum for one day, in recent times, probably capable of carrying ten thousand pilgrims."

(National Archives, UK. FO 195/1987)

Acknowledgements

The desire for this book was prompted back in 2006 when I wrote something for Singapore's Islamic Religious Council (Muis) on their role in the hajj. In particular I was struck then by an image that we reproduce here, on page 173. It was the frail determination of an old man being helped towards a hajj ship in 1953. Ever since then I fear I've been boring people by talking about wanting to produce a book that gave a kind of face to those who undertook the hajj journey by sea. But talking is not doing, so I first offer a special thanks to Mohd Raman Daud for galvanising this project. Raman researched and shaped the chapter on the very significant role within the Malay world of printing, publishing and entertainment in Singapore.

Of the organisations to acknowledge there is the wonderful resource of the online digitised Singapore newspapers under the National Library Board at NewspapersSG (http://eresources.nlb.gov.sg/newspapers/) that allowed me, far away in New Zealand, to spend hours trawling through nineteenth century ship movements and much more. But any comment acknowledging Singapore's National Library must also acknowledge people behind it and those within it: that includes the generosity of the Lee Foundation, working in memory of Lee Kong Chian, since they have given so much to culture and learning.

At the library itself I owe thanks to the librarians who are consistently helpful, especially Mazelan Anwar, Juffri Supa'at, Timothy Pwee, and a former librarian, Nor-Afidah Abdul Rahman. Thanks also to the good people of the National Archives of Singapore, especially Ms Fiona Tan; and to helpful individuals in the National Maritime Museum, London; the Merseyside Maritime Museum, Liverpool; and those individuals who have been especially helpful in providing old photographs.

For financial support we would like to acknowledge the generosity of Singapore's National Heritage Board; Muis – the Islamic Religious Council of Singapore; Mr Mohamed Halim bin Ali; and the Trustees of the Sultan Mosque. And thanks too, to AMTAS (the Association of Muslim Travel Agents of Singapore) for their help in the book's launch.

From the shipping world, the website "Ships Nostalgia" that put me in touch with retired mariners and, based in Liverpool but with members across the globe, the Blue Funnel Association. Ms Charlotte Bleasdale in Le Bons Bay, New Zealand – a lady with a long association with China Navigation – for her great help in the loan of her collection both of newsletters from China Navigation in the time of the hajj ships, and of the now, long-defunct, Blue Funnel line. In Pegasus, New Zealand, just north of Christchurch, my thanks go to Darrell Daish for explaining the "ins and outs" of the ship *Kuala Lumpur* and for connecting me with CNCo stories, and to Capt. Mohamad Salleh bin Ahmad Sarwan, Director of the Singapore Maritime Academy at Singapore Polytechnic for the message systems of flag signalling.

And so many individuals: Ibrahim Tahir of Wardah Books, a respecter of the printed word and a guardian of memory and the "loose change" of history that can be overlooked or "spent without caring." The generosity of people who sometimes let me, a stranger, wander off into the night with precious family photographs or documents to copy. Thanks to Peter Batchelor for his close reading and correcting of the text. A special thanks to Mdm Fatmah Mohamed Salim who lent me a complete set of photographs from the hajj journey made by her mother and father. Cameras were not common things among hajj pilgrims so the everyday incidents on board were not commonly captured. John Spain gave me much time and precious, coloured images of his time on *S. S. Tyndareus* in 1960. Many shared offered memories: both those who travelled or whose relatives travelled, and those who worked on the ships.

Some, sadly, have passed on since I spoke with them, and some may well have wondered if they would ever see a story in print. I owe them an apology for taking so long. All of those retired seamen – many of whom I never met in person – who sent hand-written letters to me with their memories of working on hajj ships. There are many divisions in the world but through the way they spoke or wrote they offered personal insights into this journey and into the way that the pilgrims were seen. Vernon Elliott – who I never met in person – wrote, "I applaud your decision to record for posterity the saga of the Pilgrim Voyages from the Straits and Indonesia to Jeddah so many years ago." I fear I've fallen well short of what he might have anticipated but his respect and sympathy for these pilgrims stays with me.

And my thanks to my family, especially my wife, Sajinah, for her long patience and support, waiting to see if this project would be finished. This book just seems to scratch at the surface of this story. Perhaps it's a beginning.

Epilogue:

Some thoughts about this book

In the Acknowledgments we list some of the many people and organisations who have helped in this, together with a brief comment on how this book came to be. But a word here may be appropriate about some of the learnings involved in this process.

An oral and visual history of ordinary people

The early wish in this book was not for a focus on prominent individuals or on large movements, often with "political" overtones, but to try to get a sense of the journeys of "ordinary people" for whom faith tends to be quiet and personal and whose lives would far more likely be centred on family and neighbours than on issues outside. They may be caught up, even swept up, in events but they are not themselves generally the drivers or agents of such things.

The style the book aspired to was to be a kind of oral and visual history: to try to "show" the journey with images and maps and to hear it from those "ordinary people." But, as we have said, these are people who exist in the records, at most, as a number and, again for clear reasons, very few gave any account, so there is a significant challenge in writing about them, especially in trying to approach the most important element in their journey: the "inner" dimension and what it meant.

Building a context

If a people have not told their own story; if their names almost never appear; then the direction we took was to try to build a context around them: to try to describe the other events that were taking place and elements being put in place and, just as the pilgrim view of things was missing from the detailed reports of the "Jeddah" incident, be alert to the gaps in the story and listen for the silences.

Years ago, in a television programme about killings by paramilitaries in Central America, a forensic archaeologist from the USA was digging up mass graves for the relatives of the deceased, to try to build a story for them of what had happened to their loved ones. The deceased could not speak but, he said, "You listen with your eyes." A portion of our story then has to be closer to a kind of speculation than hard fact but, as one young Malay man said to me, "Even if we don't have a picture, at least we have a silhouette."

Timing and testimonies

Another issue is timing. Are there people around who took part in this thing we're writing about or who witnessed it? On more than one occasion, meeting with some older folk who had travelled on the kapal haji the response to questions was, "Saya tak ingat" – I can't remember – and there were a number of times when you'd hear that, "my brother was the one who kept all these memories but he passed away last year" or, "my aunt was linked to this shipping company but she has dementia." So the wish often came that we'd begun twenty years ago or more. Today, then, has to be the best time to start. Yesterday might have been better but it's gone. So if many of those with first-hand experiences had passed on and few had left written records, you look for other testimonies, and a traditional letter "snail-mailed" to an interest group of retired mariners in Liverpool found its way into their newsletter and from there onto an online presence that then produced letters, often hand-written, detailing personal experiences of the hajj ships. It was a sometimes touching but also encouraging thing to receive from complete strangers, men in their seventies or eighties, letters that had taken them time to reflect on and to write. The comment from Vernon Elliott that we quote in the Acknowledgements is a good example of this.

What counts?

One more observation on timing may be worth adding. To turn up as a stranger into people's lives and jump straight into an interview seems now both a shade unrealistic and, perhaps even, unfair. In this book we quote a line from the English poet Walter de la Mare, that, "Long looking, long desiring, long loving – these win at last into the inmost being of a thing." Good things take time, and it would have been better to have been able to first build a relationship and then sit much longer with witnesses and have time to reflect on their answers and to return, to revisit or re-shape the questions. But time presses. Add to this that a tiny detail that one may feel to be important may not at first be recognised by another and that not all who are interviewed will produce responses that seem illuminating. Asked about what the spirit or feelings were on board ship, an answer like "mabuk sahaja" might come – "just seasick." You can't expect every response to be profound so I came to recognise the need to learn to listen better and question better.

The label "independent researcher"

Working from a personal interest but outside of the discipline, or perhaps support, of an academic setting I'm sure I criss-crossed territory that could have been traversed more directly by one with greater skills. I'm also sure I held back at first on the project because I felt I hadn't read some texts that might be considered "101" readings in this field; or felt that I did not know enough to produce a sufficient account. But all writing is an ordering of thought and almost never a final statement, and E M Forster's question was a valuable reminder: "How can I know what I think until I see what I say?"

If others read these comments and are coming to projects from any similar position, then perhaps the positive thought to take from this is just to start, and to realise that there was a reason for starting: you start with a sense that something in what you want to say is not being said. Leave it to others at the end as to whether you've contributed anything of value to the discussion.

Tangents and cross-currents

The ideal research ground for any work on hajj shipping from Southeast Asia would be in that part of the world, or in the centres from where the ships ran: London, Liverpool, Holland. In this case, brief visits to places in the UK were squeezed in to family reunions in the country. Inadequate, but they had to suffice. But many of the ships' logs that might document onboard incidents have not been kept and many of those that do survive now sit in Newfoundland, Canada. Direct access to records can be invaluable and ascertaining which voyages might have included a hajj passage or two is not straightforward when done online, so lacking that direct access and sitting far away in New Zealand the digitised Singapore newspapers from the National Library were a much visited resource. Simply by scanning the "Shipping in Harbour" sections for the days of sail, for example, you come to see the pattern of departures, realise the role of the monsoon and get a feel for how many months, even years, would necessarily be taken by a journey to the Hejaz.

In these nineteenth century English-language newspapers, the fact that the perspectives and priorities were colonial and expatriate – views, if you like, "from the outside" towards the people they ruled over – did not prevent them offering value. And being newspapers, the references to hajj ships often sat embedded in, or alongside, other events that offered insights into the times, as in the case in November 1866 of the "coolie" ship *"Jeddah"* (not the Alsagoff steamship) and the deathbed admission by its doctor.

> We remember the loss through fire of the English coolie ship *Jeddah* which was bound to Demerara from Amoy, and that an enquiry was held at Singapore, which terminated in favour of the Captain and Doctor of that vessel who were highly praised for their humane conduct, and courage in the affair. We hear now that the Doctor on his death bed made a solemn declaration, that the coolies were very cruelly treated on board. Putrid water was given to them to drink, which soon brought about a peculiar kind of sickness that made

> the coolies throw themselves overboard in despair. That the Captain having a suspicion that a mutiny was brewing had fifteen of the ringleaders seized and so severely flogged that five out of the number died shortly afterwards, and the remainder being so exasperated with the unkind treatment set fire to the vessel, by which two hundred coolies either lost their lives by being burnt or drowned. It is high time that this abominable traffic was put an end to. We hear that the Captain has been placed in prison in England.
> (Singapore Free Press and Mercantile Advertiser, 15 November 1866)

There is an odd – perhaps sad – reassurance in this that the dreadful conditions on board hajj ships in the first half of the nineteenth century were not exceptional; not some consequence of disorganisation peculiar to Muslims. They were more like the norm applied to those without money and, at times, those who were non-Europeans. Stories like this invite questions and further exploration.

A lack of records

What relevance might the approach taken in this book be to others?

There does seem to be an increased interest in identity and personal history; an increase in the number of questioners asking, Who am I? Where did I come from? How did I come to be here in this place? Who were my forebears? What did they go through? What was the world like in which they lived?

Many who grow up in the "western" world – (I have to include myself in that) – can often count on a degree of good fortune because detailed records of births, deaths, marriages and much more exist. Records are easily available, for example, of migrants who departed from Britain for "the colonies." For Australians who trace their ancestry back to those transported from Britain as convicts (sometimes for "crimes" like stealing a candlestick) shipping records exist that list the ships and name those who were carried, the ports they sailed from, the places where they disembarked and more. That level of detail cannot be claimed by everyone, and year after year for many in the world people's lives and deaths can feel unmarked and more like vanishings, so a story such as this "coolie" ship from Amoy relates to those who were the ancestors of many Chinese in modern-day Southeast Asia and perhaps can add some texture to an appreciation of their own past.

The assumptions of Empire

To touch on one more reflection from the process of this book, we might comment on the assumptions of Empire and the connotations that attach to the labels that come down through history.

We've remarked that throughout the nineteenth century the market prices of goods were printed at the head of the front page of Singapore newspapers. At the foot of a list that included such everyday commodities as black pepper, coffee, sago, and tin would be the price for Benares or Malwa opium, and on the inside pages you'd read updates on the quantities of opium shipped through the port. This from 1870:

> The British steamer *Statesman* arrived her yesterday morning . . . leaves again for Hongkong today. The *Statesman* carries about 1,000 chests of Benares Opium for China . . .

Set against this, it struck me that a report such as the following, from 29 July 1929, speaks to a kind of colonial blindness or indifference towards double-standards and a comfort over a monopoly on misery:

> Exemplary sentence was passed on two Chinese with being in possession of a quantity of "non-Government opium," a walking stick gun and several rounds of ammunition. They were given 15 strokes of the rotan each, plus imprisonment, for possession of the gun, and a combined fine of $7,000 fine plus imprisonment for the opium.

In the story of the hajj pilgrimage the concerns over the possibilities of the hajj as a centre for fomenting "anti-colonial sentiment" sat against other, fundamental "assumptions of Empire." So the question occurs that if there was an "anti-colonial sentiment" that was spoken of, what would a "colonial sentiment" look like, since the colonial assumption was that land was there to be purchased or simply taken. That prompted reflection on the underlying assumptions and justifications of European exploration and control and the thought that such assumptions might trace back to Papal Bulls of the fifteenth century that legitimised the taking of land from people already there and the categorising of them as merely "occupants." That, though, would be a huge diversion but throughout human history there has been that unhelpful tendency – even a need – to have an "other"; a group against which one can seek to define one's own identity and set up degrees of opposition. Examinations like this, though, are far beyond the scope of this book.

And the "failings"

Yet alongside any criticism of colonial actions and controls we come to recognise instances of a kind of self-induced chaos created by Muslim themselves, both pilgrims and others. John Slight's book *The British Empire and the Hajj: 1865 – 1956* reveals the sheer size of the Muslim community within the territories under British rule and the implications to Britain of that rule. In it he documents the practice of large numbers of pilgrims, many from the Indian sub-continent, who would arrive for the hajj with insufficient funds that resulted in a state of destitution in the Hejaz, and their sleeping in front of the British offices in Jeddah and putting pressure on authorities to provide them with return tickets to home, only to subsequently turn around and repeat that in another year. Given the cross-currents of difficulties, vanities, ambitions, fighting, and even mischief of that time through the collapse of the Ottoman Empire to the control of the region by Ibn Saud, John Slight's book prompted much thought on the need for self-criticism or critical history from within the Muslim world toward the forces and behaviours that have shaped the order that we now live with.

Closing

There are many reflections that we could add. If the book began with an interest restricted to the journey and in "simply" trying to imagine, even re-create, that journey, the realisation soon came that much more was involved in making that journey possible than was originally envisaged: more connections, more actors, more consequences.

You can begin with sympathies. Perhaps we all begin with sympathies. We've said in the Acknowledgements that this book began with the lined face in a photograph of an old man. A photograph, a word, a brief caption stirs something and you can wonder, "what is his story?" At the end that old gentleman's story stays with him – "Allahu 'alam," as Muslims say: "God Alone knows best." And we, perhaps, arrive at the end with more questions than answers. The hope is always that the questions are worth asking.

Anthony Green